# New Directions in Race, Ethnicity and Crim

The disproportionate criminalisation and incarceration of particular minority ethnic groups has long been observed, though much of the work in criminology has been dominated by a somewhat narrow debate. This debate has concerned itself with explaining this disproportionality in terms of structural inequalities and socio-economic disadvantage or discriminatory criminal justice processing.

This book offers an accessible and innovative approach, including chapters on antisemitism, social cohesion in London, Bradford and Glasgow, as well as an exploration of policing Traveller communities. Incorporating current empirical research and new departures in methodology and theory, this book also draws on a range of contemporary issues such as policing terrorism, immigration detention and youth gangs. In offering minority perspectives on race, crime and justice and white inmate perspectives from the multicultural prison, the book emphasises contrasting and distinctive influences on constructing ethnic identities.

It will be of interest to students studying courses in ethnicity, crime and justice.

**Coretta Phillips** is a Reader in the Department of Social Policy at the London School of Economics and Political Science.

**Colin Webster** is Professor of Criminology at Leeds Metropolitan University.

# New Directions in Race, Ethnicity and Crime

Edited by
**Coretta Phillips and Colin Webster**

Routledge
Taylor & Francis Group

LONDON AND NEW YORK

First published 2014
by Routledge
2 Park Square, Milton Park, Abingdon, Oxon, OX14 4RN

and by Routledge
711 Third Avenue, New York, NY 10017

*Routledge is an imprint of the Taylor & Francis Group, an informa business*

*British Library Cataloguing in Publication Data*
A catalogue record for this book is available from the British Library

*Library of Congress Cataloging in Publication Data*
Phillips, Coretta.
  New directions in race, ethnicity, and crime / Coretta Phillips and Colin
Webster.
    pages cm
  1. Discrimination in criminal justice administration–Great Britain. 2.
Crime and race–Great Britain. 3. Imprisonment–Great Britain–Social
aspects. 4. Anti-Semitism–Great Britain. 5. Racism–Great Britain. 6.
Criminology–Great Britain. I. Webster, Colin (Criminologist) II. Title.
  HV9960.G7P47 2014
  364.3'400941–dc23
          2013014038

ISBN: 978-0-415-54048-3 (hbk)
ISBN: 978-0-415-54049-0 (pbk)
ISBN: 978-0-203-10728-7 (ebk)

Typeset in Times New Roman by
Taylor & Francis Books

MIX
Paper from
responsible sources
FSC
www.fsc.org   FSC® C013604

Printed and bound by CPI Group (UK) Ltd, Croydon, CR0 4YY

# Contents

# List of Tables

# Contributors

**Mary Bosworth** is Reader in Criminology and Fellow of St Cross College at the University of Oxford, and concurrently, Professor of Criminology at Monash University, Australia. She has published widely on race, gender and citizenship in prisons and immigration detention. Her books include *Engendering Resistance* (1999), *The US Federal Prison System* (2002), and *Explaining US Imprisonment* (2010). She is currently heading a five-year ESRC Starter Grant on migration, imprisonment, and detention.

**Rod Earle** worked in youth justice in the London Borough of Lambeth in the 1980s and 1990s. He is currently academic lead for youth justice qualifications in the Faculty of Health and Social Care at The Open University. He spent two years working full-time with Coretta Phillips on a research project examining men's ethnic and social identities in prison. He is a founding member of the British Convict Criminology group that supports the development of criminological perspectives from those with first-hand experience of penal sanctions.

**Alistair Fraser** is currently Assistant Professor in the Department of Sociology, University of Hong Kong. His doctoral research involved a community ethnography in Glasgow, focusing on young people's understandings and experiences of youth 'gangs'. His research interests focus broadly, on youth crime and justice – incorporating gangs, subcultures, and street-based leisure – and qualitative research, particularly ethnography and oral history. He is currently developing an agenda for comparative qualitative research on youth, globalisation and identity.

**Paul Iganski** is Senior Lecturer in Social Justice, and Head of Department of Applied Social Science, at Lancaster University, UK. For over a decade he has specialised in research, writing and teaching on 'hate crime'. His books on 'hate crime' include *Hate Crime and the City* (2008), *Hate Crimes Against London's Jews* (2005, with Vicky Kielinger and Susan Paterson) and the edited volumes *Hate Crime: The Consequences of Hate Crime* (2009), and *The Hate Debate* (2002). He mostly conducts his research in collaboration with, or commissioned by, NGOs and the equalities sector.

**Zoë James** is an Associate Professor (Senior Lecturer) at Plymouth University. Her key research interests lie in policing issues, particularly relating to public order policing, plurality in policing and managing diversity. More recently, Zoë's research has developed understandings of diversity in policing within a rural context and as part of a consideration of 'hate' crime. Additionally, Zoë has carried out research projects on the management of anti-social behaviour, focusing particularly on the work of Family Intervention Projects. Zoë is also Chair of the South West branch of the British Society of Criminology.

**Blerina Kellezi** is a Research Fellow and study co-ordinator at the Division of Primary Care, University of Nottingham. She has previously held research positions at Freedom from Torture and Oxford University. She completed her PhD in psychology at the University of St Andrews. She has published on the impact of social identity on support, coping and well-being and is currently conducting a systematic review on interventions with torture survivors.

**Suzella Palmer** is a Lecturer in Applied Social Studies at the University of Bedfordshire. Her research interests include young black people and crime, policing and black communities, and youth gangs and she has published in these areas. Outside of academia, Suzella is engaged in activities geared towards the empowerment of young people and African/African Caribbean communities through her work with youth and community groups and organisations in London.

**Alpa Parmar** is a visiting scholar at the Institute of Criminology, University of Cambridge, UK. She was previously Principal Research Fellow at the University of Leeds prior to which she completed her post-doctoral research at the School of Law, Kings College London. Alpa has conducted research on counter-terrorist policy and the local community impact, ethnicity, racism and crime, and is involved in a transnational comparative study of policing in India and the UK. She has a forthcoming book entitled *Crime and the Asian Community: Disentangling Perceptions and Reality* (Oxford University Press 2013).

**Coretta Phillips** is a Reader in the Department of Social Policy at the London School of Economics and Political Science. She has published extensively in the field of ethnicity, crime and criminal justice, including in three editions of the *Oxford Handbook of Criminology*. She is the author of *The Multicultural Prison: Ethnicity, Masculinity, and Social Relations among Prisoners* (Oxford University Press 2012) and co-author of *Racism, Crime and Justice* (Longman 2002).

**Teresa Piacentini** is currently a Post Doctoral Research Associate based in the School of Education at the University of Glasgow. She is working on an AHRC/SFC funded GRAMNet project into the development of a pedagogical model for effective translation in intercultural health care settings. The project aims to identify and provide innovative pathways forward for challenging structural inequalities as they affect migrant service users, and for developing greater reflexivity in health care and interpreting practice. Teresa's PhD explored the associational experiences of mainly Francophone African asylum seeker and refugee-led groups in Glasgow. Her research interests lie in the broad field of migration studies, covering the various aspects of social, cultural and political life affecting experiences of 'settlement', integration and belonging. Teresa is particularly interested in engagement with grass roots experiences of migrant groups through ethnographic methodologies, developing participatory research methodologies with communities.

**Colin Webster** is Professor of Criminology at Leeds Metropolitan University and Visiting Research Fellow at Teesside University. His publications include *Poor Transitions: Social Exclusion and Young Adults* (Policy Press 2004) and *Understanding Race and Crime* (Open University Press 2007). He has a co-authored book *Poverty and Insecurity: Life in Low-Pay, No-Pay Britain* (Policy Press 2012) and is co-authoring *Youth on Religion: The Development, Negotiation and Impact of Faith and Non-Faith Identity* (Routledge 2013).

# 1    Introduction

## Bending the paradigm – new directions and new generations

### *Coretta Phillips and Colin Webster*

**Plus ça change plus c'est la même chose? The relationship between race, ethnicity and crime**

Even before the seminal work of criminology founder, Cesare Lombroso, de Gobineau (1853) had published *The Inequality of Human Races* in which he outlined the behavioural traits associated with the black, Asian and white races. Located at the bottom of the racial hierarchy, de Gobineau claimed for the lower races of Negroes, an inability to distinguish between vice and virtue, a limited intellect, tendencies of animalism, great energy, and a wild desire and will. Two decades on, Lombroso (1876) developed an anthropometric tradition which recorded a variety of physical stigmata and descriptions which were associated with the atavistic races of *Criminal Man*, including white Southern Italians, Gypsies, Aboriginal Australians and Negroes, to name but a few.[1] In his later work, Lombroso (1897) demonstrated a more subtle awareness of the effects of racism on American Negroes' patterns of offending, but he remained wedded to the idea that there were immutable features of the Negro and other so-called 'primitive' races which were biologically inferior and inextricably linked to immorality and criminality.[2]

Lombroso's (1876) preposterous ideas about cranial capacities, extra nipples, handle-shaped ears and the like, can easily be ridiculed in the twenty-first century, but remnants of race thinking within criminology and public discourse remain stubbornly present now and in the recent past (Herrnstein and Murray 1994; Eysenck and Eysenck 1970; Wolfgang and Ferracuti 1967; see Webster 2012a for a recent review). Two centuries on, calling for 'plain talking' rather than evidence, David Starkey, an Honorary Fellow of Fitzwilliam College Cambridge, suggested that the August 2011 riots could best be explained by a shared black culture that was innately criminal and violent. He told the audience of the BBC's flagship programme *Newsnight* that, 'what has happened is that the substantial section of the chavs[3] ... have become black. The whites have become black. A particular sort of violent, destructive, nihilistic, gangster culture has become *the* fashion'. When pressed by host Emily Maitlis, Starkey did emphasise that it was a particular kind of black culture that was to blame. For good measure, and thus rather undermining this qualification, he also reminded us that the language of the rioters had intruded into Britain such that 'so many of us [*presumably white Britons*] have this sense of *literally* a foreign country ... It's not skin colour, it's culture ... '. In one fell swoop, Starkey presented us with the usual tropes of black criminality – gangsta rap, Jamaican patwa, an alien wedge – but also cleverly managed to implicate members of the irresponsible and contemptuous white working class too. These are the loathed, degenerate, excessively but tastelessly consumerist, the 'lesser whites' who are marked by a stigmatising disreputability (Webster 2008). Such assertions lie at the very heart of the race and crime paradigm which we look to 'bending' in this book.

The central problematic of the contemporary race and crime debate turns on a question – some say an imponderable one (Reiner 1993) – of whether the overrepresentation of black prisoners that we see in prison populations in England and Wales is the result of a higher propensity for black people to commit crime or whether this pattern can be explained by discriminatory actions by the police and the courts (for a recent review see Phillips and Bowling 2012). Thus, in the most recent annual Ministry of Justice publication, *Race and the Criminal Justice System* (MOJ 2011), while black people aged over 10 years were just 2.7 per cent of the general population, they were 10.8 per cent of the prison population in 2010. It is thus the case, of course, that 78 per cent of those in the prison population were white, although this fact has tended to escape research attention (Webster 2008). Notwithstanding, for relative comparison, even more starkly, in 2000 when detailed incarceration rates were last published by the Home Office, 1,704 of black Caribbeans and 1,274 of black Africans were incarcerated per 100,000 of the general population. This contrasted sharply with the incarceration rates of those of white (188 per 100,000), Pakistani (329 per 100,000) and Bangladeshi (183 per 100,000) origin. Likewise, among those dealt with formally by the criminal justice system for riot-related offences, and those not officially implicated but self-reported as involved in *The Guardian*/LSE study,[4] black people were over-represented (MOJ 2012; Muir and Adegoke 2011). It is now accepted that black people may have elevated rates of certain kinds of offending, particularly theft-person and robbery (Clancy *et al.* 2001; Smith 2003), which feature prominently in public anxieties about crime, although it is important to remember that they comprise around only 3–4 per cent of police recorded and CSEW (Crime Survey of England and Wales) offences (ONS 2012a).

Starkey's position serves as one possible but implausible explanation, given scholarly insight into the permeability and fluidity of cultures and how they are influenced by local ecologies and socio-cultural systems (Barth 1969; Parekh 2006). Of more significance, perhaps, is the evidence from the quarterly unemployment figures in March 2012 indicating that 45 per cent of those aged 16–24 and black were unemployed compared to 20 per cent of young white people (Rhodes 2012). Such figures could indicate workshy fecklessness among young black men, but both the hypercyclical nature of unemployment which hits minority ethnic groups hardest during a recession (Smith 1977; but see Hogarth *et al.* 2012), the political economic dynamics associated with neoliberalist undermining of the welfare state (Wacquant 2009; Reiner 2007), and the finding of racial discrimination at the recruitment stage of employment are rather more persuasive (Wood *et al.* 2009; see also Heath and Cheung 2006). Likewise, there have consistently been methodologically sophisticated studies of decision points in the criminal justice process in which race/ethnicity is still often a predictor of a more negative, disproportionate outcome for those of black and Asian origin over and above relevant legal factors (see for example May *et al.* 2010; Feilzer and Hood 2004; Mhlanga 1997; Hood 1992; Phillips *et al.* 1998).

## What we do not know

Having set out what we know from the race and crime debate as traditionally conceived it is just as important to be clear about what we do not know or what we could easily have misunderstood. It is now well-acknowledged that the conceptual basis for the race and crime debate is on rather shaky ground. The concept of race as a meaningful analytical category (as opposed to a social construction) has long been discredited (Montagu 1943; Miles 1989; Mason 2000; Fenton 1996). Yet all official data on arrests, incarceration rates, sentencing outcomes and the like – even when as is now sometimes the case they are based on self-ascription – create somewhat artificial aggregated categories which is likely to be internally diverse. Recognising the multiple, contingent and complex ethnic identities of all ethnic groups, *including* those of white origin, is likely to be critical to subjective identity expression and the politics of affirmation. But as Prewitt (2005) notes, such categorisations can frustrate efforts to monitor and respond to discrimination. After all, do police officers decide to stop an individual who claims an identity which reflects the composite identities of, say, their maternal and paternal grandparents and parents, their nationalities of origin and residence and possibly their faith too, or do they pull over an individual as an observed member of a lower classed group typically considered homogenously as 'police property' (Reiner 2000)? Evidently, class matters, and is central to understanding any social process in which inequality is implicated (see for example Mooney and Young 2000 in relation to proactive policing; Waddington *et al.* 2004). That said, the answer to the question posed may not be a simple one and it may not hold for all of the possible encounters between citizens and officials of criminal justice agencies. Repeated occurrences like the frequent stop and search of 'famous blacks' – most recently Stephen Lawrence's brother, Stuart, a teacher[5] – suggests class may not always be the key motive force of suspicion that is often claimed. Probably more helpful is to recognise the overlapping inequalities and othering processes which position certain social groups subordinately, confirming their marginalisation through race, class and often gender (Anthias *et al.* 1992; Goldberg 2009; Rattansi 2005). This places centre stage the mechanisms of social control which envelop poor white communities who typically live alongside ethnically mixed communities too.[6] Such understandings are also more easily able to accommodate new potential Others. The largest growing ethnic group according to the 2011 census – the white Other group – up 2 per cent since 2001 is one such example (ONS 2012b); disaggregation could indicate important processes of inequality which are currently masked in the aggregated categories used in criminal justice agencies. Webster in his chapter recognises the significance of new forms of identification which overlap with self-identities formed through race and ethnicity. For young people in Bradford for example, Muslim and British identities were not mutually exclusive and young people appeared at ease with religious diversity. There remained though some less spoken of underlying issues and anxieties about racism and segregation.

Reflecting on the inadequacies of the race and crime debate, Bosworth *et al.* (2008) have been frustrated by the exclusion of social theory, political discourses of race and nation, nuanced and historically situated understandings of criminalisation and penalisation, particularly within the context of globalisation. Bosworth's chapter with Kellezi, corrects these omissions by applying theoretical examinations of border control to the experience of women detained in immigration centres in Britain. In the new global order, Britain faces its post-colonial condition by imposing new exclusionary boundaries of belonging to keep out non-citizen women. Patel and Tyrer (2011) have similarly problematised the under-theorised race and crime field, particularly with regard to the nature of power and its effect on disproportionality. Parmar's interviews with young Asian men highlight how these direct experiences of suspicion and control exerted by police officers can have fundamental effects in leading those stopped and searched to seek out those similarly marked by their subordinate, criminalised identities. As one put it, 'When I was stopped, it was a reminder, that I am British, but only up to a point'. Notwithstanding, Webster (2012b: 107) has deplored the 'obsessive, deracinated measurement of proportionality and discrimination' and its empiricism which has failed to alter patterns of prison disproportionality or acknowledge the deepening of racial inequality and injustice. This points us away from using official s.95 Criminal Justice Act 1991 statistics towards an approach which favours critical qualitative research as means of unpacking the nature and experience of discrimination by control agents such as police officers, magistrates, judges, and prison and immigration officers. However, unless we believe that we live in a post-racial state, the official data which provide a picture of victimisation and offending for public consumption, can only be completely ignored at our peril (cf. Gilroy 1987). Such data, limited though they are, provide a means to challenge the flawed and idiosyncratic views of media pundits like David Starkey who are never far from the camera or microphone.

### What gets included and what is excluded

Finally, while it is impossible not to agree that the contours of the race and crime debate, as traditionally conceived, are narrow, it is also insightful to reflect on what gets included and what is excluded, just as much as it is to point to its conceptual and analytical weaknesses. Significantly, its key referent is *offending by minority ethnic groups* rather than *race and crime per se*. Included, for example, is the worrying indication that black people are more likely to be represented among homicide victims and offenders than might be expected from their representation in the general population (MOJ 2011). This is not unreasonable given the heightened public concern about such crimes particularly within communities with large concentrations of minority ethnic groups. However, excluded is the racist and religious victimisation of families like the Alams, interviewed on BBC radio in February 2013, after they were forced to leave their home in the Nottinghamshire village of Bingham. The family had been the victims of repeated abuse and harassment, including having a wooden cross covered in ham pushed into their home when their front door was opened. Against those marked by their race, ethnicity, religion, or culture, 41,318 incidents were recorded by the police as hate motivated in 2010, but this was rather lower than the 136,000 estimated in the 2010/11 British Crime Survey, of which 61 per cent involved personal as opposed to household crimes (Smith 2012). Reminding ourselves that there remain areas of Britain in which minorities may be spatially and violently excluded is what the *race and crime* debate should also be about (Virdee 1997; Garland and Chakraborti 2004; Tyler 2003). Iganski's contribution explores elements of this 'hatred' which has historically and in the contemporary period been directed at Jewish people. Often assumed to be connected to the Israeli-Palestinian conflict, Iganski identifies a deeply embedded and visceral racism which is far more banal than extremist. Similar sentiments were voiced by the white prisoners studied by Earle in his chapter, despite denials of their racist meanings.

Moreover, included in debates about race and crime is the disproportionate black involvement in 'mugging' and robbery across police BCUs (Smith 2003; Clancy *et al.* 2001), but excluded are the claims of racist brutality by the police which are reported by the media and referred to the Independent Police Complaints Commission with startling regularity. Yet this tells us something very important about how a fundamental democratic principle, fairness and equality before the law (Stenson 2011), operates in a less inclusionary way for some social groups. In James' chapter on Gypsies and Travellers, we hear of their harsh treatment in surveillance and enforcement actions by the police and local authorities which problematises the nomadism of these groups as a particular threat to settled communities. Similarly, Palmer's chapter notes that the time when this was not so, during slavery, remains a potent reminder for those young black people in contemporary London whose daily experiences are similarly marked by deep economic and social inequalities. Likewise, Parmar's research with young Asian men points in a similar direction with regard to painful interactions with control agents whose suspicions are racialised. It will only be when these interrelated and connected elements of the race and crime field are given equal thought and critical attention that it will make sense to talk about a moribund or theoretically inadequate race and crime field within criminology. We move forward in this new direction in the chapters of the book that follow this Introduction.

## New directions

By 'new directions', the book sets out to capture social, cultural and demographic change over the last two decades which has reconfigured the boundaries of the race and crime debate as originally conceived. Because of these changes the debate has become wider in scope and deeper in analytical reach. There are a wider range of groups and situations to take into account and the meaning of race and ethnicity and associated racialisation processes have in some ways changed form. Therefore a reassessment of concepts and theories is required beyond a narrower focus on effectiveness, efficiency and fairness regarding equality before the law and in the criminal justice system, important as these are. Taking the criminological study of race, ethnicity and justice in new conceptual, methodological and theoretical directions we have three aims: first, to incorporate new empirically-informed understandings of ethnicity, crime and justice, which draw more deeply on sociological accounts of complex configurations of identity and difference; second, to consider the experiences, uncovered through current empirical research, of a new and diverse generation of migrants and minority ethnic groups; and finally, to provide a vehicle for the dissemination of the work of a new generation of scholars who have recently entered the field. By 'bending the paradigm' traditionally associated with the race, ethnicity and crime debate we engage with several emerging issues and themes, which the chapters in this book in their different ways exemplify.

First, we do not intend to ignore or abandon the 'facts' of continuing or worsening racial and ethnic disparity in Britain. The context of relatively recent demographic and other changes and a supposed accompanying change in racial attitudes have led some to interpret change as presaging life in a 'post-racial' Britain. The 2011 Census has for instance shown that the largest 'minority' is 'white other', thus disarming the myth of 'race swamping'; there has been large scale new migration and declining religiosity and very significant growth in mixed heritage people; Poles are the second largest foreign community in Britain, and so on.[7] Rather, we ask why in a climate said to point to decline in racism, racial and ethnic disparities in policing, the courts and the wider social structure stubbornly endure? We doubt for example, along with writers asking similar questions in America (Bush 2011), that white racism has completely disappeared – even among the middle classes. The seemingly widespread belief that we are entering a 'post-racial' situation serves only better to rationalise and mask inequality and discrimination through the important role that ideology plays in distorting our views about, and denying the existence of, race and class as markers of group membership. Like ideology itself, these aspects of group identity are deemed obsolete.[8] This leads to our second theme, in which we draw away from describing racial disparities towards the changing role of racism in forming identity on one hand, and the 'cultural turn' from race to ethnic identity (and sometimes religious identity) on the other. This shift is partly mirrored in the book's contributions that capture more qualitative conceptualisations of race, ethnicity and crime while recognising demographic changes to Britain's ethnic makeup that ideologically shift contemporary constructions of race, racism and ethnicity. These ideological shifts have increased the opaqueness and obliqueness of ethno-racism in neoliberal societies like Britain. They point to the formation of a popular and apparently racially and ethnically tolerant 'liberal individualism' (see for instance, Webster's and Earle's chapters in this volume), which has encouraged racial tolerance while at the same time denying the continued significant existence of racism, disavowing and disapproving of overt public expressions and practices of racism. Liberal individualism does this by means of ideological devices such as individualising ethno-racism on one hand (racism as individual failure) and coding race by projecting cultural difference onto groups on the other (cultural racism). It is these sorts of blurring, conflation or confusion of visible (physical) race and subtle ethnicity that our contributors attempt to capture in their accounts of race, ethnicity and justice. In essence, in this collection we argue that because the formation of identity and constructions of race, ethnicity and crime in our neoliberal societies are indirect, subtle and 'cultural', their understanding and study require a more nuanced and subtle approach than perhaps has been the case previously in criminological studies. It is similarly worth noting that it is important to attempt to go beyond official racial and ethnic categories (Stenson 2011). Our third bending of the race and crime paradigm is to examine the construction of marginalised white ethnicities (see Fraser and Piacentini's and Earle's chapters) as well as visible and minority ethnicities as a threat to social and symbolic order. To be clear, in addressing these three general themes here and variously addressed by our contributors, we are emphatically *not* saying that the enduring effects of racism today in wider society as well as law enforcement have significantly decreased or disappeared. What we *are* saying is that the nature and nomenclature of how race and ethnicity are socially constructed and understood are more varied, more complex, subtle, and contingent on particular settings, interactions and places – as well as being less explicit – than was perhaps the case in the past.

### New racism?

Some writers in the United States have claimed that previous explicit and direct forms of racial discrimination have been supplanted by a 'new racism'. Before consideration of whether a similar process of change has occurred in Britain, which we do in the conclusion to this book, it seems legitimate to delineate the 'old' racism and ask what, if anything, appears *not* to have changed. For a start, the cruel and brutal mistreatment and criminalisation of young black men by the police in 1970s and 1980s Britain – often through treating suspected drug users as criminals – is well known. An early study – Wolfgang and Cohen's (1970: 112) prescient *Crime and Race* – concluded that 'Treating drug users as criminals serves no useful social function', which was precisely what the police treatment of black people amounted to at the time. Since then, the police's reluctance to, and resentment towards reform, and the patchiness and lack of real progress made in persuading the police to treat young black men fairly as suspects and victims, since Scarman and after the Lawrence Inquiry, are well known. This 'old' style of policing – shown by a copious literature[9] – didn't disappear, it suffered a crisis of legitimacy. Therefore police reform has not resulted in significant changes in stop and search, arrests and other substantive outcomes of police processes, contact and conflict with minority and marginalised groups (Miller 2010; Shiner 2010). For instance, Loftus (2008), for her part, found that, in spite of the many years of diversity politics and efforts to change the values of police officers, ethnic discrimination and intolerant attitudes had not diminished in the British police force. The arenas where discrimination appeared had become fewer and more consciously restricted to the kind of 'safe environments' represented by 'white' spaces 'where the white majority feel comfortable enough to resist and subvert aspects of the diversity agenda' (Loftus 2008: 764).

Following from this there is perhaps an older historical argument that policing in Britain has involved social relationships between themselves and subordinate groups such as the white working-class and visible minority groups that are intrinsic to how British policing should be understood – as relationships of power and domination (Lea 2000). Although not inevitable these sorts of relationships seem likely and there is something ubiquitous about how individuals and groups with little power and lower social and economic status are policed. On this argument, if these fundamental power relationships remain a central feature of the policing of subordinate groups then in ethnically and socially divided and stratified societies like Britain then we can expect such groups to have negative experiences of the police. Some argue that the policing of minorities is essentially based on class as much as racial prejudice. The inferior treatment of minorities is likened to that of any group perceived by the police as being of lower social status (minorities are predominantly working-class, the working-class are perceived of lower status and therefore minorities too are policed in authoritarian and discriminatory ways). There remain discernible and definite patterns of disadvantage among people from minority ethnic groups to be sure. Evidence shows that poverty is higher among all black and minority ethnic groups than among the majority white population, and men and women from some ethnic groups are paid less on average than those from other groups who have similar qualifications, skills and experience. These patterns cannot however, be explained by class alone (Barnard and Turner 2011). Racial and ethnic stratification is complicated and crosscut within and across ethnic groups by other aspects of identity such as gender, age, religion and location. Broad patterns start to break down due to the enormous variation between minority ethnic groups of which some such as British Bangladeshi people have the smallest spread of incomes and the highest poverty whereas others such as British Indian people contain such variation of income as well as other factors they hardly constitute a unitary group at all. In addition, as Barnard and Turner (2011) state, information about people from some ethnic backgrounds – particularly white minorities, newer migrants and small groups – is not separately available in many official datasets and research. It is difficult overall then to sustain the argument that minorities are policed differently only because of their perceived social status just as it is to argue that they are only because of their ethnicity.

We have repeatedly said that while it is important to recognise societal change it is also important to recognise continuities of context in which the race and crime debate has been and continues to be conducted and to which it refers. We wish to avoid therefore exaggerating novelty and change while ignoring continuities in race, ethnicity and justice. Our contention nevertheless – and the context in which our contributor's work may be placed – is that while discriminatory treatment and racism in the police, courts and other places of institutional authority have far from disappeared, discrimination and racism may have taken new and different forms. This contention – following parallel debates in the United States about the existence of 'new racism' and how best to study or uncover this apparently novel development – offers the paradoxical situation that racist and discriminatory attitudes and behaviours appear to have declined while their effects of racially and ethnically-based outcomes of disparity, disproportion and inequality have not.

To begin to address this apparent conundrum in both Britain and America one claim is that we are entering a 'post-racial society' or alternatively, that we are entering a different phase of the historical development of racism. In the United States, although the language is often more strident – perhaps reflecting a more racially polarised society – these claims are made in the context of an increasing political polarisation of American society and penal populism (reflected in the election of judges and prosecutors there) resulting in an uncompromising vindictiveness (Garland 2010). This is reflected for instance in Alexander's (2010) somewhat bleak work, *The New Jim Crow: Mass Incarceration in the Age of Colorblindness.* The essence of claims about the emergence of a 'new racism' in the United States is a sharp decline in racism there because of a growing reluctance to express in public, racism which is no longer considered socially acceptable, whilst private racism remains widespread and continues to motivate discrimination. This debate has hardly begun in Britain and we give it a passing review here so as to raise questions about 'new racism' in Britain.[10] We also pursue this a little further in the conclusion.

Extensive survey research on white racial attitudes on the one hand and ethnographic studies of the meaning of white ethnicity on the other have found that contemporary white racism in the United States is more likely than in the past to be based on 'colour-blind racism' whereby whites think racially but manage to avoid explicitly referring to race (Bonilla-Silva 2006). Hartigan (2010: 190) summarises this position thus:

> Though race continues to affect discrepant life chances and alternately to limit and to open access to social resources, it is increasingly difficult to find explicitly 'racist' components in much of what whites say and do. Instead there is a profusion of 'nonracial' discourses that seemingly strive to obscure the real racist sentiments, perceptions, and interests of whites, who now cautiously and conscientiously police their public comments to efface any mention of race.

As well as the methodological implications of how this sort of racism might be studied and uncovered, Hartigan (2010) goes on to say that what counts as 'race' is less certain and more negotiable than perhaps it has been in the past; that what is racial slides in and out of view according to local contexts and contingent conditions; and depends on the ways that racial identities are performed, responded to, or interpreted as having explicit or implicit racial meanings. In a wider sense, the key issue for the race and crime debate is whether we belong to an era in which there has been a genuine decline of racism or, whether 'colour-blind' racism, associated with the growth of 'colour-blind' free markets and individualism has replaced explicit public forms of racist expression and practice. We return to this crucial question in the conclusion. Meanwhile, Goldberg's (2009) delineation of what he calls 'racial neoliberalism' is that racism and its causes have become obfuscated and denied as incompatible with market freedoms, individualism and meritocracy, and that where remaining this remnant takes personal and individualising rather than institutional or systemic forms. Here, it is claimed, 'race' is no longer relevant because we are all 'just people', 'everyone is an individual', and as sovereign individuals we do not belong to groups such as 'classes', 'genders' or 'races'. Occurrences of racism must then be expressions of some sort of personal failure on the part of individuals. Colour-blind racism then serves as an ideology mirrored in individualism, which in turn has great difficulty perceiving group circumstances and therefore racial discrimination. At the same time our membership of projected group identity 'may be mutable – at one moment framed by class, in turn by gender, at another moment by race, then by generation, region, or neighbourhood or other affiliations' (Hartigan 2010: 11, 14; see also MacLeod 2009; Sampson 2012; Phillips 2012).

Finally, we can expect the claims made for the existence of 'new racism' to have been reflected and inflected in the criminal justice system. Michael Tonry (2011: x) asks how and why it is possible that special damage to black Americans has been and continues to be done through criminal justice policies 'in a country in which few whites any longer believe in white supremacy or black inferiority'? Using surveys of 'racial resentments and public opinion',

Tonry (2011: 92) shows that 'Few whites, however, believe that the [criminal justice] system treats blacks unfairly.' Tonry (2011) addresses this dilemma of enduring or worsening racial injustice while at the same time racism appears to be declining by suggesting that in actuality, at one level white Americans resent efforts to overcome the legacy of racism while on another, stereotyping black criminality and unthinkingly supporting policies that advantage whites and disadvantage blacks. Can the same be said of Britain or has racism indeed declined?

## Structure of the book

Reminding ourselves that racist victimisation should be central to the race and crime debate, Chapter 2, focusing on anti-Jewish incidents as a case study, argues that we need to understand the motivating impulses behind so-called 'hate crime' against Jews. Paul Iganski critically evaluates the appropriateness of labelling such incidents 'anti-Semitic', 'hate crime', 'religiously aggravated' or 'faith hate crime'. He argues that if the now common use of such terms is fundamentally flawed then this will influence the political and legal challenges involved in countering, and the legislative and criminal justice responses to, the problem.

Exploring new forms of living diversity, Colin Webster draws upon a large study of how young people negotiated their identities in multi-faith, multi-ethnic and multicultural locations in London and Bradford to critically examine concerns about, and how we might understand community cohesion. These concerns, since the inception of community cohesion as a concept and policy informing the governance of race relations in Britain, have recently turned from race to religion. Chapter 3 focuses on young people's views about and contacts with religious difference and the role religion plays in the problem of social order.

Alistar Fraser and Teresa Piacentini in their chapter find commonalities as well as differences between two seemingly unrelated contemporary folk-devils – the 'asylum-seeker' and 'gang-member' in Glasgow. The authors reflect on convergences and divergences in the experiences of economic and political marginalisation among young white men developing gang identities, and African refugee and migrant populations and individuals negotiating the process of asylum dispersal and settlement. Sharing neighbourhoods in the context of global mobility and immobility and local socio-economic deprivation we are shown how novel ethnicities emerge and the ways in which localities and identities are invested with meanings at odds with how they are perceived by others outside these locations. This is also one of the themes of Mary Bosworth and Blerina Kellezi's chapter which draws on interviews conducted in Britain's primary immigration removal centre for women, to explore the racialised logic of citizenship and British nationality that underpin border control. Using women's testimonies, the authors sought to 'give voice' to an otherwise silenced custodial population. In doing so, they seek to enrich the theoretical literature on border control and challenge its pessimistic view of such places merely as 'zones of exclusion'. Again, and consistent with the book's overriding theme of new directions, they demonstrate the salience of detention centres – and migration – for criminological research on race and ethnicity.

Suzella Palmer's chapter critiques the ethnocentric approach of contemporary mainstream criminology in Britain. It calls for a greater recognition of minority perspectives in criminological research and critical reflections on the nature of 'whiteness' and its influence on criminological discourses. Drawing on the author's own research with three generations of black people in London, it demonstrates how the relationship between Black young males and crime can be understood by exploring 'Black perspectives', on race, crime and justice which contributes to a more multidimensional understanding. Palmer concludes that the group history of black people and their distinctive perspectives imprinted by slavery and colonialism should be forefronted to understand race, crime and justice. Alpa Parmar's chapter shows how stops and searches under counter-terrorist legislation in London in labelling and criminalising British Asian Muslims constructs and reconfigures ethnic identity. Being subject to police suspicion and attention forces a re-examination of ethnic group boundaries and differences among those affected. Zoë James' chapter turns to a previously much neglected aspect of race, ethnicity and crime in Britain by identifying how Gypsies and Travellers are policed as offenders in part because they live in ways that are deemed inappropriate by sedentary society and how they are policed as victims of 'hate' crime. The chapter goes on to explore the implications, which are how Gypsies and Travellers pose a problem to policing agencies that perceive them as offenders but fail to recognise their victimisation.

In our final contribution Rod Earle uses his personal experience and research in English men's prisons to explore how some white ethnicities are shaped by ethnic resentments that emerge in the face of the powerful strategies of the prison regime to eradicate unfair differential treatment of minority ethnic prisoners. The prison setting, with its highly managed spaces and sensibilities, provides a lens through which to analyse tensions in the ways in which ethnicity is formally recognised and directly experienced.

## Notes

1 Lombroso was more magnanimous about other tribal groups. For example he acknowledged that the native Yuris of America had a high respect for property.
2 Lombroso (1897: 647) went on to claim that 'were it not for the Negro population, the crime of homicide would be almost as rare in the United States as it is in the most civilized countries in Europe'.
3 Starkey makes passing reference here to the work of co-panellist Owen Jones, whose book *Chavs: The Demonization of the Working Class* (2012) describes the pathologisation of white working class cultures (see also Webster 2008).
4 Of the 270 rioters interviewed by *The Guardian* and the LSE, 50 per cent were black, 27 per cent were white, 18 per cent of mixed race and 5 per cent Asian, although this varied across the study's sites.

5 The Metropolitan Police Service referred his complaint of racist harassment to the Independent Police Complaints Commission.

6 It is certainly true that London may also be muddying the waters as its patterns of stop and search are higher than most other police forces, and thus exposure to it is more likely among the large proportion (58 per cent) of the black Caribbean and black African population that live there.

7 Bakalar, A. (2012) 'Polish People are Britain's Invisible Minority', *The Guardian*, 18 December. The 2011 census confirmed Poles as the second-largest foreign community in Britain. Simon Rogers (2012) 'Census 2011: religion, race and qualifications – see how England & Wales have changed', *The Guardian Datablog*, 11 December, available at www.guardian.co.uk/news/datablog/2012/dec/11/census-2011-religion-race-education. Robert Booth (2012) 'Census reveals decline of Christianity and rise in foreign born to one in eight', available at www.guardian.co.uk/uk/2012/dec/11/census-religion-decline-rise-born-abroad?intcmp=239.

8 By 'ideology' we simply mean ideas and meanings that legitimate or promote the power of a dominant social group or class (see Eagleton 2007).

9 Phillips and Bowling (2012); Webster (2012a, 2012b); Burnett (2012); Dixon (2010); Hall (1999); Hall *et al.* (2009); Holdaway and O'Neill (2007); House of Commons (2009).

10 A useful review of the American debate is found in Quillan (2006). Bobo (2001) after extensively reviewing the empirical literature and different theories explaining recent changes in racial attitudes and race relations found a complicated situation of a significant decline in explicit racism but not of race thinking amidst considerable pessimism and alienation among African Americans that racist attitudes and practices had changed significantly. This seemed to be particularly the case in respect of the police and the criminal justice system and the courts among blacks *and* whites. At the level of interpretation and theory though, Bobo suggested there was evidence of the replacement of the old overt Jim Crow racism with what he calls 'laissez faire racism' – inconclusive racism simultaneous with racial polarisation. In contrast in the UK the evidence seems more straightforward of a strong decline in racist attitudes and prejudice among the young (a 'generation effect') while there was little evidence that this had been replaced by cultural prejudices or racism, according to Ford (2008).

# References

Alexander, M. (2010) *The New Jim Crow: Mass Incarceration in the Age of Colorblindness.* New York: The New Press.

Anthias, F., Yuval-Davis, N. and Cain, H. (1992) *Racialized Boundaries: Race, Nation, Gender, Colour and Class and the Anti-Racist Struggle.* London: Routledge.

Barnard, H. and Turner, C. (2011) *Poverty and Ethnicity: A Review of Evidence.* York: Joseph Rowntree Foundation.

Barth, F. (1969) *Ethnic Groups and Boundaries: The Social Organisation of Culture Difference.* Long Grove, IL: Waveland Press.

Bobo, L. D. (2001) 'Racial Attitudes and Relations at the Close of the Twentieth Century', in N. J. Smelser, W. J. Wilson and F. Mitchell (eds) *America Becoming: Racial Trends and Their Consequences, Volume 1.* Washington, DC: The National Academies Press.

Bonilla-Silva, E. (2006) *Racism without Racists: Color-Blind Racism and the Persistence of Racial Inequality in the United States.* Second Edition. Lanham, MD: Rowman & Littlefield.

Bosworth, M. (1999) *Engendering Resistance: Agency and Power in Women's Prisons.* Aldershot: Dartmouth Publishing Company Limited.

Bosworth, M., Bowling, B. and Lee, M. (2008) 'Globalization, Ethnicity and Racism: An Introduction', *Theoretical Criminology*, 12 (3): 313–31.

Burnett, J. (2012) 'After Lawrence: Racial Violence and Policing in the UK', *Race & Class*, 54 (1): 91–98.

Bush, M. (2011) *Everyday Forms of Whiteness: Understanding Race in a 'Post-Racial' World.* Second Edition. Lanham, MD: Rowman & Littlefield.

Clancy, A., Hough, M., Aust, R. and Kershaw, C. (2001) *Crime, Policing and Justice: The Experience of Ethnic Minorities; Findings from the 2000 British Crime Survey. Home Office Research Study 223.* London: Home Office.

Dixon, L. (2010) 'Tackling Hate by Driving Diversity: A New Labour Success Story?', *Probation Journal*, 57 (3): 314–21.

Eagleton, T. (2007) *Ideology: An Introduction.* London: Verson.

Eysenck, S. B. G. and Eysenck, H. J. (1970) 'Crime and Personality: An Empirical Study of the Three-Factor Theory', *British Journal of Criminology*, 10: 225–39.

Feilzer, M. and Hood, R. (2004) *Differences or Discrimination?* London: Youth Justice Board.

Fenton, S. (1996) 'Counting Ethnicity: Social Groups and Official Categories', in R. Levitas and W. Guy (eds) *Interpreting Official Statistics.* London: Routledge.

Ford, R. (2008) 'Is Racial Prejudice Declining in Britain?', *British Journal of Sociology*, 59 (4): 609–36.

Garland, D. (2010) *Peculiar Institution: America's Death Penalty in an Age of Abolition.* Cambridge, MA: Belknap Press of Harvard University Press.

Garland, J. and Chakraborti, N. (eds) (2004) *Rural Racism.* Cullompton: Willan Publishing.

Gilroy, P. (1987) 'The Myth of Black Criminality', in P. Scraton (ed.) *Law, Order and the Authoritarian State.* Stratford: Open University Press.

Gobineau, A. D. (1853) *The Inequality of Human Races.* New York: Howard Fertig.

Goldberg, D. T. (2009) *The Threat of Race: Reflections on Racial Neoliberalism.* Oxford: Wiley-Blackwell.

Hall, N., Grieve, J. and Savage, S. P. (2009) *Policing and the Legacy of Lawrence.* Cullompton: Willan Publishing.

Hall, S. (1999) 'From Scarman to Stephen Lawrence', *History Workshop Journal*, 48: 187–97.

Hartigan, J. (2010) *Race in the 21st Century: Ethnographic Approaches.* Oxford: Oxford University Press.

Heath, A. and Cheung, S. Y. (2006) *Ethnic Penalties in the Labour Market: Employers and Discrimination, Research Report No. 341.* London: Department for Work and Pensions.

Herrnstein, R. J., and Murray, C. (1994) *Bell Curve: Intelligence and Class Structure in American Life.* New York: The Free Press.

Hogarth, T., Owen, D., Gambin, L., Hasluck, C., Lyonette, C. and Casey, B. (2012) *The Equality Impacts of the Current Recession. Equality and Human Rights Commission Research Report 47.* London: EHRC.

Holdaway, S. and O'Neill, M. (2007) 'Where Has All the Racism Gone? Views of Racism within Constabularies after Macpherson', *Ethnic and Racial Studies*, 30 (3): 397–415.

Hood, R. (1992) *Race and Sentencing.* Oxford: OUP.

House of Commons Committee, (2009) *The Macpherson Report – Ten Years On. Twelfth Report of Session 2008–09*. London: The Stationery Office.

Jones, O. (2012) *Chavs: The Demonization of the Working Class*. London: Verso.

Lea, J. (2000) 'The Macpherson Report and the Question of Institutional Racism', *The Howard Journal*, 39 (3): 219–33.

Loftus, B. (2008) 'Dominant Culture Interrupted: Recognition, Resentment and the Politics of Change in an English Police Force', *British Journal of Criminology*, 48 (6): 756–77.

Lombroso, C. (1876) *L'uomo Delinquente [Criminal Man]*. Turin: Fratelli Bocca.

——(1897) 'Why Homicide Has Increased in the United States', *The North American Review*, 165 (493): 641–48.

MacLeod, J. (2009) *Ain't No Makin' It: Aspirations and Attainment in a Low-Income Neighbourhood*. Third Edition. Boulder, CO: Westview Press.

Mason, D. (2000) *Race and Ethnicity in Modern Britain*. Oxford: Oxford University Press.

May, T., Gyateng, T. and Hough, M. (2010) *Differential Treatment in the Youth Justice System, EHRC Research Report 50*. London: EHRC.

Mhlanga, B. (1997) *The Colour of Engllish Justice: A Multivariate Analysis*. Aldershot: Avebury.

Miles, R. (1989) *Racism*. London: Routledge.

Miller, J. (2010) 'Stop and Search in England: A Reformed Tactic or Business as Usual', *British Journal of Criminology*, 50 (5): 954–74.

MOJ (2007) *Offender Management Caseload Statistics 2006*. London: Ministry of Justice.

——(2011) *Statistics on Race and the Criminal Justice System 2010*. London: Ministry of Justice.

——(2012) *Statistical Bulletin on the Public Disorder of 6th to 9th August 2011 – September 2012 Update*. London: MOJ.

Montagu, A. (1943) *Man's Most Dangerous Myth: The Fallacy of Race*. Walnut Creek.

Mooney, J. and Young, J. (2000) 'Policing Ethnic Minorities: Stop and Search in North London', in A. Marlow and B. Loveday (eds) *After Macpherson: Policing after the Stephen Lawrence Inquiry*. Lyme Regis: Russell House Publishing.

Muir, H. and Adegoke, Y. (2011) 'Reading the Riots: Were the Riots About Race?', *The Guardian*, Thursday 8 December 2011.

ONS (2012a) *Crime in England and Wales, Year Ending September 2012*. London: ONS.

——(2012b) *Ethnicity and National Identity in England and Wales 2011*. London: ONS.

Parekh, B. (2006) *Rethinking Multiculturalism: Cultural Diversity and Political Theory*. Basingstoke: Palgrave Macmillan.

Patel, T. G., and Tyrer, D. (2011) *Race, Crime and Resistance*. London: Sage.

Phillips, C., Brown, D., James, Z. and Goodrich, P. (1998) *Entry into the Criminal Justice System: A Survey of Police Arrests and Their Outcomes*. London: Home Office.

Phillips, C. (2012) *The Multicultural Prison: Ethnicity, Masculinity, and Social Relations among Prisoners*. Oxford: Oxford University Press.

Phillips, C. and Bowling, B. (2012) 'Ethnicities, Racism, Crime and Criminal Justice', in M. Maguire, R. Morgan and R. Reiner (eds) *The Oxford Handbook of Criminology*. Fifth Edition. Oxford: Oxford University Press.

Prewitt, K. (2005) 'Racial Classification in America: Where Do We Go from Here?', *Daedalus*, 134 (1): 5–17.

Quillan, L. (2006) 'New Approaches to Understanding Racial Prejudice and Discrimination', *Annual Review of Sociology*, 32: 299–328.

Rattansi, A. (2005) 'The Uses of Racialization: The Time-Spaces and Subject-Objects of the Raced Body', in K. Murji and J. Solomos (eds) *Racialization: Studies in Theory and Practice*. Oxford: Oxford University Press.

Reiner, R. (1993) 'Race, Crime and Justice: Models of Interpretation', in L. R. Gelsthorpe (ed.) *Minority Ethnic Groups in the Criminal Justice System*. Cambridge: The Institute of Criminology, Cambridge University.

——(2000) *The Politics of the Police*. London: Harvester Wheatsheaf.

——(2007) *Law and Order: An Honest Citizen's Guide to Crime and Control*. Cambridge: Polity.

Rhodes, C. (2012) *Unemployment by Ethnic Background. Sn/6385*. London: House of Commons Library.

Sampson, R. J. (2012) *Great American City: Chicago and the Enduring Neighbourhood Effect*. Chicago, IL: The University of Chicago Press.

Shiner, M. (2010) 'Post-Lawrence Policing in England and Wales: Guilt, Innocence and the Defence of Organizational Ego', *British Journal of Criminology*, 50 (5): 935–53.

Smith, D. J. (1977) *Racial Disadvantage in Britain*. Harmondsworth: Penguin.

Smith, J. (2003) *The Nature of Personal Robbery*. Home Office Research Study 254. London: Home Office.

Smith, K. (2012) (ed.) *Hate Crime, Cyber Security and the Experience of Crime among Children: Findings from the 2010/11 British Crime Survey. Supplementary Volume 3 to Crime in England and Wales 2010/11*. London: Home Office.

Stenson, K. (2011) 'Review of Race, Crime and Criminal Justice: International Perspectives', *Global Crime*, 12 (1): 87–92.

Tonry, M. (2011) *Punishing Race: A Continuing American Dilemma*. Oxford: Oxford University Press.

Tyler, K. (2003) 'The Racialised and Classed Constitution of English Village Life', *Ethnos*, 68: 391–412.

Virdee, S. (1997) 'Racial Harassment', in T. Modood, R. Berthoud, J. Lakey, J. Nazroo, P. Smith and S. Beishon (eds) *Fourth National Survey – Ethnic Minorities in Britain: Diversity and Disadvantage*. London: PSI.

Wacquant, L. (2009) *Punishing the Poor: The Neoliberal Government of Social Insecurity*. Durham, NC: Duke University Press.

Waddington, P. A. J., Stenson, K. and Don, D. (2004) 'In Proportion: Race, and Police Stop and Search', *British Journal of Criminology*, 44 (6): 889–914.

Webster, C. (2008) 'Marginalized White Ethnicity, Race and Crime', *Theoretical Criminology*, 12 (3): 293–312.

——(2012a) 'Different Forms of Discrimination in the CJS', in K. Sveinsson (eds) *Criminal Justice V Racial Justice: Over-Representation in the Criminal Justice System*. London: Runnymede Trust.

——(2012b) 'The Discourse on 'Race' in Criminological Theory', in S. Hall and S. Winlow (eds) *New Directions in Criminological Theory*. London: Routledge.

Wilson, D. (2003) "Keeping Quiet' or 'Going Nuts': Some Emerging Strategies Used by Young Black People in Custody at a Time of Childhood Being Re-Constructed', *Howard Journal of Criminal Justice*, 42 (5): 411–25.

Wolfgang, M. and Ferracuti, F. (1967) *The Subculture of Violence: Towards an Integrated Theory in Criminology.* London: Tavistock.

Wolfgang, M. E. and Cohen, B. (1970) *Crime and Race: Conceptions and Misconceptions.* New York: Institute of Human Relations Press.

Wood, M., Hales, J., Purdon, S., Sejersen, T. and Hayllar, O. (2009) *A Test for Racial Discrimination in Recruitment Practice in British Cities. Research Report No 607.* London: DWP.

# 2 'Antisemitism' and anti-Jewish 'hatred'

## Conceptual, political and legal challenges

*Paul Iganski*

Probably, most readers of this essay[1] will be familiar with, or at least will have heard of, the term 'hate crime'. It is a term that has now infused the lexicon of criminal justice policy and practice, the campaigning language of NGOs working against racism and other forms of human rights abuses and oppression, and even the news and entertainment media. The term probably means different things to different people. But one thing is for sure. The notion of 'hate crime' is fundamentally flawed. Most 'hate crime' scholars would agree that the term is a misnomer and the idea of 'hate crime' a misconception. That is because in most offences labelled as 'hate crimes', 'hate' as a sentiment only infrequently appears to serve as the offender's motivating impulse.

Despite this conceptual malady, a field of 'hate crime' studies has bloomed, growing from its roots in scholarship in the United States in the 1990s to more recent scholarship in Australia, Canada, the United Kingdom and elsewhere in Europe such as Germany and Sweden. The field is one in which there is now an analytical convergence at the edges of once entirely separate domains of study concerned with discrimination and oppression. Scholars have emerged from different substantive fields concerned with racism, sexism, heterosexism, and disablism, and from different disciplines in the humanities and social sciences, to stepover the boundaries to engage in an analytical conversation centring on the problem of so-called 'hate crime'. Although this scholarly movement is in its nascent period we might perhaps envisage some analyses exploring the synergies and intersections between different forms of oppression and discriminatory violence. This is the task that this essay seeks to undertake by focussing on the conceptualisation of 'hate crimes' against Jews. The essay unfolds understandings about such crimes and engages with how they might be conceptualised. The analysis that is offered is inspired by four fundamental questions concerning the offenders. What are their characteristics? What are the motivating impulses behind offences? What are the consequences of offenders' actions? And what are the political and legal challenges in responding to their actions?

## Trends in antisemitic 'hate crime'

It is instructive to set the context for the analysis presented in this essay by briefly discussing the evidence of 'hate crimes' against Jews. In Europe, there is a considerable lack of publicly available data on racist crimes across EU Member States, and the same applies to data about violence against Jews. Despite this, there has been a consensus and concern in the EU policy community that racist crime and violence has been on the rise. There has also been a concern about a perceived rise in extremism, and especially the activities of far-right groups (ECRI 2010: 9; ENAR 2009: 18; FRA 2010: 35–38). In the context of such concerns, and given the limited official data on racist crimes across EU Member States, a recent study of racist violence in Europe undertaken for the European Network Against Racism (ENAR) aimed to produce an experiential analysis of the problem using evidence and perspectives provided in country reports by ENAR network members who work to support victims of such violence (Iganski 2011). On the basis of the country reports, the study drew attention to pan-European patterns of racist violence, noting that ... in different European countries some minority communities – Roma/Gypsies/Travellers; Muslims; Jews; and other visible minorities, such as migrant workers, refugees and asylum seekers – are consistently targeted in racist attacks'. The study noted though that the '... contexts and patterns of such attacks differ, however, across the communities targeted' (Iganski 2011: 19). A particular context for attacks was noted in the case of racist violence against Jews whereby '... it is clear that the numbers of recorded incidents appear to rise and fall in relation to tensions in the Israel-Palestine conflict and conflicts elsewhere' (Iganski 2011: 27). A peak in incidents was noted in France, for instance, in late 2008 and early 2009 associated with the Israel Defence Force attack on Gaza – operation Cast Lead (Camus 2010). Likewise in Britain, there was also a peak at the time in incidents against Jews. The Community Security Trust (CST), an NGO which advises and represents Britain's Jewish communities on matters of antisemitism, terrorism and security, recorded its highest level of reported incidents in January and February 2009. Before then there had similarly been notably high peaks in incidents in 2006 during the war between Israel and Hizbollah in Lebanon, the Israel Defence Force actions in Jenin in 2002, and in 2000 when the second Palestinian Intifada began. According to the CST, such peaks have punctuated an otherwise underlying upward trend of street-level racism against Jews. In the United States, increases in anti-Jewish incidents and crimes have also been evident following upsurges in the conflict in the Middle East (Levin 2002: 14) and even after the September 11 attacks which some blamed on Jewish influence over U.S. foreign policy (Gerstenfeld 2004: 153).

The apparent association of spikes in 'hate crimes' against Jews with conflicts involving Israel, might be regarded as a tragic irony. A Jewish homeland – now in its modern incarnation as the State of Israel – was seen by early Zionist thinkers before the Holocaust as a necessary refuge from a Judeophobia seen to be intractably rooted in many nations around the world and manifest by centuries of hostility against Jews, and centuries of religious persecution and oppression. Since the late 19th century such hostility towards Jews has become firmly racialised, and since the Holocaust the 'Nazi-card' (Iganski and Sweiry 2009) is frequently played in abuse against Jews whereby Nazi references are wielded in the daubing of swastikas on synagogue walls or on the gravestones of Jews for instance. And the Nazi-card is now also employed against Israel when comparisons are drawn between the Israeli State and Nazi Germany. Since the Holocaust some Jews undoubtedly see the State of Israel as an 'insurance policy' (Cohn-Sherbok 2006: xi) against further genocidal anti-semitism. Paradoxically though, some have also seen Israel as a cause of antisemitism through the hostility against Jews evoked by its military policies and practices (cf. Avnery 2002; Finkelstein 2005). And at the very least, while not condoning such proxy violence against Israel, others have seen it as 'hardly surprising' that the violence of the conflict between the Israeli State and Palestinians and other Arabs spills over into hostility against Jews in Europe and elsewhere, given that many Jews outside of Israel align themselves with the Jewish state (cf. Klug 2003).

The apparent association of spikes in 'hate crimes' against Jews with conflicts involving Israel might suggest that such crimes represent a unique phenom-enon compared with other types of 'hate crime'. The evidence of racist attacks against Jews suggests that in some cases Jews on the streets of Europe are targeted as representatives for the State of Israel. The conflict between Israelis and Palestinians and other Arab communities has therefore become a global phenomenon spreading from Gaza and the Occupied Territories of the West Bank into some of Europe's major cities. Jews in London, Manchester, Amsterdam, and Paris are attacked as proxies for Jews in Tel Aviv and Jer-usalem and elsewhere in Israel. It is a crude and indiscriminatory form of political violence as many Jews within and outside of Israel are opposed to Israel's military practices and many are also opposed to Zionism. But that would have no bearing on offences against Jews, because as with 'hate crimes' in general, they are not personal. The victims are attacked arguably not for who they are, but for what they represent to the attacker.

Given this political context for some incidents, how are hate crimes against Jews to be interpreted? Are they indeed acts of political violence? Are the perpetrators street-level activists exercising their sympathy for Palestinians through violence on the streets against Jews who are targeted as proxies for Israelis? Might they also perhaps be outpourings of outrage about the plight of Palestinians by people not normally disposed to violent conduct? Or are they simply manifestations of an underlying centuries-long bigotry against Jews which is brought to the surface by news media reporting of the conflict in the Middle East? And is it appropriate to label such 'hate crimes' against Jews as 'religiously aggravated' crimes? These questions can only begin to be answered by developing understandings about the characteristics and motivations of the perpetrators of 'hate crimes' against Jews. Before engaging with these questions directly in the analysis offered in this chapter, it is informative to examine how 'hate crimes' against Jews have been interpreted in some of the leading contributions to the 'hate crimes' literature to date to consider whether they might shed any light on the questions just posed.

## Anti-Jewish incidents and the 'hate crimes' literature

Discussion of the problem of 'hate crimes' against Jews has by no means been absent from the field of 'hate crime' studies – although it has not been a substantial concern. In the foundational study of the field, and one of the most influential works, Levin and McDevitt (1993) drew attention to a number of anti-Jewish manifestations in the United States. Of particular note were sentiments expressed by some publicly prominent religious leaders and political figures in the 1980s. Such sentiments were manifest in racial and religious insults (1993: 37–38, 138–39); allegations that Jews and Israeli interests were a powerful force in the Congress of the United States (1993: 39–40) which dragged the U.S. into the Persian Gulf war; public expressions of scepticism about the extent of Nazi genocide against Jews during the Second World War, and; allegations of Jewish complicity in the slave trade. Levin and McDevitt also discussed a number of manifestations of anti-Jewish incidents and crimes, and notably: an apparent rise in anti-Jewish incidents, including the sexual harassment of Jewish women, on U.S. college campuses in the early 1990s, and; the notorious episode in the Crown Heights area of Brooklyn in 1991 when longstanding hostility between the Black and Jewish communities erupted into violence on the streets in which an Australian rabbinical student was killed following the accidental killing of a Black child pedestrian by an Orthodox Jewish driver (1993: 138–39 and 188–89). Levin and McDevitt refer to the Anti-Defamation League's annual *Audit of Anti-Semitic Incidents* compiled since 1979 (1993: 200 and 206), the year after the National Socialist Party for America sued with the assistance of the American Civil Liberties Union to hold a demonstration in Skokie, Illinois (a town with a large Jewish population – of whom many were Holocaust survivors) (Gerstenfeld 2004: 23). However, in the absence of empirical study of anti-Jewish incidents at the time in the United States their observations were necessarily mostly informed by news media reports. In a later foundational work in the field of 'hate crime' studies, Jenness and Grattet (2001) provided some of the data compiled annually by the ADL, but as their work was primarily concerned with social movement formation around the problem of 'hate crime' rather than the problem itself, little analysis is offered about anti-Jewish incidents.

The longstanding conspiracy theories about Jewish power and Jewish influence in the United States over government and foreign policy, and the centrality of antisemitism to the ideologies of White supremacists, anti-state extremists and organised hate groups in the United States, provide key themes in later influential 'hate crimes' texts where anti-Jewish hostility is discussed (cf. Perry 2001). Possibly one of the most sustained discussions of these themes and their historical provenance is provided by Gerstenfeld (2004: 96, 104, 115, 124–25, 151–56). Commentary in these texts on anti-Jewish 'hate crime' necessarily relies on the FBI's Uniform Crime Report 'hate crime' data (which began to be collated following the passage of the 1990 Hate Crime Statistics Act) in which crimes against Jews are categorised as hate crimes on the basis of religion, and the ADL's annual audits of anti-semitic violence. However, it is difficult to appreciate the qualitative dimensions of such incidents from such data, and that certainly applies to trying to find clues about the motivations of offenders. Accordingly, Gerstenfeld noted that: 'Although there is ample literature on anti-Semitism, few studies have focused specifically on anti-Jewish hate crimes. Those that have are primarily the work of advocacy organizations such as the ADL rather than independent scholars. Therefore ... we do not know how common hate crime victimization is among Jews or how often it gets reported' (2004: 156).

In Jack Levin's later work on hate crime, when discussing the problem of antisemitism, he refers to the unique political context for some incidents against Jews – the Israel-Palestine crisis. Levin suggests that the conflict triggered a latent 'hate' against Jews:

> Hate can remain dormant in the culture, emerging without warning from the darkness in response to a threatening but enlightening episode. In October 2000, as conflict between Israelis and Palestinians began to reach a fever pitch, Jews around the world became targets of violence. In the United States alone, the number of anti-Semitic acts reached a peak, with some 259 incidents occurring during a 30-day period.
>
> (Levin, 2002: 14)

And in relation to such triggers, Gerstenfeld asked: 'Do events like September 11 and the Middle-East crisis really increase anti-Semitism, or do they merely serve as a vehicle for rationalizing anti-Semitism that already exists? These are only a few of the questions that remain unanswered' (2004: 156).

Among the leading hate crime texts in the United Kingdom, hate crimes against Jews are discussed fleetingly by Nathan Hall as an instance of 'religiously motivated offending' (Hall 2005: 57) and alternatively as 'faith hate' crime, alongside 'Islamophobia'. A more sustained discussion of 'religiously motivated hate crime' is provided by Neil Chakraborti and Jon Garland (2009: 36–54). Chakraborti and Garland cast 'antisemitism' as an example of 'religious intolerance', a 'faith-related' issue, involving 'attacks upon religious identity' and 'religious-based animosity'. Informed by, and echoing, Gerstenfeld's earlier discussion of antisemitic hate crime, Chakraborti and Garland briefly draw attention to 'confusion between anti-Zionism and anti-semitism'. They suggest that such confusion 'may be an especially telling factor behind the rise in levels of prejudice directed towards Jews.' Chakraborti and Garland explain that:

While those opposed to the basic proposition of Zionism – namely, support for a political movement to establish a national homeland for Jews in Palestine – should be distinguished from those who are opposed to Jewishness *per se* or who advocate the persecution of or discrimination against Jews, in practice the two positions may often become conflated. Consequently, Jewish people may commonly be the victims of attack where the perpetrator in fact has nothing against Jewishness, just the principles of Zionism.

(2009: 49)

To date, the scholarly 'hate crimes' literature has only offered short discussions of the problem of contemporary 'hate crimes' against Jews. However, they are a considerable step forward when compared with what it seems fair to describe as a lack of attention to antisemitism and anti-Jewish 'hate crimes' in the disciplines from which hate crime scholars have emerged.

## The problem of extremism and hate crimes against Jews

Given the questions posed about the perpetrators of 'hate crimes' against Jews in opening this essay, it is useful to progress to the questions about their characteristics and motives. The recent *Antisemitism Worldwide 2011* report produced by the Kantor Centre at Tel Aviv University provides some unequivocal answers to these questions. The report states that:

On the basis of eye witness reports and other evidence accumulated in recent years, perpetrators of antisemitic violence can be categorized roughly into two ethnic and ideological groups: young Islamists, and racists from the extreme right. They are not necessarily members of any specific organization, although they frequently identify with the ideology and goals of one or more extremist movements.

(Kantor Centre 2012: 13)

Likewise a recent working paper on antisemitism produced by the European Union Agency for Fundamental Rights (FRA 2012), which offers a review of data sources about antisemitic incidents, noted in a review of the country monitoring work of the European Commission against Racism and Intolerance (ECRI) that one conclusion that can be drawn is that: 'The main perpetrators of antisemitic incidents are neo-Nazis, sympathisers of the far right and far left, Muslim fundamentalists and the younger generation' (FRA 2012: 11).

For short-hand, such conclusions about the perpetrators of 'hate crimes' against Jews might be called the 'extremism thesis'. It is a thesis that has been prevalent on a number of occasions in the international policy literature in the last decade. One controversial contribution to this policy literature was a report published in 2003 commissioned from the Centre for Research on Antisemitism at the Technische Universität Berlin by the European Monitoring Centre on Racism and Xenophobia (EUMC) (now the European Agency for Fundamental Rights [FRA]). Informed by information provided by the EUMC's 15 national focal points of its Racism and Xenophobia Network (RAXEN) the report pointed to the culpability of extremists in relation to incidents against Jews but it also drew attention to the social exclusion encountered by young Muslims as providing a context for some of the violence:

> ... from the perpetrators identified, or at least identifiable with some certainty it can be concluded that the antisemitic incidents in the monitoring period were committed above all either by right-wing extremists or radical Islamists or young Muslims mostly of Arab descent, who are themselves potential victims of exclusion and racism.
>
> (Bergmann and Wetzel 2003: 7)

And specifically in relation to the culpability of Muslim youths, the report noted in the case of France, Belgium, the Netherlands and the United Kingdom that:

> The observers agree that these are disaffected young men who themselves are frequently targets of racist attacks, i.e. here the social problems of these migrant minorities are obviously an essential factor for their propensity to violence and susceptibility to anti-Semitism.
>
> (Bergmann and Wetzel 2003: 27)

Such attribution of culpability to Muslim youths, with the finger not only pointed at extremists, was controversial and was alleged to have been behind the EUMC's decision not to publish the report. For its part, the EUMC claimed that the research for the report was inadequate given that it covered a short monitoring period and commissioned a further report (EUMC 2004) to review evidence over a longer period. That second report was equivocal about whether Muslim youths had by then joined extreme right-wing offenders as the typical perpetrators of antisemitic crimes.[2]

## Portraits of antisemitic hate crime offenders

It would seem fair to note that few of the assertions in the policy literature about the perpetrators of 'hate crimes' against Jews are supported by the presentation of systematic research evidence, and they mostly rely upon observations that Arab-looking or Muslim youths were involved in some incidents and in other incidents Nazi-references were employed, and in some cases both of these. Unless offenders are apprehended, such evidence rests upon the testimony of victims' and witnesses' observations about the offender's ethnic appearance and recollections of what might have been said to them by the offender. As incidents will generally be disturbing and often traumatic for the victims, their testimony will inevitably be less than precise (CST 2012: 22).

While relying on the testimony of victims and witnesses to draw conclusions about the motives and characteristics of perpetrators can indeed be a less than reliable task, applying the label 'hate crime' to anti-Jewish crimes potentially confuses further rather than illuminates the matter about offenders. That is because as a notion, 'hate crime' perhaps conjures up an image of hate-fuelled individuals who consciously act out their hate in premeditated attacks. But given what was proposed at the beginning of this essay, this would arguably be a misconception. Most offenders that are known about do not seem to hate their victims. And most offenders that are known about are not specialist hate crime offenders, or even committed bigots. Practitioner experience in the UK and elsewhere in the case of racist crime suggests that many offenders are generalists who are involved in a variety of offending activity over time. Practitioner experience also suggests that 'hate crime' offenders' actions are fuelled by a variety of impulses – anger, resentment, frustration, retaliation, revenge, thrill-seeking or fun – rather than being solely, or even mostly, motivated by animus against their victim. And practitioner experience of working with hate crime offenders also suggests that many offenders have chaotic and disadvantaged lives and that such disadvantage often provides the context for their offending. The understandings that practitioners have developed are also echoed in the limited scholarly literature on 'hate crime' offenders (cf. Gadd and Dixon 2011: 51–76).

In short, from what is known about 'hate crime' offenders, albeit it must be acknowledged that the evidence is still limited, they seem in general to be much more like other offenders than unlike them in their characteristics and in the attitudes and beliefs they express. On occasion these attitudes are expressed as hostility or violence in situations of emotional arousal and threat. There is no single type of offender, of course. But the limited research evidence suggests that there is a tendency for offenders to be young males for whom violence and aggression are acceptable and normal modes of interaction and problem-solving, and the translation of hostility into action is often fuelled by a sense of grievance, perceived slights, or the dynamics of acting out in front of friends and peers.

But are the perpetrators of 'hate crimes' against Jews somehow different to what practitioner experience and the limited research on the matter suggests about many racist offenders? This question is particularly pertinent given that news media reporting of upsurges in the Israel-Palestine conflict uniquely provides the context for spikes in incidents against Jews and also given the long history of right-wing animus towards Jews. Unfortunately there is little publicly available information on the conviction by courts of anti-Jewish 'hate crimes' to properly inform the matter.

In the case of France, the FRA working paper notes that the National Consultative Commission on Human Rights' (Commission nationale consultative des droits de l'homme, CNCDH) 2011 annual report indicates that out of 129 violent antisemitic acts recorded that year, about one in seven 'could be imputed to persons of "Arab origin or Muslim confession"' and the

Nazi-card was played in about one in eight incidents 'mainly consisting of displaying swastikas'. Of the 260 antisemitic threats recorded, '15% related to neo-Nazi ideology, with another 14% imputable to persons of "Arab origin or Muslim confession"' (FRA 2012: 27).

FRA's working paper on antisemitism also provides a few anecdotal 'snapshots' of offenders. It is reported that in Denmark, for instance:

- On 2 April 2010, a man reported to the police that two 'Arabic men' had thrown stones at his dog, threatened to shoot him and made disparaging remarks about his Jewish background;
- On 1 May 2010, a Jewish man reported to the police that he had been hit in the face by two 'Arabic men' who had called him a 'Jewish pig'.

And in the case of Germany, it is reported that:

- During the night of 21 April 2011, three young adults between 18 and 20 years of age desecrated 30 gravestones with Nazi symbols in a Jewish cemetery in Essen (North-Rhine Westphalia);
- During the night of 25 August 2011, a group of 10 youths attacked a 15-year-old boy in the Jewish community of Stuttgart (Baden-Württemberg). Two of the youths, one a 12-year-old, kicked the boy in the head and stomach, calling him 'dirty Jew' (Scheiss Jude). The boy had to be hospitalised.

Unfortunately, beyond such anecdotal information in the policy literature there is little systematic and robust empirical research evidence to inform answers to the questions raised in this essay about the perpetrators of hate crimes against Jews. The 2005 study *Hate Crimes Against London's Jews* (Iganski, Kielinger and Paterson 2005) still stands therefore as a key source of research evidence especially given that there is a paucity of more recent scholarly analysis of the problem of 'hate crimes' against Jews. At a time when the 'extremism' thesis was being promoted in the policy literature, the study analysed London's Metropolitan Police Service crime reports of incidents flagged as 'antisemitic' to seek to develop and share understanding of the contexts for such incidents – which included seeking to determine the extent to which extremism might have been involved. The research team concluded early on that the motivating impulses in offenders' minds could not be determined from the information recorded in crime reports. However, it was also concluded that the situational contexts and dynamics of incidents recorded in the crime reports – in terms of the degree of apparent premeditation on the part of offenders and the circumstances in which the encounters between offenders and victims occurred – when considered in the light of other information about offenders such as words they used, or discourse conveyed by other means such as graffiti, along with any information about the visible characteristics of offenders reported by victims or eye-witnesses – could provide clues about offenders' motivating impulses. Upon applying such an approach to the analysis of records of reported antisemitic incidents, it could not be ruled out that offenders affiliated with extremist groups or supporting extremist ideologies were responsible for some of the incidents. However, there seemed to be little apparent evidence of extremism at work.

The researchers concluded in consultation with police and security specialists on extremism that extremist offenders would be more likely to be involved in premeditated violent attacks than other offenders. Such offenders were influentially characterised as 'mission offenders' by Levin and McDevitt in their analysis of hate crime records of the Boston, Massachusetts, Police Department (Levin and McDevitt 2002; see also McDevitt, Levin and Bennett 2002). On the basis of their research Levin and McDevitt concluded that mission offenders accounted for approximately only 5 per cent of the reported hate crimes they analysed. Informed by the methodology of Levin and McDevitt's research, the analysis of the Metropolitan Police Service records of antisemitic incidents similarly indicated that such mission offenders seemed to account for only a small proportion of reported incidents against Jews in London. Only about one in 12 incidents involved direct face-to-face interaction between offenders and victims in which the offenders had appeared to engineer the encounter. In over a quarter of the incidents analysed in the Metropolitan Police Service research, while clearly premeditated and engineered by the offenders, there was no face-to-face contact between offenders and victims, and such offenders were consequently characterised as 'indirect' mission offenders. The more recent FRA working paper provides some anecdotal examples of such incidents:

- On 1 December 2010 in Larnaca … an unknown perpetrator spray painted a Menorah – the symbol of Hanukkah – putting a swastika next to it (FRA 2012: 21).
- On 21 December 2010, a man of undefined religious affiliation reported to the police that a swastika had been drawn on his front door along with the following caption: 'We hate Jews.' (FRA 2012: 25).
- On 5 August 2011 in Levallois-Perret, graffiti of swastikas were found on the walls and grounds of the synagogue, along with a letter addressed to the rabbi (FRA 2012: 29).
- On 2 October 2011 in Gonesse in the Ile-de-France region, an advertising leaflet was found in the mailbox of the synagogue to which the following handwritten text was added: 'Death to Jews. Long live Palestine.' (FRA 2012: 29).
- During the night of 14 May 2011 in Volos, unidentified perpetrators painted antisemitic graffiti on the inside and outside walls and doors of the synagogue of the Jewish community (FRA 2012: 33).

The remainder of the reported incidents that were analysed in the Metropolitan Police Service research seemed to occur for a variety of other reasons and not in circumstances that were planned by the offenders. Among them, over one in six incidents seemed to involve the spur-of-the-moment, or opportunistic, targeting of victims where the offender took the opportunity to vent hostility against Jews. Again a number of such instances are provided in the more recent FRA working paper on antisemitism:

- On 4 April 2011, the *Tiroler Tageszeitung* reported that a young man who was wearing, visibly, a Star of David was attacked while sitting on a bus in Innsbruck by two men he thought were of Turkish origin. The young man was not himself Jewish but wore the Star of David as a show of his support for Israel. The aggressors, after punching the young man twice in the face, allegedly told him that 'Hitler should have finished the Jews off, Israelis are child murderers and Turkey will sweep Israel away' (FRA 2012: 15).
- On 1 March 2011 in Antwerp, two Orthodox Jewish men and an Orthodox Jewish woman were refused service upon entering a cafe. The bartender shouted 'No Jews!' at them and said that the cafe was closed although it was full of customers (FRA 2012: 19).

In other cases in the *Hate Crimes Against London's Jews* study, about one in seven of all incidents, the offenders and victims were already involved in some form of altercation, a commonplace conflict arising from the routine incivilities of everyday life, which then became aggravated by the offender who vented anti-Jewish bigotry in an apparent expressive act – perhaps after believing that a wrong had been inflicted upon them and their expressed antisemitism was a retaliation intended to hurt the victim in return.

The research showed that this pattern of victimisation was also the case in periods of peaks of recorded incidents associated with upsurges in the Israel-Palestine crisis. By comparing separate sub-samples of incidents from months where there were high, low and average rates of reported antisemitic incidents, the profile of the alleged offenders appeared to be largely similar across all months. Likewise, in considering the level of injury sustained by the victims of incidents as a possible indicator of whether there was a different intensity to the incidents in the peak months of reports, there were only negligible differences between high, average and low months. The suspects appeared to differ little too between the months in terms of their ethnic appearance. On the basis of information provided by victims and witnesses, 'White European' suspects accounted for the same proportions of suspects in the high and the low months, suggesting that Muslim youths – from London's Bangladeshi, Pakistani, Middle Eastern and African communities – were not significantly more likely to be represented among offenders when there was news media reporting of upsurges in the Israel-Palestine crisis.

However, the research did reveal a clearly discernible difference in the reported discourse of offenders between the high months of April and May 2002 and the other samples of incidents from the low and average months. In approximately one in five incidents in the 2002 peak there was evidence of anti-Israeli sentiment in the discourse of the offenders, and in some instances sentiment drawing more broadly on the Arab-Israeli conflict, compared with just less than one in 20 incidents in other periods with lower rates of reported victimisation. Some of the anti-Israeli sentiment manifest in incidents clearly constituted political criticism, albeit of a rather crude form. When directed at evidently political targets, it would arguably be difficult to characterise it as 'antisemitic' despite it being flagged as such in Metropolitan Police Service records, or as 'religiously aggravated'. For instance, in an incident that ostensibly involved clear political action and with a political target, a group of young people forced their way into the offices of the Israeli tourist board and sprayed the word 'Terrorists' in large black letters. In another recorded incident, anti-Israeli stickers were found on a number of lamp posts in Oxford Street. Given their location, they were clearly targeted at the general public, which would of course include Jewish shoppers in the area, although Jews were not specifically targeted.

But as was evident, recorded incidents against Jews which involved anti-Israel discourse were still only a minority of incidents even in the peak months. Many of the rest of the incidents conveyed an everyday visceral racism about Jews. Such findings suggest that arguably, the majority of incidents against Jews provide an indicator of the banality of antisemitism, of particular attitudes towards Jews: the type of intractable antisemitism which the early Zionist thinkers believed was interminable, the type of antisemitism for which the early Zionists believed there needed to be a Jewish homeland to provide a refuge. It is banal in that it is woven into the ideological and cultural structure which lies beneath the surface of everyday conscious cognition for many people. Particular attitudes about Jews rise to the surface for some people when the opportunity arises to express them.[3] For others, their rise to the surface is often triggered by a grievance, an irritation, a conflict, a frustration. For some people, such instances present a particular opportunity, or trigger a particular reflex, when a Jewish person is involved in the situation, and the research literature indicates that this is not dissimilar to the situational dynamics of 'hate crime' more generally. And there is little evidential basis, from the types of incidents against Jews discussed and the discourse used by offenders, that they might be cast as 'religiously aggravated' or 'faith hate' crimes. While religious symbols, such as the wearing of a kippah or the Star of David, for instance, might identify the person to be targeted as Jewish, offenders are arguably expressing a visceral racism against Jews rather than religious hatred. Even in incidents where synagogues are daubed with graffiti, or menorahs damaged, there is little evidence that it is the religious tenets of Judaism that are being targeted. Therefore, just as the notion of 'hate crime' is a misnomer in many instances, the notion of 'religiously aggravated' or 'faith hate' crime in the case of anti-Jewish incidents is a misleading misconception.

## How 'hate' hurts

Most victims of crime suffer some psychological and emotional trauma, and in the case of 'hate crime' a body of evidence has accumulated from research in a number of countries which has evidenced in-depth the harms and impacts felt by victims (for instance, for evidence from research carried out in Latvia see: Dzelme 2008; for Sweden see Tiby 2009; and for the UK see: Victim Support 2006). Research evidence also clearly indicates that on average victims of 'hate crime' are more likely than other victims to report such effects. Early research on the matter published in a number of studies across the 1990s began to illuminate the particular psychological and emotional impacts of 'hate crimes' (cf. Barnes and Ephross 1994; Hershberger and D'Augelli 1995; Otis and Skinner 1996). However, due to the design of the research concerning a lack of sufficient control and comparison with victims of parallel crimes (the same types of crime, but occurring for other reasons than the victim's identity), the findings were equivocal on the question of whether 'hate crimes' actually do hurt more. Towards the end of the 1990s Herek, Gillis and Cogan (1999) took a significant step forward by comparing a purposive sample of lesbians and gay men who had been victims of 'hate crime' with a sample who had been victimised on other grounds than their sexual identity. It was observed that the 'hate crime' victims recorded statistically significant higher scores on measures of depression, traumatic stress, and anger – although generalisation of the findings was limited by the use of purposive samples of 'hate crime' victims and victims of parallel crimes.

At the beginning of the last decade, one of the most comprehensive studies by that time on the psychological harms of 'hate crime' was conducted by Jack McDevitt and colleagues (McDevitt *et al.* 2001). The study involved a mail survey of a sample of victims of assaults reported to the Boston Police Department and victim advocacy agencies and included victims of both 'hate crime' and parallel crimes. Statistically significant differences between victims of 'hate crime' and victims of parallel crimes were observed on a number of measures of psychological post-victimisation impacts. 'Hate crime' victims reported stronger reactions on measures of depression, nervousness, lack of concentration, unintentional thinking about the incident, and thoughts of futility regarding their lives (McDevitt *et al.* 2001). The design of the study had some limitations, however, as McDevitt and colleagues acknowledged. Chiefly, a low response rate to the mail survey and the purposive nature and the sources of the sample potentially introduced selection bias.

These methodological limitations were later overcome by a secondary analysis of British Crime Survey data for England and Wales which showed that victims of racist crime were more likely, when compared with victims of parallel crime, to report feelings of 'shock', 'fear', 'depression', 'anxiety', 'panic attacks', 'loss of confidence' and 'feeling vulnerable' (Iganski 2008: 82, Table 4.2). The same pattern of difference between victims of racist crime and victims of parallel crime was shown to hold even when controlling for the type of crime experienced (Iganski 2008: 12–13, Tables 1.4 and 1.5). More recently, further analyses of British Crime Survey data have indicated that on average, all victims of 'hate crime' as a group are more likely to report a range of emotional impacts compared with victims of parallel crimes (Smith, Lader,

Hoare and Lau 2012: 22, Table 1.2) and that such differences hold even when controlling for crime type (Botcherby *et al.* 2011).

The psychological impacts upon victims of 'race-hate crime' are unfolded in depth by Kellina Craig-Henderson (2009) who suggests that while victims of crime in general are encouraged to 'take comfort in knowing that what happened to them could have happened to anyone', 'hate crime' victims come to recognise that what happened to them happened because of who they are. After an initial shock period this painful realisation will begin to sink in. And for victims of 'hate crime' from minority communities, this realisation will closely resonate with, and be compounded by, their knowledge of the stigmatised and marginalised status of their group, increasing their sense of alienation and 'feelings of deviancy'.

While it is likely that there would have been some Jewish respondents in the studies just briefly reviewed, none of the studies focused on Jewish victims specifically. In the case of such victims of 'hate crime' we might expect particular harms to be inflicted in particular circumstances, and especially when the Nazi-card is played against Jews in instances of verbal abuse, daubings and graffiti. The playing of the Nazi-card hurts by invoking painful collective memories for Jews and by using those memories against them. Deep wounds are scratched hard (Iganski and Sweiry 2009: 26). The depth of the consequences for the immediate victims, and for other Jews who come to hear about such incidents, are frequently captured in media reporting: in September 2012 'shock waves' were reportedly sent through Germany's Jewish community by news of a violent attack in daylight against a Rabbi on a Berlin street;[4] in October 2012, following acts of desecration at a Jewish cemetery in Avignon, the Jewish community was reported to be 'living in a state of constant tension and uncertainty caused by antisemitic incidents';[5] and an incident in Auckland, New Zealand in October 2012, in which Jewish graves were 'spray-painted with large black swastikas or inscriptions reading "f*** Israel" and "don't f*** with us"', was branded as 'very alarming' by a senior rabbi from the Auckland Hebrew Congregation.[6] While recognising that many types of crime have a 'ripple effect' in terms of their impacts (Noelle 2001, 2009), one 'hate crimes' scholar, Phyllis Gerstenfeld, has written that 'I am Jewish, and when I have read about a synagogue having been spray-painted with swastikas, it has had an emotional impact on me that ordinary graffiti would not have had' (Gerstenfeld 2004: 18).

## Against 'hate crime'

In opening this essay, it was proposed that a conceptual malady afflicts the heart of the field of 'hate crime' studies. It was argued that the very notion of 'hate crime' is fundamentally flawed as most so-called 'hate crime' offenders do not hate their victims, but instead among a variety of impulses and motivations for their actions, many offenders emotionally express sentiments of prejudice that are intricately woven into the socio-cultural fabric rather than manifest persistent and enduring sentiments of hatred. The essay has attempted to offer a case study of this phenomenon by conceptualising anti-Jewish 'hate crime' in the context of the banalisation of particular, and well known, sentiments about Jews.

The challenge presented by the infirmity of the notion of 'hate crime' is not only conceptual. There are also political and legal challenges. At the core of these challenges is the problem that the term 'hate crime' homogenises offenders into a single category of 'haters'. This is highly problematic for a number of reasons:

- The diversity of impulses and motivations behind offenders' actions are masked by the conceptual foregrounding of 'hatred'. Offenders are effectively dehumanised, stripped of their social and emotional deficits, their disadvantages, frailties, weaknesses and needs, which often provide the context for their offending, and instead they are pathologised as being beyond reason and redemption.
- Offenders' impulses are dramatised and marginalised. Hatred is an extreme sentiment. It is hardly surprising, therefore, that offenders might be regarded as extremists, an aberration, confined to the margins of society. This is arguably illustrated by the tendency that has been in evidence, as discussed in this essay, to label the perpetrators of 'hate crimes' against Jews as 'extremists'. It might be argued that it is sound reasoning to posit that after the experience of genocidal antisemitism in Europe in the twentieth century, it must only be extremists, those beyond reason, who can continue to hold and express anti-Jewish sentiment. However, such reasoning about the characteristics of offenders cannot be sustained on the basis of the empirical evidence about anti-Jewish incidents which has been unfolded in this essay.
- A retributive response is encouraged towards offenders. In a number of jurisdictions the criminal law provides for harsher penalties in cases of racially and religiously aggravated crimes (which include anti-Jewish crimes) compared with parallel crimes. In Europe, the European Council (2008) Framework Decision on 'combatting forms and expressions of racism and xenophobia by means of criminal law' seeks to harmonise the criminalisation of racially motivated conduct by specifying that: 'Member States shall take the necessary measures to ensure that racist and xenophobic motivation is considered an aggravating circumstance, or, alternatively that such motivation may be taken into consideration by the courts in the determination of the penalties.' The wielding of greater punishment in cases of so-called 'hate crimes' is an acknowledgement of the greater hurts inflicted by such crimes and it applies the liberal principle of providing offenders with the just deserts for their actions. But it also indicates that the politics of retribution has prevailed over movements to rehabilitate 'hate crime' offenders.

The provenance of the notion of 'hate crime', and the legislative response to the problem, can be traced to the activism of an anti-hate crimes movement which emerged in the United States in the 1960s. Civil rights movements coupled with victims' rights movements to construct 'hate crime' as a contemporary social problem (Jenness and Grattet 2001: 17ff). A similar social movement has been in evidence in the UK in recent years in the construction of disablist 'hate crime' as particularly requiring a punitive response. The notion of 'hate crime' has served as a powerful banner for such movements behind which have rallied coalitions of civil society and governmental actors seeking to challenge discriminatory violence and crimes.

In the context of the politics of recognition for the rights and needs of 'hate crime' victims, there is a sensitive political challenge to be encountered when advocating recognition of the needs of offenders and recognition of the value of alternative interventions beyond the courts. A legal challenge lies in the advocacy of flexibility in the management of hate crime offenders. It is a challenge which requires an acknowledgement of the limitations of the courts in reducing re-offending and recognition of the potential effectiveness of non-punitive interventions. Some such innovative interventions have been taken with the perpetrators of anti-Jewish incidents. In a demonstration in Amsterdam in January 2009 against Israeli military actions in Gaza, a number of young males, some of whom were minors, were arrested for carrying a banner with depictions of mutilated and dead Palestinian children with a swastika and Star of David superimposed on them. Some of the young men were arrested after chanting the slogan 'Hamas, Hamas, all Jews should be gassed' during a minute's silence declared by the organisers. While the public prosecutor demanded a fine for the adults involved, an alternative intervention was proposed and subsequently adopted for the offending boys (van der Geest 2009). With the support of the Anne Frank Foundation, they were taken on a guided tour of the Anne Frank House in Amsterdam and were required to write an assignment related to the visit which was submitted to the public prosecutor and the Council for the Protection of the Child. The aim was for the boys to begin to appreciate the seriousness and the consequences of antisemitism. In another innovation, a restorative justice partnership between Greater Manchester Police in England, and the Community Security Trust along with the local Jewish community, was launched in 2011. A community advocate of the scheme proposed that the 'concept of restorative justice whereby restitution is coupled with remorse and a plea for forgiveness is basic to Jewish law. There cannot be closure for any crime against the person whether verbal or physical or for any act of damage to a person's property or reputation without a genuine regret for one's actions and a sincere apology to the victim' (CST 2011).

Practitioners working with offenders report that sometimes the perpetrators of racially aggravated crimes deny that they are 'racist' (this has been echoed in the scholarly literature, cf. Smith, Ray and Wastell 2002). Accepting such a claim might be a difficult challenge for some, and especially those who are deeply committed to advocating for victims' rights. A perhaps understandable inclination might be to condemn offenders and label their defensiveness as 'denial'. However, acceptance that it might be a genuinely held view of many offenders, and the adoption of a non-judgemental attitude, opens up an opportunity for working with them (Lindsay and Danner 2008). Some practitioners believe that early intervention which helps offenders develop insight into the consequences of their acts and fosters empathy for victims might potentially inhibit re-offending more effectively than would criminal prosecution. While it would be fair to argue that such a hypothesis has yet to be adequately tested, it seems to be a humanistic principle for the management of offenders and if effective it offers an alternative means to achieve social justice than solely retribution by the courts.

## Notes

1  The arguments offered in this essay were tested in a number of presentations: 'The concept and definition of "hate crime" in relation to Jews', symposium on Defining and Conceptualising Antisemitism. Institutions and the Law, Pears Institute for the Study of Antisemitism, Birkbeck, University of London, 28 September 2012; 'Global Antisemitism', Global Racisms Conference, University of Leeds, 5 October 2012, and; 'From the extreme to the everyday: understanding racist offenders', Lancashire Constabulary Symposium on Extremism and Radicalisation, 14 November 2012. The author is very grateful for the questions, debate, and the ideas which ensued and have informed the thinking offered in this essay.
  The author is also grateful to Spiridoula Lagou for research assistance provided for the preparation of this essay.
2  For a discussion of the controversy and this episode of the 'extremism thesis' see Iganski 2009: 138–41.
3  The author of this essay was reminded about the banality of antisemitism while reading through a final draft of the text on a train journey from Lancaster to London in December 2012. One of a group of men in the carriage, who were drinking beer at breakfast time, took out his sandwich and announced to his travelling companions that he had a 'kosher special', 'roast rabbi with piccalilli'. His announcement was met with howls of laughter from others in the group.
4  www.icare.to/articleHC.php?id=40984&lang=en.
5  http://alephprd.tau.ac.il/F/B58XYC6KGRPI5QBEVGHS1KIEMYCB9EG49BSGI SLKR2GM226NR1–15131?func=direct&local_base=ASMLB&doc_number=0002 40402.
6  www.kantorcenter.tau.ac.il/jewish-graves-desecrated-new-zealand.

## References

Avnery, U. (2002) 'Manufacturing Antisemites', *Haaretz*, 28 September 2002.
Barnes, A. and Ephross, P. H. (1994) 'The impact of hate violence on victims – emotional and behavioural responses to attacks', *Social Work*, 39 (3): 247–51.
Bergmann, W. and Wetzel, J. (2003). *Manifestations of Anti-Semitism in the European Union*. First Semester 2002, Synthesis Report on behalf of the European Monitoring Centre on Racism and Xenophobia. Berlin, Germany: Zentrum für Anti-Semitismusforschung/ Center for Research on Anti-Semitism, Technische Universität Berlin.
Botcherby, S., Glen, F., Iganski, P., Jochelson, K. and Lagou, S. (2011) *Equality Groups' Perceptions and Experience of Crime: Analysis of the British Crime Survey 2007–08, 2008–09 and 2009–10*. Manchester: Equality and Human Rights Commission.

Camus, J. Y. (2010) *Racist Violence in France*. Brussels: European Network Against Racism/Open Society Foundations.

Chakraborti, N. and Garland, J. (2009) *Hate Crime. Impact, Causes and Responses*. London: Sage.

Cohn-Sherbok, D. (2006) *The Paradox of Anti-Semitism*. London: Continuum.

Community Security Trust (CST) (2011) 'CST supporting Restorative Justice in Manchester', http://blog.thecst.org.uk/?p=2456.

——(2012) *Antisemitic Incidents Report 2011*. London: Community Security Trust.

Craig-Henderson, K. (2009) 'The psychological harms of hate: implications and interventions', in P. Iganski (ed.) *Hate Crimes. The Consequences of Hate Crimes*. Westport, CT: Praeger.

Dzelme, I. (2008) *Psychological Effects of Hate Crime*. Riga: Latvian Centre for Human Rights.

European Commission against Racism and Intolerance (ECRI) (2010) Annual Report on ECRI's Activities covering the period from 1st January to 31st December 2009. Strasburg: ECRI.

European Council (2008) Council Framework Decision 2008/913/JHA of 28 November 2008 on combating certain forms and expressions of racism and xenophobia by means of criminal law, http://eurlex.europa.eu/LexUriServ/LexUriServ.do?uri=OJ:L:2008:328:0055:0058:EN:PDF.

European Network Against Racism (ENAR) (2009) *Racism in Europe. ENAR Shadow Report 2008*. Brussels: ENAR.

European Union Agency for Fundamental Rights (FRA) (2010) *Annual Report 2010*. Vienna: FRA.

——(2012) *Antisemitism. Summary Overview of the Situation in the European Union 2001–2011*. Working paper, June 2012. Vienna: FRA.

European Union Monitoring Centre (EUMC) (2004) *Manifestations of Anti-Semitism in the EU 2002–2003*. Vienna: EUMC.

Finkelstein, N. G. (2005) *Beyond Hutzpah. On the Misuse of Anti-Semitism and the Abuse of History*. London: Verso.

Gadd, D. and Dixon, W. (2011) *Losing the Race. Thinking Psychosocially about Racially Motivated Crime*. London: Karnac Books.

Gerstenfeld, P. B. (2004) *Hate Crimes. Causes, Controls and Controversies*. Thousand Oaks, CA: Sage.

Hall, N. (2005) *Hate Crime*. Cullompton: Willan.

Herek, G. M., Gillis, J. R. and Cogan, J. C. (1999) 'Psychological sequelae of hate-crime victimization among lesbian, gay, and bisexual adults', *Journal of Consulting and Clinical Psychology*, 67 (6): 945–51.

Hershberger, S. L. and D'Augelli, A. R. (1995) 'The impact of victimization on the mental health and suicidality of lesbian, gay, and bisexual youth, *Developmental Psychology*, 31: 65–74.

Iganski, P. (2008) *Hate Crime and the City*. Bristol: Policy Press.

——(2009) 'The banality of anti-Jewish "hate crime"', in R. Blazak (ed.) *Hate Crimes. Hate Crime Offenders*. Westport, CT: Praeger.

——(2011) *Racist Violence in Europe*. Brussels: European Network Against Racism/Open Society Foundations.

Iganski, P., Kielinger, V. and Paterson, S. (2005) *Hate Crimes Against London's Jews*. London: Institute for Jewish Policy Research/Metropolitan Police Service.

Iganski, P. and Sweiry, A. (2009) *Understanding and Addressing the 'Nazi Card'.
Intervening Against Antisemitic Discourse.* London: European Institute for the Study
of Contemporary Antisemitism.

Jenness, V. and Grattet, R. (2001) *Making Hate a Crime. From Social Movement to
Law Enforcement.* New York: Russell Sage Foundation.

Kantor Centre (2012) *Antisemitism Worldwide 2011.* Tel Aviv: Kantor Centre for the
Study of Contemporary European Jewry.

Klug, B. (2003) 'The collective Jew: Israel and the new antisemitism', *Patterns of
Prejudice,* 37 (2): 117–38.

Levin, J. (2002) *The Violence of Hate. Confronting Racism, Anti-Semitism, and other
Forms of Bigotry.* Boston, MA: Allyn and Bacon.

Levin, J. and McDevitt, J. (1993) *Hate Crimes. The Rising Tide of Bigotry and
Bloodshed.* New York: Plenum.

——(2002) *Hate Crimes Revisited: America's War against those who are Different.*
Boulder, CO: Westview Press.

Lim, H. A. (2009) 'Beyond the immediate victim: understanding hate crimes as message crimes', in P. Iganski (ed.) *Hate Crimes (Volume 2). The Consequences of Hate
Crimes.* Westport, CT: Praeger, 107–22.

Lindsay, T. and Danner, S. (2008) 'Accepting the unacceptable: the concept of acceptance in work with perpetrators of hate crime', *European Journal of Social Work,* 11
(1): 43–56.

McDevitt, J., Balboni, J., Garcia, L. and Gu, J. (2001) 'Consequences for victims: a
comparison of bias and non-bias motivated assaults', *American Behavioral Scientist,*
45 (4): 697–713.

McDevitt, J., Levin, J. and Bennett, S. (2002) 'Hate crime offenders: an expanded
typology', *Journal of Social Issues,* 58 (2): 303–18.

Noelle, M. (2001) 'The ripple effect of the Matthew Shepard Murder: impact on the
assumptive worlds of members of the targeted group', *American Behavioral Scientist,*
46 (1): 27–50.

——(2009) 'The psychological and social effects of antibisexual, antigay, and antilesbian
violence and harassment', in P. Iganski (ed.) *Hate Crimes (Volume 2). The
Consequences of Hate Crimes.* Westport, CT: Praeger, 73–105.

Otis, M. D. and Skinner, W. F. (1996) 'The prevalence of victimization and its effect on
mental well-being among lesbian and gay people', *Journal of Homosexuality,* 30: 93–122.

Perry, B. (2001) *In the Name of Hate. Understanding Hate Crime.* New York: Routledge.

Smith, D., Ray, L. and Wastell, L. (2002) 'Racist violence and probation practice',
*Probation Journal,* 49 (1): 3–9.

Smith, K., Lader, D., Hoare, J. and Lau, I. (2012) *Hate Crime, Cyber Security and the
Experience of Crime among Children: Findings from the 2010/11 British Crime
Survey.* London: Home Office.

Tiby, E. (2009) 'Homophobic hate crimes in Sweden: questions and consequences', in
P. Iganski (ed.) *Hate Crimes. The Consequences of Hate Crimes.* Westport, CT:
Praeger, 31–48.

van der Geest, T. (2009) 'Anne Frank als alternatief. Een nieuwe leerstraf?', *Oppor-
tuun,* 15 (5): 6–8.

Victim Support (2006) *Crime and Prejudice. The Support Needs of Victims of Hate
Crime: A Research Report.* London: Victim Support.

# 3   Negotiating identities

## Ethnicity, religion and social cohesion in London and Bradford

*Colin Webster*

### Introduction

The British prime minister's recent criticisms of supposed 'state multi-culturalism' as a source of separation between ethnic, cultural and faith groups and as a threat to community cohesion and shared national identity are disingenuous.[1] David Cameron stated that 'Under the doctrine of state multiculturalism, we have encouraged different cultures to live separate lives, apart from each other and apart from the mainstream' (Cameron 2011). His pronouncement that 'multiculturalism' as a state endorsed policy governing ethnic and religious relations in Britain in a way that encourages segregation is not new. Previous British governments too set themselves against a policy of 'separatist' multiculturalism in favour of the integration of cultures and values around 'one nation' (Parekh 2000; Cantle 2001, 2004). Rather, the reason occasioning this repeated charge is its connotation of a pervasive obsession with the vulnerability of young Muslims as a group to 'Islamist extremism', as evidenced in Cameron's speech. According to this perspective the worry is of isolation, of segregation, of a lack of contact, interaction and understanding between different faith and ethnic groups. The key issue explored in this chapter then is whether these worries are justified and to understand and draw together evidence about them. A supplementary aim is to attempt to bring clarity to the often muddled theoretical and conceptual thinking about social cohesion and the nature and role of religion in contributing to cohesion.

The chapter draws on the findings of the Youth On Religion (YOR) study[2] (Madge *et al.* 2013) about the meaning of religion and religious identity among young people living in religiously and ethnically contrasting places – the city of Bradford in West Yorkshire and the London Boroughs of Hilling-don and Newham. Among other questions the study asked about young people's perceptions of their own religious identity, how important religion is to them, and 'What can young people, schools/colleges and the government do to make sure that people from different religions get on well together?' In asking these questions we sought young people's views about, and experiences of, contact and understanding between people of different ethnicity and religion within their neighbourhoods and more generally. This chapter focuses on some of the implications of their answers for personal safety and neighbourhood relations.

## Cohesion and criminology

One way of thinking about the relevance of religion and cohesion to criminological concerns is through young people's perceptions of their safety and local order in multi-faith and multi-ethnic situations, which we discuss in the final section before concluding. Here, and as will be shown, religion and cohesion are intimately linked to the problem of order. Another is that the criminological study of community, disorder and crime, hinges upon the theme of declining community and yearning for renewal underlying community cohesion discourse. With its roots in the Judeo-Christian tradition, the concept of social cohesion informs and is informed by a sociological tradition arguing that large population size, density, and ethnic heterogeneity were socially disintegrative features that characterised rapidly changing cities (Wirth 1938). This old language of 'social disorganisation', crime and disorder posited that social ties bound 'collective civic engagement', and countered disorder. Alternatively, dense personal neighbourhood ties may *both* inhibit *and* generate crime and disorder. So, although dense local ties do promote social cohesion, they simultaneously foster crime (Sampson 2012). These negative *and* positive consequences of dense social ties questioned the supposed benefits of social or community cohesion.

Sampson (2012) has shown how social control is a major source of variation in crime rates and general wellbeing across and within neighbourhoods. Cohesion and control depends on some level of working trust (shared expectations) and social interaction and the capacity of residents to exercise informal social control. Providing a person perceives trust and infers shared expectations about public behaviour people don't actually have to know one another for there to be cohesion. Sampson (2012) concludes that in communities that are otherwise similar in composition, those with higher levels of cohesion and control exhibit lower rates and fear of crime and disorder. Concentrated disadvantage and segregation between and within neighbourhoods however, isolate minority and immigrant groups. Identity comes particularly to the fore whenever people become uncertain about where they belong, and how to go on in each other's presence (Bauman 2001). Community cohesion would seem to be inextricably linked to the dynamics and negotiation of identity, sometimes negatively in community cohesion policy that distrusts what it perceives as overly strong identifications with ethnic, religious and other groups which cause conflict and the wrong sorts of solidarities (Wetherell *et al.* 2007).

Drawing together some of the theoretical discussion and data presented below, the role that faith, race and ethnicity play in the public life of young people in face-to-face contact with each other in a range of settings from the mundane to the unsettling, will be a main focus. We take the *idea* of social cohesion seriously and wish to give it substance. Shorn of its premature dismissal of the facts of multicultural diversity, social cohesion as a major source of public order needs to be recognised. Goffman (2010 [1971]) has shown in his microstudies of public order, that although normally we can rely on unremarkable, predictable and routine exchanges between strangers, when this sense of normality is made fragile and trust is broken we become aware of our own vulnerabilities. At such times the processes whereby social order is negotiated rather than imposed come to the fore. This is shown many times in what young people told us about their everyday encounters with diversity, encounters they on the whole relished and celebrated. Some disagreed with and distrusted identity-based conflict and segregation while a few were actively engaged in this sort of behaviour. The prevailing discourse however, was of what we call 'liberal individualism' (Madge *et al.* 2013). By 'liberal individualism' is meant identity orientated to a self-reliant emphasis on personal choice and action, human rights, human agency, equality and respect for the positions of others, and importantly in our context more accepting of the rights of faith and ethnic groups to self-expression within the framework of a shared state.

They lived with 'hyperdiversity' mostly comparatively comfortably or rather, though this could also mean living fairly segregated lives. The pressure points at which this negotiated order became fragile and identity vulnerable were around a complex association between visible race and faith. At the level of their everyday encounters with race and religion, awareness, tolerance and some understanding of religious difference seemed to serve as a sort of etiquette easing the conduct of relations in public. Richard Sennett's (2012: 221) study of the ritual and politics of co-operation and community points to the crucial role that 'everyday diplomacy' plays in dealing with 'people they don't understand, can't relate to or are in conflict with …' because '… in all cultures people learn how to relate to one another through deploying tact or giving hints, while avoiding blunt statement.' Durkheim's (2001) discussion of rites and rituals found in religion, in which the former involves homage and close interchange and the latter violation and avoidance, can be likened to Goffman's (2010) observation that rites are a central organising aspect of public order. He goes on to argue that local order is maintained, provided for and ensured by individuals maintaining the 'right relationship' to universal norms of interaction such as respecting 'personal space', 'taking turns' in receiving a benefit, 'summoning', respecting privacy as well as territorial claims and 'boundary markers'. Conversely, social order in everyday relations in public can be threatened through various sorts of 'violations' and 'territorial offences'.

## Studying religion

Unlike the study of race and ethnic relations the study of religion – whether as an aspect of ethnicity or cohesion or more generally – is comparatively neglected. Because of this neglect some rudiments of the sociological study of religion are brought to the reader's attention here to introduce its importance for understanding ethnicity, cohesion and identity in multicultural settings. This sort of study is about the relationship of the individual to society ('negotiating identities'), how this relationship is linked to the possibilities of social and community cohesion, and how cohesion is intrinsically about the problem of order, i.e. what unites and divides society. The specific issue of social order and its connection to cohesion and religion is the main thread running through this chapter. By the 'problem of order' is meant how human beings manage to create regular and recurrent patterns of interaction with one another, and more particularly what motivates them to interact and achieve consensus on common goals. According to Wrong (1994) the problem of order merges into the issue of the relations between the individual and society and cannot ignore the processes by which human nature is formed through contacts with other cultures, or patterns of belief and symbolic expression. This chapter then contributes theoretically and empirically informed debates about cohesion that move beyond a previous sole concern with whether people from different ethnic or religious backgrounds get on or not – whether they integrate or segregate – to its underpinning in the problem of order. The often close interrelationships between ethnic, cultural and local identities have been joined by a growing interest in religious or faith-based identities, while refocusing interest on 'interactive multiculturalism' (Parekh 2005a, 2005b) and 'interculturalism' (Cantle 2008, 2012), discussed later. In particular, drawing from the sociology of religion, the role that religious identity plays in how members of ethnic groups negotiate, construct and maintain social and moral order (Berger 1967), while sociological theory has long been concerned with the problem of personal existence and the negotiation of identity in society of which the social form of religion was a key element (Luckmann 1967).

The importance of religious identity for cohesion is found in the fundamentally social or group nature of religion. According to Durkheim (2001) 'sociability should be made the determining cause of religious sentiment' rather than individual, private or personal belief.[3] In helping its adherents make sense of the meaning of the world it is the *social* nature of religion that binds each individual to his and her fellow-citizens and it is this social sentiment that is most manifest within community settings and day-to-day relationships, that 'include the sentiments of honour, respect, affection and fear which we may feel towards one another' (Giddens 1972: 219). Conventional understandings of religious beliefs and practices tend to be based on the notion that they are individually held by all the members of the group. Rather, it is that they unify and bind members in a common, single 'moral community', and it this collective and social dimension to religion that is important for cohesion as it 'expresses a tenuous unity already there and then enhances it' (Introduction, Durkeim, 2010: xx). This is not of course to deny religion's more commonly acknowledged transcendent properties connected to the sacred and profane (Durkheim 2001: 46), nor to deny the subjective experience of religion and the nature of different religious beliefs, but to recognise the common features religion may bring across these differences (Weber 1978). Religiosity is a bulwark and security against excessive and isolated individualism. Indeed, through regularly repeated common acts and rituals (perhaps evoking feelings of inner peace, serenity and security) religion expresses collective ideals. The paradox of religiosity is that while transcendent feelings become individualised they at the same time show something essentially social – a grasp of society and social relations.

These classical sociological views arguing that religion has a key role in understanding society have been lost in a narrow, parochial concern with the decline of religious institutions. Religious decline (in Europe at least) assumed the identification of church and religion so that the shrinking reach of the churches was taken as proxy for the decline of religion in modern societies. This prognosis was reinforced by ignoring the 'subjective' aspects of religiosity. Simply pointing to the decline in church attendance ignored how religiosity (a wider sentiment than religious practice) continued to locate the individual in society, integrate the routine meanings of everyday life and legitimise its crises, and offered 'transcendent', overarching structures of shared meaning (Luckmann 1967). Today, a resurgent and fierce debate about the status and meaning of religious values and identity within social philosophy and ethics also goes to the heart of the nature of ethnic as well as religious identity. Writers such as Alain Badiou (2001) and Terry Eagleton (2009, 2010) are once again raising important questions about the universal versus contingent nature of religious and cultural values and beliefs, specifically, whether the existence of universal values can be denied in the name of cultural difference and secularity, and whether moral values rather than merely customs and beliefs can really be said to fundamentally differ between ethnicities. Eagleton (2009: 152) argues that they cannot:

> The fundamental moral values of the average Muslim dentist who migrates to Britain are much the same as those of an English-born plumber ... They may well have different customs and beliefs: but what is striking is the vast extent of common ground between them on the question of what it is to live well.

## Resurgent religion?

Beyond the confines of institutional analysis and secularisation theory, the study of religion returns us to questions about the social origin of self and the relationship between society and individual. Renewed interest in the study of religious identity in part reflects a popular belief that religiosity is resurgent, especially outside Europe but also among some young people in western societies. Various general reasons for this claimed resurgence of religion as an aspect of identity and group conflict have been proffered. First, that modernity undermines taken-for-granted certainties; second, the imposition of an elite, metropolitan secularity is resented by many; third, human existence bereft of transcendence is an impoverished and finally untenable condition (Berger 1999). At this level of generality evidence pointing one way or another is difficult to establish. The studies there are add complexity and confound any simple conclusions about resurgent religiosity versus secularisation. Findings tend to be paradoxical and offer the conclusion that there is qualitatively and quantitatively both more and less religiosity in western societies across groups. For example, Putnam and Campbell's (2010) large survey of religion and public life in the United States shows that there is secularisation *and* resurgence, religious polarisation *and* pluralism taking place at the same time in America. Importantly, for our findings, this resurgence is taking place most among minorities and secularism most among the young. There is increasing polarisation along religious lines with the highly religious at one pole, and the avowedly secular at the other. The co-existence of polarisation and pluralism is explained in part by growing ethnic and racial diversity while America's high religiosity is in sharp contrast to low religiosity in Britain. Generally, the linkage between ethnic and religious identification is strong and growing in the United States. Putnam and Campbell (2010: 160) describe generational changes in religiosity using the terms 'switching, matching, and mixing' to convey the increasingly likelihood that individuals now choose their religious affiliations and beliefs rather than following their parents' religious commitments.

In terms of the role religion plays in cohesion, religiously based conflict in the US is muted, religious bridging through friendships is common and the effects of social contact are greater levels of tolerance and acceptance both towards their own diverse social networks and towards people of different or no religion generally. This – the largest recent US study of its kind – concluded that 'geographic segregation by religion has largely ended, while social segregation along religious lines is also mostly a thing of the past' (Putnam and Campbell 2010: 550). These findings are not generally replicated in our London and Bradford study, particularly Bradford where segregation is far from being a thing of the past. This potentially negative ethnic and religious aspect of identity for cohesion also retains its resonance in public and political debate. This has more to do with a rise of interest *in* the influence of religion on politics than it has to do with a possible resurgence *of* religiosity *per se*. In particular, it seems, in the supposed role assigned to Muslims and Islam maintaining community cohesion and social order while at the same time standing accused of fomenting fragmenting disorder (Thomas 2011). Much of the source of these confusing positions among politicians and policy makers that wish to distinguish radical Islamism from Islam has sprung from the radical Right of the political spectrum.

These concerns go beyond the possibilities of terrorist attacks resulting from the 9/11 Wars (Burke 2011) to the 'unprecedented scale of recent immigration' said to pose a severe threat to the identity and integrity of European societies, and in particular the threat posed by Muslims because Islam is deemed inassimilable to European societies (Caldwell 2009). A well known version of this thesis is Caldwell's *Reflections on the Revolution in Europe* in which he argues that a withdrawal from an initial and new 'partial embrace' of national identity to religious identity has occurred within later generations of young Muslim people in European societies. Islam is painted as a 'hyper-identity' taking precedence over, and dominating other aspects of identity such that 'Europe was not dealing with an ordinary immigration problem at all, but with an adversary culture' (2009: 139). It is in the context of these sorts of ethnocentric arguments that a 'religious resurgence' and advancing segregation is said to be taking place through cultural mores and traditions forbidding interethnic marriage, encouraging divisive dress codes, and opposing the relativistic and hedonist host culture. In short, Islamic and European culture appears incompatible bordering on mutual hostility. A similar sort of argument appears at the more mundane level of whether faith schools in Britain are divisive for, or agents of, community cohesion (Conway 2009). His ethnocentric conclusion was there is a need for assimilation and acculturation at a fundamental level of existing immigrants and a severe restriction of new immigration and that faith schools teach shared nationality. Interestingly, and by contrast, the young people in our study – of all faiths and none – seemed unequivocal in their views that faith schools discouraged religious and ethnic mixing, which they saw negatively. Compare this to the previous and current government's policies that have seen a large growth in the number of faith schools.[4] As Cantle (2012: 123–24) states:

> The large proportion of faith schools also exacerbates this trend [towards separate educational experiences] and the UK government has recently developed new policies that have served to increase the number and range of faith schools.

How odd that governments otherwise committed to cohesion are so busily encouraging a 'resurgent' religiosity in schooling.

## Social cohesion and the turn from 'race' to religion

The question 'What accounts for social cohesion?' is perhaps the fundamental, obvious and necessary starting point for social theory itself. For us cohesion is about the problem of how social and moral order is accomplished, social integration achieved, and whether societies become divided or united, albeit seen at the level of neighbourhoods in our study. According to Wrong (1994: 3) the problem of order becomes resolved in everyday associations that maintain regular social life rather than there being only minimal and occasional contacts. These associations however are underpinned by certain universal aspects of moral conduct and the existence of moral rules.

Cohesion concerns that once focused on ethnicity and race have increasingly focused on the role of religious identity as a source of conflict and division.

Further to the reasons outlined above, Cantle (2008: 17) notes that the turn from 'racism' to 'the same dogma' of a belief in the superiority of a particular faith, ethnicity 'or some other identifiable group characteristic' rests on 'the same unfounded and irrational belief systems.' According to Cantle (2012: 49–50) however:

> The transposition to faith has, to some extent, been no more than a continuation of the racial vilification [of the past], by using faith as a proxy for race in which the Muslim communities bear the brunt of the attacks by the Far Right and where Muslims are readily identified as a visible and largely non-White minority and as 'others'.

For Cantle, the supposed problem of a lack of community cohesion is that much legislation over the last fifty years has been devoted to ensuring equal opportunities, or preventing discrimination, while ignoring the more urgent task of changing attitudes and values. Thus legislation has been of limited effect with racism and religious bigotry simply either rising or falling depending on particular conditions and factors but the influence of these remains. For Cantle (2008: 18), the solution to racism and bigotry found in segregation is much greater 'cross cultural contact', understood as 'natural inter-group contact in the course of daily life'. Other writers have shared Cantle's early and influential claims (2001, 2004) that there is a 'crisis' in community cohesion accompanied by growing 'self-segregation' between ethnic and religious groups (Flint and Robinson 2008) without there being convincing evidence that segregation on the basis of ethnicity rather than class is actually chosen or taking place in British cities (Finney and Simpson 2009).

Consistent with the starting point of this chapter, Burnett (2008: 35) in his discussion of community cohesion in Bradford argues that the 'community cohesion agenda' marks a shift in the governance of race relations, from the values of multiculturalism in which different cultural legacies are encouraged to prosper side by side, to the assimilation and integration of different cultural traditions and ethnicity to 'a set of core British values'. Burnett (2008: 35) suggests this nationalist notion of citizenship – predicated upon an essentially racialised emphasis on culture and identity – has to be understood in the context of a climate of hostility towards Muslims said to pose a threat to 'national security, stability and identity'. At the same time while being seen as part of the problem, religion and religious identity are simultaneously seen as part of the solution, as source of *both* conflict *and* 'strong communities'. Thus according to Dinham *et al.* (2009) a claimed religious resurgence, especially among non-Christian religion in Britain, has been paralleled by a growing policy interest and government support that prescribes the role of faith in the creation of 'consensual social glue'. Whether and in what ways faith or non-faith organisations, beliefs and practices may or may not contribute to community cohesion it is somewhat ironic that the relation between religion and the state in a liberal democracy like Britain is becoming blurred.

Religion, once seen as a matter of private or personal belief formally separate from public or political citizenship, is increasingly expected to socially engage and somehow contribute to cohesion. Levey and Modood's (2009: 1) discussion of the complex relationships between secularism, religion and multicultural citizenship, concedes that until recently the prevailing view was that religiosity in western democracies 'would attenuate with each generation', as secularisation and consumerism increasingly held sway. Further, that 'This attenuation ... would parallel the expected eclipse of ethnic identities more generally.' However, as their collection makes clear 'such expectations have been roundly shaken.'

Other commentators have pointed to the positive aspects of retaining 'community cohesion' as a policy and conceptual framework for governing ethnic diversity and conflict as well as it, resilience in remedying and improving political participation and civic involvement (Ferlander and Timms 1999; Wetherell, *et al.* 2007; Arneil 2006; Thomas 2011). In these senses the concept and ideal deserves most consideration, especially when it is said to embody common vision, a sense of belonging and shared valuing of the diversity of people's different backgrounds, who it is said, *should* have similar life opportunities. Even the Local Government Association (2006: 5) in its account of cohesive communities talks about 'Strong and positive relationships' based on extensive contact between groups of different backgrounds in work, in schools and within neighbourhoods. The availability of plenty of 'bridging social capital' (community networks of support and trust) (Putnam 2000; Halpern 2010) within neighbourhood settings that connect across groups rather than strengthen exclusive ties within groups is taken as defining of cohesion. If individuals find their social identity through group associations, social networks and connections then social cohesion requires that participation extends *across* the confines of area, class, faith and ethnically based local communities, 'knitting them together into a wider whole' (Ferlander and Timms 1999: 9). Without social cohesion societies find that their individual members are disconnected from society whereas cohesive societies are based on values of solidarity, individual and collective rights and responsibilities and active citizenship. In some versions of these scenarios cohesive societies are said to privilege social values and social justice over private and economic interests and values. Halpern (2010: 119) uses terms such as 'wellbeing', 'true reciprocity', 'greater trust' and 'mutual respect' to capture systems of mutual recognition associated with cohesion.

Ted Cantle is the most comprehensive and consistent advocate and defender of community cohesion as a basis to govern religious and ethnic difference in urban Britain. He also most emphasises the turn from 'race' to religion in these discussions, to which we return later. Cantle's (2012) argument is that coded racism has substituted for religion, and ethnicity or culture for race, while at the same time, the salience of 'race' remains as an important aspect of identity it has also been dissipated and diffused by a much wider range of social, national and language groups. In Cantle's view young people have foregone these obsessions with identity politics as they are greatly more able than before to choose their identity. They are also more likely than ever before to come into contact with people from different national, religious and ethnic backgrounds and to develop personal relationships that challenge communal structures and pure forms of race or faith identity and recognise that these have been socially and culturally constructed in the first instance. For Cantle, the real reason that 'multiculturalism' has 'failed' is because it has been essentially about 'race', and the concept of race and racial difference has 'failed the test of time' and no longer has popular appeal whereas other differences such as ethnicity or faith may remain of importance. We turn now to some of the criticisms of community cohesion as a concept and as a policy – particularly its premature abandonment of multiculturalism – and how this brings something of a false dichotomy to debates about cohesion.

## Community cohesion and the turn from multiculturalism to 'interculturalism'

On the few occasions when community cohesion has been subject to systematic empirical scrutiny, an important insight to emerge from this evidence-based approach seems to be that perceptions of neighbourhood are complicated and differ according to class, age, ethnicity, gender and, most significantly, in relation to policing and crime, whether a neighbourhood is poor or affluent (Cooper and Innes 2009). Critics often make the point that although the *idea* of community cohesion is an appealing one; aspects of the *policy* have actually served to antagonise Muslim communities. In part, as Chakraborti (2007) argues this is because it serves to sideline other important contributory factors to neighbourhood fragmentation such as discriminatory policing, far-right political fear-mongering and residential segregation. Community cohesion as a 'solution' to fragmentation is overly simplistic, condoning and excusing white community instability while condemning Muslims as representative of their unwillingness to accept the norms of national identity. In a related context studying racist violence, Gadd and Dixon (2011: 164) found that rejection of ethnic diversity is a more typical response within beleaguered neighbourhoods.

> ... people who feel themselves to be unfairly judged, derided, or ostracized will have psychological difficulty in perceiving *strength in diversity*, be resistant to being touched *emotionally* by the plight of others, and find it much easier to manage their feelings of persecution by establishing greater social distance between themselves and those who they deem to be culturally different and morally inferior.

Not only might it be the case that those most socially and economically marginalised are ill-placed to relinquish their isolation and racism, they may be least suited to the seductions of community cohesion discourse. This is especially likely if ethnic segregation was really quite insignificant compared to entrenched ethnic and class disadvantages and inequalities which segregation reflects rather than causes (Dorling 2010; Finney and Simpson 2009). Against community cohesion's essentially conservative, nostalgic and Christian narrative of the redemptive possibilities of a fall from grace redeemed by civic unity and shared norms (Arneil 2006; Putnam and Campbell 2010), critics locate civic decline in recent social, economic and demographic change. Barbara Arneil (2006) in particular asks whether community cohesion is possible without addressing what she calls 'multicultural justice' and diversity, by which she means the return to questions of equality and power, in a context in which community decline is felt much more by some groups than others. In this view, struggles for mutual recognition among ethno-racial identities implies 'multicultural justice' as well as cohesion. Among other critics, cohesion represents a retreat to failed policies of coercive assimilation (Back *et al.* 2002), a racialisation of economic and social marginalisation and a resulting blaming of Asian communities (Alexander 2004), a misplaced obsession with 'segregation' (Finney and Simpson 2009; Kalra 2002), and a factually wrong insistence on the 'death of multiculturalism' (Kundnani 2002) in Britain, the latter having been particularly perverse as Britain's multicultural approach to ethnic diversity has been so lauded in much more ethnically fractious European societies. Whether this shift from multiculturalism to cohesion means abandoning or denying minority groups' struggle 'for equal participation in political life where their minority ethno-racial identities can be maintained rather than assimilated into the majority culture, essentially challenging for a multicultural rather than a monocultural state' (Phillips 2012: 36) is considered next.

Of most significance for debates about social and community cohesion is the shift from concerns about racial harmony to those of interfaith harmony, while also echoing a conceptual shift from multicultural to 'intercultural' concerns. Cantle's (2012) view is that faith identity once again looms large as the world is increasingly divided between religions. As faith identity increasingly becomes wedded to the illusion of unique identity, the relevance of other ways in which people see themselves diminishes, while this illusion is challenged by the confusion and confounding of nationality, faith, culture and ethnicity. In reality we are entering an age of 'super diversity', of hyphenated and multiple identities, growth in mixed-race people and an increasing irrelevance of single identities, predefined groups and ethnic categories themselves. Paradoxically, policy responses to 'super diversity' have often served to help bolster single religious identities despite the fact that people identify less and less with single identities or group allegiances. Policy has been particularly deleterious for Muslim communities reinforcing negative identity, privileging pure or single forms of identity enumerated in ethnic classification and monitoring, and all in the face of different issues and more pressing concerns of newer migrant groups (Cantle 2012). If this echoes Cameron's mythical 'multicultural state' said to promulgate separate ethnic identities, Cantle

(2012) argues that an exclusive focus on the needs, identities and concerns of each separate ethnic group (multiculturalism), then *interculturalism* and community cohesion 'recognises a renewed focus on commonality and on community relations and is recognised and supported on the ground' (Thomas 2011: 195). Interculturalism is about encouraging interaction and contact, discouraging faith and other sorts of segregation, especially school segregation and by extension, residential segregation (Harris 2011). Echoing Wrong's (1994) view of the problem of order, from the perspective of interculturalism, resolves and somehow overcomes class and ethnic segregation through contact between groups that is likely to increase mutual understanding, though it needs to be close and meaningful contact.

### 'Mixing' and 'getting along': Ethnicity, religion and social cohesion in London and Bradford

Despite criticisms, considerable scepticism and many doubts about the efficacy of community cohesion, particularly the policies derived from it that target Muslim communities and individuals, empirical studies of its workings on the ground seem to show considerable acceptance and embracing of diversity without there being any apparent need to assimilate or integrate difference. Similar to findings from the YOR study, Thomas' (2011) empirical study of community cohesion and identity among Muslim and non-Muslim young people in Oldham, Rochdale and Manchester, did not support fears that support for community cohesion meant a return to the assimilation of cultural, ethnic and faith differences into some sort of amorphous 'British' identity. On this basis Thomas (2011) suggests that some of the criticisms of community cohesion are misplaced because they ignore the limitations of previous 'multicultural' policy that often stressed differences and distinctions rather than commonalities and tolerance between all ethnic groups. Although community cohesion as a policy, when narrowly understood and implemented, has been harmful to Muslim identity, Muslim young people are clearly positive about being British and Muslim, and about ethnic diversity. According to Thomas' findings, if white working class young people are less positive about diversity this is because of what they see as an exclusive focus on visible minorities rather than on what young people have in common. Dilwar Hussain (2004, 2007) came to similar conclusions about how young British Muslims had embraced the idea of community cohesion in Leicester, bringing, for example, members of different faiths into shared dialogue while denying the premise that Muslims are homogeneous and are to be 'cohered' into white British communities. Consistent with these, our findings were that the three main things young people suggest would help improve community cohesion are better integration, better education (at school, in the community, through the media) and improved equality and respect (Madge *et al.* 2013).

The findings from our study in Bradford and London are particularly interesting in respect of Bradford because this city is often perceived as polarised along ethnic and religious lines (Ouseley 2001). The Youth On Religion (YOR) study asked what can be done to ensure that people from different religions get on and shows a consistent overall support for the benefits of social interaction between people of different religious, ethnic and cultural backgrounds. It was felt that groups from different religions meeting and mixing would help improve community relations. The role of ethnically mixed and multi-faith schools was important in accomplishing understanding and awareness about, and respect and tolerance towards, differences and similarities between groups. Despite much optimism about the benefits of mixing, interaction cannot be forced and sometimes differences will remain. A few expressed some resentment about the 'equal' status Islam had been 'given' to Christianity but this was very much a minority view. The main problem though, it was felt, that hindered harmonious community relations was racism, bullying and religion (which are linked in complex ways).

The qualitative data collected by the YOR study confirmed that in effect, in practice, and on the ground, young people were engaged in a sort of 'interactive multiculturalism', which 'is about opening up oneself to others, learning from their insights and criticisms, and growing as a result into a richer and tolerant culture' (Parekh 2005b). There was widespread agreement that mixing across cultures was to be encouraged to enable different belief systems to be understood. A generalised prohibition on racism shared by most young people in our study, accompanied by apparent tolerance towards religious and other sorts of difference, was however, far from complete when tensions and caveats at points of local public controversy arose, such as the siting of new mosques. Situations such as these could lead young Muslims to feel that there was intolerance and misunderstanding of their religion.

When asked to tell us about the extent and nature of their contact with people of the same, a different or no faith to them, reinforced by asking them what their understanding of others' faith or non-faith was and how they had come by this understanding, the same theme repeated itself. There was considerable agreement that faith schools insofar as they encouraged adherence to a single religion will also discourage ethnic and faith mixing while encouraging segregation. An issue in Bradford was that school intake tended to reflect the segregated localities in which many young people lived, and it was widely felt that this in itself could be a factor leading to religious misunderstanding. Young people in all study areas reinforced the benefits of mixing as early as possible to enable greater knowledge of different religions and cultures and to prepare them for growing up in a multicultural society. Having friends from a range of backgrounds was commonly reported to be beneficial.

> Often the area around the faith school is largely built up of that particular faith, again meaning that the children from that area are not mixing with other children outside of school, in their home area. Although there is the possibility of children mixing with other children from different

backgrounds, in extra-curricular activities which they may partake in, it can generally be said that children spend most of their time in school and playing in the area they live in.

(Annette: female, no religion, religion not very important)

Young people were asked whether different faiths got along, and most were positive in saying that they did. In the main, they said they liked the experience of living in a multicultural and multi-faith place and having the opportunity to engage in open discussion and debate about religious mores. One white Christian male contrasted different faiths according to personal knowledge of friends' practices and beliefs. Apart from describing lessons learned from his Muslim friends, he described his atheist friend's family as having

> ... a laid back life and it was refreshing to see how they led more of a guilt-free life without religion. However, they were still good and nice to others, obviously, as you don't need religion to do that – just basic human morals and kindness.
>
> (Leon: male, Christian, religion important in some ways but not others)

Asked about whether individuals of different faiths mixed within their area answers obviously depended on the ethnic and religious mix of where the young person lived. But here again the pattern of answers is generally that where areas are of mixed faith and ethnicity there would seem to be a lot of cross-ethnic and cross-faith contact. Some respondents suggested that within local areas overt conflict between people of different backgrounds was avoided but nevertheless tensions remained.

Looking at the findings overall across the range of data, religious pluralism, although seemingly accepted and admired by many of the young people we spoke to across all the research sites in Bradford as well as London, in actuality there were underlying anxieties about differences and segregation especially in Bradford. At the level of attitudes there was an active dislike of ethnic or religious segregation whether this was perceived as occurring in school or neighbourhoods. In terms of how young people actually behaved the situation seemed less sanguine than the impression we were given on the basis of what we were told by young people. One young female Muslim talked about residential segregation in ways that suggested a complicated interconnection between class, ethnicity and religion:

> ... I think the majority of the time it's not a conscious decision you know, I think it's a more subtle sort of subconscious segregation that happens. People of the same culture tend to live in the same areas and they tend to share the same religion and I think that's something that's inevitably built over time ... I think religion only really becomes a factor when you make

conscious decisions like moving house. And that's when you kind of notice everybody's religion and you really start to take it into account.

(Naihla: female, Muslim, religion very important)

When we asked about personal safety and local relations, religion was of lesser importance compared to 'race' in the minds of some young people as a source of tension or conflict *insofar* as these arose in the first place. Nevertheless the relationship between faith, visible ethnicity and place were sometimes ambiguous, uncertain and complicated in respect of personal safety as among other aspects of life in multicultural settings. It was apparent that most young people preferred to spend time in areas they were familiar with and alongside people they knew and who knew them.[5]

## Concluding discussion

The everyday negotiation and ordering of identity by young people in multi-faith, multi-ethnic and multicultural localities – often ignored or unknown in discussions about social cohesion – tells a more or less benign story of tolerance between young people of different ethnic and religious backgrounds in their interactions. Our study (Madge *et al.* 2013) is sceptical that this tells the whole story in that an endorsement of liberal individualism at the level of attitudes and what we were told may not necessarily translate into benign behaviour. After all we found significant ethnic and religious segregation, less in Newham, more in Bradford. The problem of order – what unites and divides society – is resolved in these everyday encounters and negotiations rather than in abstract debates about cohesion versus multiculturalism, although these too are real enough. In this chapter the emphasis has been to explore some theoretical and conceptual issues to study and understand the nature and contribution of religiosity to identity and cohesion. Although only scraping the surface of our data about young people and religion, the influence of faith and non-faith identity on social and community cohesion in multi-ethnic places is apparent and can be characterised as usually benign, and it is encouraging that among young people at least there is plentiful evidence of diversity and tolerance towards difference in Britain's urban, multicultural places.

## Notes

1 Disingenuous because combining 'state' with 'multiculturalism' serves to discredit both by their association while expressing an almost wilful ignorance of the contested and different possible models of multiculturalism, cohesion and difference available within and between polities. These may range from 'nationalist', in which 'the state promotes a single national culture and expects all to assimilate to it' to 'liberal' (diversity is limited to the private sphere), plural (communities and identities overlap and are interdependent), and finally, 'separatist' (the state largely confines itself to maintaining order and stability while each community remains

separate from the others) (Parekh 2000: 42). The point is that assertions like Cameron's open rather than close a debate about the empirical facts of the existence of different 'cultures', the nature of the values and loyalties associated with citizenship they assume, their advocacy of a political programme, and the balance to be struck between equal treatment, different treatment and maintaining social cohesion.

2 The author wishes to acknowledge that the research outlined in this paper is funded by the AHRC/ ESRC Religion in Society programme, Grant Number AH/ G014086/1. The research was carried out by a team named as authors of a book summarising the overall findings: Madge *et al.* (2013) *Youth On Religion: the development, negotiation and impact of faith and non-faith identity*, London: Routledge. The study involved a large school survey of around 10,000 school students and an in-depth follow-up study of around 160 17-year-olds.

3 Durkheim (2001: 46) was clear about this in his definition of religion as 'a unified system of beliefs and practices relative to sacred things, that is to say, things set apart and surrounded by prohibitions – beliefs and practices that unite its adherents in a single moral community … religion must be something eminently collective.'

4 See Copson, A. 'Should we allow faith schools at all?' *The Guardian* 1 May 2012, available at www.guardian.co.uk/commentisfree/belief/2012/may/01/should-we-allow-faith-schools

5 Sometimes it was difficult disentangling the precise reasons why young people tended to avoid or visit areas. Reasons such as an area being 'run down', 'having or not having a nice atmosphere', 'not standing out', 'feeling like a vulnerable minority' and so on blurred into each other.

## References

Alexander, C. (2004) 'Imagining the Asian gang: ethnicity, masculinity and youth after "the riots"', *Critical Social Policy*, 24 (4): 526–49.

Arneil, B. (2006) *Diverse Communities: The Problem with Social Capital*. Cambridge: Cambridge University Press.

Back, L., Keith, M., Khan, A., Shukra, K. and Solomos, J. (2002) 'New Labour's white heart: politics, multiculturalism and the return of assimiliationism', *Political Quarterly*, 73 (4): 445–54.

Badiou, A. (2001) *Ethics: An Essay on the Understanding of Evil*. London: Verso.

Bauman, Z. (2001) *Community: Seeking Safety in an Insecure World*. Oxford: Polity Press.

Berger, P. (1999) *The Desecularization of the World: Resurgent Religion and World Politics*. Grand Rapids, MI: William Eerdmands.

Berger, P. (ed.) (1967) *The Sacred Canopy: Elements of a Sociological Theory of Religion*. New York: Anchor Books.

Burke, J. (2011) *The 9/11 Wars*. London: Allen Lane.

Burnett, J. (2008) 'Community cohesion in Bradford: neoliberal integrationism', in Flint, J. and Robinson, D. (eds) *Community Cohesion in Crisis? New Dimensions of Diversity and Difference*. Bristol: Policy Press.

Caldwell, C. (2009) *Reflections on the Revolution in Europe: Can Europe Be The Same With Different People In It?* London: Penguin.

Cameron, D. (2011) 'PM's Speech at Munich Security Conference', 5 February 2011, available at www.number10.gov.uk/news/pms-speech-at-munich-security-conference/.

Cantle, T. (2001) *Community Cohesion: A Report of the Independent Review Team*. London: Home Office.

——(2004) *The End of Parallel Lives? Final Report of the Community Cohesion Panel.* London: Home Office.

——(2008) *Community Cohesion: A New Framework for Race and Diversity.* Basingstoke: Palgrave Macmillan.

——(2012) *Interculturalism: The New Era of Cohesion and Diversity.* Basingstoke: Palgrave.

Chakraborti, N. (2007) 'Policing Muslim communities', in Rowe, M. (ed.) *Policing Beyond Macpherson.* Cullompton: Willan.

Conway, D. (2009) *Disunited Kingdom: How the Government's Community Cohesion Agenda Undermines British Identity and Nationhood.* London: Civitas.

Cooper, H. and Innes, M. (2009) *The Causes and Consequences of Community Cohesion in Wales: A Secondary Analysis.* Cardiff: UPSI, Cardiff University.

Dinham, A., Furbey, R. and Lowndes, V. (eds) (2009) *Faith in the Public Realm: Controversies, Policies and Practices.* Bristol: Policy Press.

Dorling, D. (2010) *Injustice: Why Social Inequality Persists.* Bristol: Policy Press.

Durkheim, E. (2001) *The Elementary Forms of Religious Life.* Oxford: Oxford University Press.

Eagleton, T. (2009) *Reason, Faith, and Revolution: Reflections on the God Debate.* New Haven, CT: Yale University Press.

——(2010) *On Evil.* New Haven, CT: Yale University Press.

Ferlander, S. and Timms, D. (1999) *Social Cohesion and On-Line Community*, Luxembourg and Brussels: European Commission and Centre for Research and Development in Learning Technology. Sterling University.

Finney, N. and Simpson, L. (2009) *'Sleepwalking to Segregation'? Challenging Myths about Race and Migration.* Bristol: Policy Press.

Gadd, D. and Dixon, B. (2011) *Losing the Race: Thinking Psychosocially About Racially Motivated Crime.* London: Karnac Books.

Giddens, A. (ed.) (1972) *Emile Durkheim: Selected Writings.* Cambridge: Cambridge University Press.

Goffman, E. (2010 [1971]) *Relations in Public: Microstudies of the Public Order.* London: Transaction.

Halpern, D. (2010) *The Hidden Wealth of Nations.* Cambridge: Polity.

Harris, R. (2011) '"Sleepwalking towards Johannesburg"? Local measures of ethnic segregation between London's secondary schools, 2003–8/9', paper cited in Cantle, T. (2012) *Interculturalism: The New Era of Cohesion and Diversity.* Basingstoke: Palgrave.

Hussain, D. (2004) 'British Muslim identity', in Seddon, M. S., Hussain, D. and Malik, N. (eds) *British Muslims Between Assimilation and Segregation.* Leicester: The Islamic Foundation.

——(2007) 'Identity formation and change in British Muslim communities', in Wetherell, M., Lafleche, and Berkeley, R. *Identity, Ethnic Diversity and Community Cohesion.* London: Sage.

Kalra, V. S. (2002) 'Extended view: riots, race and reports: Denham, Cantle, Oldham and Burnley Inquiries', *Sage Race Relations Abstracts*, 27 (4): 20–30.

Kundnani, A. (2002) *The Death of Multiculturalism.* London: Institute of Race Relations.

Levey, G. B. and Modood, T. (2009) *Secularism, Religion and Multicultural Citizenship.* Cambridge: Cambridge University Press.

Local Government Association (2006) *Leading Cohesive Communities: A Guide for Local Authority Leaders and Chief Executives.* London: LGA.

Luckmann, T. (1967) *The Invisible Religion*. London: Macmillan

Madge, N., Calestani, M., Goodman, A., Hemming, P., King, K., Kingston, S., Stenson, K. and Webster, C. (2013) *Youth On Religion: The Development, Negotiation and Impact of Faith and Non-faith Identity*. London: Routledge.

Ouseley, H. (2001) *Community Pride Not Prejudice: Making Diversity Work in Bradford*. Bradford: Bradford Vision.

Parekh, B. (2000) *The Future of Multi-Ethnic Britain: The Parekh Report*. London: Profile Books.

——(2005a) *Rethinking Multiculturalism: Cultural Diversity and Political Theory*. Basingstoke: Palgrave.

——(2005b) 'Multiculturalism is a civilised dialogue', *The Guardian*, 21 January.

Phillips, C. (2012) *The Multicultural Prison: Ethnicity, Masculinity, and Social Relations among Prisoners*. Oxford: Oxford University Press.

Putnam, R. D. (2000) *Bowling Alone: The Collapse and Revival of American Community*. New York: Simon & Schuster.

Putnam, R. D. and Campbell, D. E. (2010) *American Grace: How Religion Divides and Unites Us*. New York: Simon & Schuster.

Sampson, R. J. (2012) *Great American City: Chicago and the Enduring Neighborhood Effect*. Chicago, IL: The University of Chicago Press.

Sennett, R. (2012) *Together: The Rituals, Pleasures and Politics of Cooperation*. London: Penguin.

Thomas, P. (2011) *Youth, Multiculturalism and Community Cohesion*. Basingstoke: Palgrave.

Weber, M. (1978) *Economy and Society*. Berkeley: University of California Press.

Webster, C. (2007) *Understanding Race and Crime*. Maidenhead: Open University Press.

Wetherell, M., Lafleche, M. and Berkeley, R. (2007) *Identity, Ethnic Diversity and Community Cohesion*. London: Sage.

Wirth, L. (1938) 'Urbanism as a way of life', *American Journal of Sociology*, 44 (3): 3–24.

Wrong, D. H. (1994) *The Problem of Order: What Unites and Divides Society*. Cambridge, MA: Harvard University Press.

# 4 We belong to Glasgow

## The thirdspaces of youth 'gangs' and asylum seeker, refugee and migrant groups

*Alistair Fraser and Teresa Piacentini*

### Introduction

In recent years, the figures of the 'asylum seeker' and the 'gang member' have become central to depictions of social problems in the UK. The construction of these twenty-first century folk-devils, while tapping into well-established and divergent popular fears relating to immigration and working-class youth, also indicate contemporary points of convergence relating to ethnicity, identity and difference in modern Britain (Alexander 2008: 14). Beyond these constructions, moreover, there are interesting and important points of intersection between youth 'gangs' and asylum seekers that bear further investigation. In very different ways, both groups are staking claims to space and articulating a desire for belonging, home-making and security in the context of limited and limiting social environments. In their own way, individuals within both groups articulate a powerful statement of identity and emplacement: 'we belong'. In this chapter, drawing together two separate ethnographic projects in the city of Glasgow – one focusing on young people's understandings of youth 'gangs', the other exploring community organisation among refugees and asylum seekers – we reflect on the local, national, and global forces that shape the lived experiences of these 'hidden communities'. In so doing, we aim to move beyond simplistic categorisations of 'gang member' and 'asylum seeker' to understand some of the common characteristics of the 'human consequences' of – and human responses to – globalisation (Bauman 2000).

The chapter is structured in two sections. In the first, engaging with the concepts of thirdspace (Soja 1998) and neighbourhood nationalism (Back 1996) in the context of global (im)mobilities, we explore the forces that shape the contemporary experiences of youth 'gangs' and adult asylum seeker, refugee and migrant populations in Glasgow.[1] In the second, we introduce our respective fieldsites, and engage with the concept of thirdspace to conceptualise the 'real and imagined' (Soja 1998) nature of lived space in Glasgow, drawing together the experiences of young people and new migrants in spaces of socio-economic deprivation. In the conclusion, we highlight some of the temporal aspects of these experiences and point to the concept of 'transitioning identities' to bring this to the fore.

## Global (im)mobility, space and identity

The interlocking processes that have developed under the heading of 'globalisation' – namely 'the progressive enmeshment of human communities with each other over time and ... the complex social, economic and environmental processes that stretch across their borders' (Held 2000: 394) – have posed a series of challenges for criminological research. On the one hand, the increasingly borderless nature of crime and crime control has brought into question the 'methodological nationalism' (Aas 2011) that has traditionally characterised the discipline, prompting movement towards more comparative, transnational, and globally-informed research. On the other, development of migration patterns from the global South to North that have significant racialised dimensions – with refugees constituting 'perhaps the most rapidly swelling of all the categories of world population' (Bauman 2002: 343) – has resulted in configurations of identity, citizenship and belonging that necessitate new vocabularies of critical scholarship outside of mainstream criminology. Specifically, attention has been paid to the 'repatriation' of colonialism (Blagg 2008), and the criminalisation of migration – so-called 'crimmigration' (Stumpf 2006) – through techniques of surveillance, monitoring and control (Schuster 2003, 2005).

These developments draw attention to the new geographies of mobility and immobility that exist in the global era, and their implications for crime and crime control. Bauman, for example, explores the intersections between social class and mobility in this context:

> Alongside the emerging planetary dimensions of business, finance, trade and information, a 'localizing', space-fixing process is set in motion ... freedom to move ... fast becomes the main stratifying force of our late-modern or postmodern times.
>
> (Bauman 2000: 2)

Globalisation is not a system of equal participation but is in reality marked by processes of inclusion and exclusion (Bauman 2004). Gated communities and urban ghettoes, for example, represent concrete manifestations of a new global stratification, in which physical, social, and geographical mobility is a central motif. It is in this sense that the compression of time and space occurring in a globalised order has to be seen as a class-stratified phenomenon (Bauman 2000): some are free of the tyranny of place ('tourists'), whilst others are constrained by their lack of resources and poverty ('vagabonds'). For some, globalisation is *de*-territorialising, resulting in weakened ties between people, culture and place (Bauman 2000); for others globalisation is *re*-territorialising, resulting in strengthened ties between identity and territorial space (Massey 1994; Brun 2001). In this latter context, Hagedorn (2008) has argued for an understanding of youth 'gangs' as a form of 'resistance identity' (Castells 1996) to processes of socio-spatial marginalisation.

Wacquant (2007) has drawn attention to the role of 'race' and ethnicity in the context of these developments. For Wacquant, urban areas characterised by the retrenchment of the welfare state, and subsequent development of informal economies – the ghettoes of Chicago and the banlieues of Paris – are also areas populated overwhelmingly by non-white groups, for whom socio-spatial marginality is coded with racial prejudice and discrimination. For Wacquant, these areas are subject to processes of 'territorial stigmatisation', in that they are 'perceived by both outsiders and insiders as social purgatories, leprous badlands at the heart of the post-industrial metropolis where only the refuse of society would accept to dwell' (Wacquant 2007: 67); a blemish of place that houses contemporary urban outcasts (Wacquant 2007, 2008). Whilst Wacquant tends to focus on racially-defined others, Rhodes (2012) – writing in a British context – argues that this process of spatial stigmatisation can also be directed towards white working class populations. Scholarship has drawn attention, for example, to the development of 'estate reputations' that are inscribed with class prejudice (Damer 1974; Hanley 2007) and the construction of a white Other (Webster 2008; Nayak 2009), witnessed most recently in the construction of 'chavs' in England (Hayward and Yar 2006; Nayak 2006), and 'neds' in Scotland (Law, Mooney and Helms 2010).[2]

It is no coincidence, in this context, that two of the most prominent 'folk devils' of the twenty-first century – the 'gang-member' (Alexander 2008) and the 'asylum-seeker' (Cohen 2002) – are spatially located in the most deprived and marginalised communities in the UK (Deuchar 2011). Although asylum seekers and youth 'gangs' embody a set of fears about the 'stranger next door' and the 'enemy within' which have existed throughout modern European history (Bauman 2000; Pearson 2011), there are points of intersection between these disparate populations that speak to the new configurations of space and identity in the global age. Through differing sets of structural constraints, both young people and asylum seekers living in disadvantaged communities experience territorial immobility and stigma, and seek out strategies for creating belonging and security within these confines, though these efforts are themselves coded with othering and difference. In the following section, we introduce two key concepts that speak to these intersections and differences: thirdspace and neighbourhood nationalism.

## Thirdspace and neighbourhood nationalism

Soja's conceptualisation of thirdspace (1998) – a re-working of Lefebvre's distinction between *perceived* and *conceived* space – represents an effort to conceptualise the complex modalities of space in the (post)modern era. Moving beyond modernist notions of 'lived' and 'imagined' spaces – the city as experienced and constructed – Soja draws attention to the liminal spaces *between* these modalities, conceptualising thirdspace as 'a simultaneously real and imagined, actual and virtual locus of structured individual and collective experiences and agency' (Soja 1998: 11). This configuration draws attention to the complex relationship between the 'real', lived, experience of space – for example that of everyday life in a housing estate – and the 'imagined', perceived, meaning of space – for example the friends, relatives and associations with particular locales. Thirdspace therefore combines spatiality with both sociality and historicality; it emplaces identity and culture, and is characterised by resistance to the 'either-or' world of urban planners (Soja 1998: 10). As we will argue, the lived experiences of young people and asylum seekers, co-located in areas of social and spatial marginalisation, are marked by the lived experience of thirdspace. For young people – in a liminal 'waiting room' between childhood and adulthood (Miller 2005) – the streets become imbued with deep-seated meaning and potential, enacted through the performance of 'gang' identities. For individuals seeking asylum – in a liminal legal status, with limited socio-spatial volition – the tower-block becomes a space for home-making, belonging and identity-formation. For both groups, the experience of marginality and liminality cohere in gradations of scalar belonging and territoriality.

Back (1996) develops the concept of neighbourhood nationalism as a means of capturing the new identities, ethnicities, and affiliations that have emerged in the 'multiculture' of contemporary London. Though racial discrimination and prejudice remains an everyday occurrence, Back identifies a process through which differences based on 'race' or ethnicity are subordinated to a collective loyalty to a geographical area. In short, neighbourhood nationalism 'attempts to banish the racial referent and replace it with a simple commitment to local territory' (Back 1996: 55), in a pattern similar to the 'Established-Outsider' relations described by Elias and Scotson (1994). Crucial to this formulation of territorial collectivism is the lived experience of class and place. As Robins and Cohen (1978: 73–74) argued of territoriality in the 1970s:

> What we refer to as 'territoriality' is a symbolic process of magically appropriating, owning and controlling the material environment in which you live, but which in real terms is owned and controlled by 'outsiders' … Territoriality is, therefore, deeply engrained in most working-class parent cultures, even if its functions are diffused through a number of institutions … But the kids have only one institution to support this function … the 'gang'.

The concept of neighbourhood nationalism develops this resistance identity to incorporate a form of territorial inclusivism that supersedes, but does not erase, distinctions on the basis of ethnicity.[3] The concept has become a relatively accepted aspect of sociological work on ethnicity and difference in working-class communities in the United Kingdom (Webster 1996; Phillips 2008); although, in the context of gang research, Hagedorn (2006) has drawn attention to the problematic nature of deracinating 'gang' rivalries. The collectivism inherent in neighbourhood nationalism, nonetheless, captures well the potentialities and problems associated with life in thirdspace.

In this chapter, we wish to develop the concept in the context of territorial loyalties to both community and city, arguing that not only are there different scales and grains of 'neighbourhood' but also different forces and impacts of neighbourhood nationalism in different geographical locales. Specifically, we wish to suggest that sociocultural, economic and political factors in Glasgow may predispose communities to neighbourhood nationalism. However, we also seek to locate the idea of neighbourhood nationalism within the context of everyday experiences of racialised othering in the Scottish context, engaging with multiple layers of belonging based on a wide range of social differences, including 'whiteness' (Virdee *et al.* 2006; Webster 2008). As we will argue, within the thirdspaces of young people and asylum seekers there are distinctive points of intersection that relate to a search for belonging and identity in limiting social environments. However, within these spaces there remain processes of othering and difference. In the following section, we explore the background, context and methodology of the two studies drawn on in the chapter.

## We belong to Glasgow ...

Although Scotland has traditionally been characterised by emigration (Macdonald 2012),[4] there have been several waves of immigration into the country, predominantly different groups of Irish, Jewish, Italian, Chinese, East European and Indian subcontinent immigrants, the latter group forming the largest ethnic minority in Scotland (Croall and Frondigoun 2010: 112–13). The ethnic composition of Scotland is summarised in Table 4.1, below:

*Table 4.1* Scottish population by ethnic group – all people

|  | % of total population | % minority ethnic population | Base |
|---|---|---|---|
| White Scottish | 88.09 | n/a | 4,459,071 |
| Other White British | 7.38 | n/a | 373,685 |
| White Irish | 0.98 | n/a | 49,428 |
| Any other White background | 1.54 | n/a | 78,150 |
| Indian | 0.3 | 14.79 | 15,037 |
| Pakistani | 0.63 | 31.27 | 31,793 |
| Bangladeshi | 0.04 | 1.95 | 1,981 |
| Chinese | 0.32 | 16.04 | 16,310 |
| Other South Asian | 0.12 | 6.09 | 6,196 |
| Caribbean | 0.04 | 1.75 | 1,778 |
| African | 0.1 | 5.03 | 5,118 |
| Black Scottish or any other Black background | 0.02 | 1.11 | 1,129 |
| Any mixed background | 0.25 | 12.55 | 12,764 |
| Any other background | 0.19 | 9.41 | 9,571 |
| All minority ethnic population | 2.01 | 100 |  |
| All population | 100 | n/a | 5,062,011 |

Source: Scottish Executive (2004: 5).

As is evident, Scotland remains an overwhelmingly 'white' nation, with approximately 2 per cent of the population categorised as belonging to a 'minority ethnic population' compared to 9 per cent in England (ONS 2002). Crucially, however, statistics indicate a relatively proportionate representation of minority ethnic groups in the Scottish criminal justice system, and that 'race' and ethnicity play a less significant role in victimisation in Scotland than in other jurisdictions (Croall and Frondigoun 2010). For some, this attenuation of the race-crime relationship reflects a particular form of civic lib-eral nationalism in Scottish identity (McCrone 2001), which Miles (1993: 78) has argued is focused on perceived economic and political disadvantages of the Union without reference to 'race'. Nonetheless, there is evidence that racialised hate crimes are under-reported (GARA 2009; de Lima 2005),[5] linked to a lack of confidence in police to recognise the 'racist' elements in offences. Regardless of the underlying reasons and whilst less visible when compared to England, crime victimisation of BME populations remains a largely under-researched area (Croall and Frondigoun 2010; de Lima 2005).

Within this broad picture, however, there are significant local variations. With the implementation of dispersal through the Immigration and Asylum Act Glasgow became, and remains, the only 1999 local council in Scotland to receive thousands of asylum seekers: from 2000–2010, more than 22,000 asylum seekers have been housed across the city, the highest number of state sup-ported asylum seekers in the UK.[6] Glasgow now has the highest concentra-tion of minority ethnic groups in Scotland, accounting for 31 per cent of the total population in Scotland (Scottish Executive 2004).

The dominant national trend for housing-led resettlement of asylum seekers (Robinson 2003; Anie *et al.* 2005; Schuster 2005; Wren 2007) has led to the majority of asylum seekers being forcibly dispersed to vacant high rise accommodation in areas of multiple deprivation in Glasgow (COSLAa 2011).[7] In Glasgow, these areas are often the same communities that experience issues with territorial youth 'gangs'.[8] In certain circumstances, this co-location has led to heightened tensions, discrimination and conflict. For example, a recent survey of young people in dispersal areas highlighted an increased sensitivity to difference and potential conflict (Ross, Hill and Shilton 2008). Whereas in England this has led to racialised conflict (Runnymede 2009), in Scotland, although the perception exists over conflict for resources, this has not led to racialised conflict and confrontation (Wren 2007; Deuchar 2011). On the contrary, in some of these communities there has been strong local support for 'We Belong to Glasgow'-led campaigns that resisted forced deportations.

Despite a comparative absence of racialised conflict, as Croall and Fron-digoun (2010) point out, there do remain deep-seated social divisions and histories of discrimination in Scotland – in relation to Roma Gypsy commu-nities, Irish Catholics and white working-class youths, labelled 'neds' (Poole and Adamson 2008; Croall and Frondigoun 2010) – that might mask the lived experiences of prejudice and othering that exist on a day-to-day level. In this context, engagement with the emergent field of 'critical whiteness studies' (Nayak 2007; Webster 2008) may reveal a more complex patchwork of identity and othering than is revealed by statistics. In the following section, we reflect on our respective qualitative research projects, which aim to move beyond simplistic categorisations of 'asylum seeker' and 'gang member' to emphasise the complex and contingent processes through which processes of othering and difference are played out in contemporary Glasgow.

## Methodology

Adopting and adapting the 'extended case method' advocated by Burawoy (2000), this chapter draws on two separate ethnographic studies conducted over a similar time frame in the city of Glasgow. The first study (2006–9) explored the understandings, experiences, and meanings of 'gang' behaviour for children and young people in an urban community in Glasgow, called Langview (a pseudonym). Alistair worked as a community youth worker, outreach worker, and high-school tutor as part of the fieldwork, as well as living in the area for a period of 18 months. In addition, he carried out a series of eighteen discussion groups with different groups of young people between these locations, focusing specifically on a group of young men – the 'Langview Boys' – who identified, with varying degrees of meaning, with the local 'gang', 'Langview Young Team'. For many, however, this identification had a mainly symbolic value – representing belonging, communitas and solidarity – in the context of the street culture of Langview.

The second study (2007–10) explored the associational experiences of mainly Francophone African asylum seeker and refugee-led groups in Glasgow. Teresa's fieldwork involved a similarly diverse range of roles: volunteer member, sympathiser, volunteer interpreter, volunteer admin. support worker, trainer, note-taker, active participant and observer.[9] The research studied processes of community and identities formation and the development of social structures that influence the nature and quality of social survival, solidarity and struggle in exile. As Africans settling in Glasgow since 2000, research participants saw themselves as a newly establishing migrant population, both highly visible, but with little history in the city. Moreover, the spatial emplacement of asylum seekers in dispersal areas across the city meant that as 'black Africans' they were immediately categorised as asylum seekers, regardless of whether this reflected their immigration status. Lastly, although their collective identities reflected a national or 'African' identity, they were each classed as 'refugee community organisations' by various external actors, the significance being that the dominant categorisations of such populations come to be framed around immigration status, and thus become focused on 'refugeeness', rather than claims to other social identities.

While there are important parallels between the two studies, there are also important differences that pertain to the argument presented. Alistair focused on the micro site of Langview, a single neighbourhood in the city of Glasgow, and thus explored identity and belonging at a primarily local level. Teresa's study was not geographically grounded in or bounded to one neighbourhood, but covered the city of Glasgow. This was largely dictated by the implementation of dispersal policy, whereby the individuals taking part were accommodated across the city to wherever vacant housing was available. Consequently, belonging was articulated more at a city-wide level, although local-level belonging was expressed, as will be discussed later in this chapter. While ethnicity was not central to these respective studies, in what follows we seek to 'extend out' from our respective projects to shed some light on what is an under-researched area.

## Young people, gang identity and thirdspace

Langview was built as a working-class community in the nineteenth century, when Glasgow was at its apogee as 'Second City of the Empire', and represents something of a microcosm of the wider currents of change that have occurred in Glasgow since this time. Though the area encompasses a number of pockets that fall within the 5 per cent 'most deprived' areas in Scotland by the Scottish Index of Multiple Deprivation, there have been successive waves of regeneration and gentrification, resulting in a mixture of class demographics. Moreover, the area has also become one of the dispersal sites for asylum seekers in Glasgow. Table 4.2, below, summarises the ethnicity of Langview, relative to Glasgow and Scotland. As illustrated, there is a small proportion of minority ethnic groups, with the largest single group being Pakistani and other South Asian.

Though these proportions are greater than the national average, they are below the city average. While the vast majority of young people involved in Alistair's research were of white Scottish descent, there was a small but significant population of minority ethnic youth attending the youth project that constituted the primary fieldsite. Though racial insults were a common occurrence, there was a distinctive feeling of neighbourhood nationalism, evidenced, for example, in divisions based on neighbourhood fortnightly football tournaments. In what follows, the concept of neighbourhood nationalism is used as a means of exploring the thirdspaces of young people in Langview.

*Table 4.2* Ethnicity of population of Langview, Glasgow and Scotland (2002)

|                                  | *Langview* | *Glasgow* | *Scotland* |
| -------------------------------- | ---------- | --------- | ---------- |
| White                            | 97.3%      | 94.5%     | 98.0%      |
| Indian                           | 0.3%       | 0.7%      | 0.3%       |
| Pakistani and other South Asian  | 1.2%       | 3.0%      | 0.8%       |
| Chinese                          | 0.4%       | 0.7%      | 0.3%       |
| Other                            | 0.7%       | 1.0%      | 0.6%       |

Source: Scottish Census Results Online Warehouse (www.scrol.gov.uk).

As Childress argues, young people are characterised by their 'neither-nor' status:

> Teenagers have limited ability to manipulate private property. They can't own it, can't modify it, can't rent it. They can only choose, occupy and use the property of others. This limitation is true in their communities, it's true in their schools, and it's true in their homes.
>
> (Childress 2004: 196)

Matthews *et al.* (1998), analysing children's geographies in public space, describe the ways in which different groups seek out hidden spaces in the urban environment – looking for a safe haven of identity away from home and school (Leonard 2006). In the context of limited space and resources, young people create 'microgeographies' and 'microcultures', gaining spatial autonomy from adults' control, and a sense of individual and group identity (Matthews, Limb, and Percy-Smith 1998; Matthews, Limb, and Taylor 2000). 'Ownership' of space is demonstrated, for example, through the construction of 'dens' (Percy-Smith and Matthews 2001), or through the use of graffiti (Ley and Cybriwsky 1974; Childress 2004). In this context, thirdspace represents a search for individual and collective agency and autonomy in the midst of an adult world. The street therefore represents a space in which young people can gain some degree of autonomy, and create 'rules of engagement' (Leonard 2006: 232) on their own terms, away from both home and school. In lived environments characterised by limited resources and socio-spatial marginality, the street becomes *the* site through which daily life is constructed and understood. As Matthews *et al.* argue:

> urban poverty need not give rise to a childhood of environmental impoverishment ... some of the poorest areas had the most vivid and varied experience of place ... The harsh and violent nature of the place produced ambivalent feelings in young people; a co-existence of fear and excitement.
>
> (Matthews *et al.* 1998: 199)

The Langview Boys grew up within a very small geographical area, and spent much of their childhoods within the space of these few streets. During the fieldwork period, the Boys were aged 14–16, and spent much of their time in the thirdspace of the street, bored and restless, seeking diversions from the mundane everyday: light fittings, found in bins, became jousting sticks; large sticks became fighting poles; cardboard boxes the site of a game of hide-and-seek; smashed-up telephone boxes the goals in a game of scratch football; eggs were thrown at passers-by from a hidden space near the main street; shopping trolleys used as racing cars. The Langview Boys' use of public space was a perpetual repetition of group activities in the same public spaces – while constantly searching for a new excitements, dares, and risks through which to test individual distinction and masculinity, and reaffirm group cohesion. In this way, the Boys build up a powerful and deep-seated attachment to both the 'real' and 'imagined' space of Langview – both the physicality of the streets and relationships themselves, and the imaginary of the creative landscape they construct from these surroundings. In a sense, the 'neighbourhood' of Langview became their 'nation'.

This form of identification was embodied, crucially, through the performance of 'gang' identity. The gang-name, for example, would be used interchangeably with the name for the area – when asked where they are from, the Boys might say '*Ah'm Langview*' (I am Langview) or '*Ah'm LYT*' (I am the Langview Young Team). In this way, space is transformed into self-identity; the gang name, used as a shorthand for this space, becomes a symbol of self-identity. In 'protecting' the area, therefore, an individual is protecting all that they hold dear, kith and kin. In the following excerpt, Kev and James discuss the performance of physical violence in this way:

AF:   What makes a gang then?
KEV:  See, people from Swigton try tae come in Lang St tae walk aboot, they jist start fightin wi' them.
JAMES:  They don't like people walking through Lang St.
AF:   Why not?
KEV:  Cos it's their community.

Urban faultlines that cross-cut the city – train-lines, motorways, rivers, parks, pathways – demarcate the boundaries of young people's street-life, confining this connection to a specific geographical area. As Robert articulates: '*It's jist an invisible boundary that every'bdae knows. Once you cross that boundary, you know you're in Lang St, you know you're in Swigton. Don't know how it came aboot.*' This boundary represents, in symbolic terms, the concentration of emotional attachment and community solidarity *within* the boundary, with a corresponding lack of positive emotional attachment to communities *outwith* the boundary. These processes of inclusion and exclusion, crucially, create a sense of neighbourhood nationalism amongst young people that can be viewed as a 'defence of place' (Castells 1996) in the context of socio-spatial marginalisation.

It is important to highlight that the neighbourhood nationalism in the South East London that Back (1996) talks about *included* white and black young people but *excluded* Vietnamese young people. As young refugees specifically, their exclusion suggests that claims to belonging or being seen as belonging could in fact be linked to length of residency and immigration status, which in turn reveals how immigration status becomes coded in their social/spatial location. Back does not explore this in any depth, although he does suggest that neighbourhood nationalism can result in particular racisms being muted whilst others flourish. Nonetheless this offers an interesting starting point of inquiry into how belonging is articulated for asylum seekers and refugees in Glasgow, despite their relative 'newness' in dispersal neighbourhoods. In the following section, though located within a differing set of structural constraints, we argue that asylum seeker, refugee and migrant groups create a similar set of localised collective identities.

## Asylum seeker, refugee and migrant groups and thirdspace

The spatial concentration of asylum seekers in Glasgow since 2000 has significantly altered its demographic and cultural landscape. Up-to-date statistics on asylum seekers arriving are extremely difficult to access, however there are some figures available on nationalities. In 2005, the most significant four groups of asylum seekers coming to Glasgow were from Turkey, Pakistan, Somalia and Iran (Wren 2007, citing unpublished NASS figures). In 2007, over one-third (34 per cent) of the asylum seekers sent to Glasgow were nationals of Iran, Pakistan, Democratic Republic of Congo and Somalia (COSLAa 2011).[10] In March 2011, almost 60 per cent of all asylum seekers in Scotland were nationals of just five countries: People's Republic of China, Pakistan, Iran, Nigeria and Iraq (COSLAb 2011).[11] This diversity has contributed to a 60 per cent increase in the black and minority ethnic population in the city, which presents new challenges for support agencies providing services for the BME population (Joshi and Wright 2004; Wren 2007: 395).

The Immigration and Asylum Act 1999 also established, for the first time, a nationally co-ordinated system for the resettlement and welfare support of asylum seekers, the National Asylum Support Service (NASS) (Wren 2007). Provided through various housing providers, NASS accommodation is offered on a no-choice basis in vacant housing in areas dominated by social housing estates. In Glasgow, the Home Office five-year accommodation contracts (2000–6, 2006–11) specified that 81 per cent of asylum seekers would be accommodated by Glasgow City Council (in partnership with Glasgow Housing Association), with the remaining 19 per cent being shared between Y-People (formerly YMCA, a voluntary sector provider), and the Angel Group (a private sector provider) (COSLAa 2011).[12] According to Home Office/UKBA quarterly statistics, as at September 2010, 10 per cent of all asylum seekers in the UK were living in Scotland.[13]

Against this backdrop, the key concerns underpinning contemporary asylum seeker incorporation regimes in the UK can be largely framed around restrictions, monitoring and control of relocation, education, work, and a fuller participation in civil society (Schuster 2005). Consequently, whilst awaiting a decision on their claim, asylum seekers exist in a status void, a liminal space. One outcome of this suspended social existence has been the emergence of community-level associations that have grown out of social contact between asylum seekers in dispersal neighbourhoods across Glasgow, and indeed the UK (see also Zetter and Pearl 2000; Griffiths *et al.* 2005). The main site of this collectivism has been NASS flats which this chapter argues represent a potent example of the creation of community level thirdspaces.

As a form of thirdspace, NASS flats are provided by the local authority, but the conditions of temporary stay are different to other social housing tenants, especially in the type of tenancy agreement available to asylum seekers, the lack of rights they have to protection from eviction compared to other tenants, and that housing is compulsory and provided on a no-choice basis, which Hynes (2006) describes as a 'bed-space'-led policy. NASS flats are unremarkable in many ways: their standardised décor has a homogenising effect whereby all NASS accommodation looks and feels the same. Attempts to personalise these spaces are thwarted by regulations that mark out both flats and their asylum seeker tenants as different to other tenants. For example, the almost identical furniture and décor, lack of name-plates on doors, restrictions on redecoration, and absence of a tenancy agreement all emphasise the lack of 'ownership' in the home space. These conditions illustrate some of the ways in which their structural positioning pervades their private sphere whilst also publicly reinforces their liminal status in these 'temporary' home spaces. Nonetheless, and despite their unsettled social positioning and very limited capital, there are clear attempts made by asylum seekers to communicate to themselves, and to guests to their homes, that they are 'rooting in'.

Many occupants have added their own 'homely' touches such as photos, religious pictures and plastic flowers. Photos are a particularly interesting public expression of 'belonging' and 'home-making': they act as a daily testimony to a settled life elsewhere before being categorised by the UK state as 'unsettled' asylum seekers. Photos of the new 'home' are also testimony to a kind of 'settlement' in the UK, an expression of belonging to life in Glasgow. Formal school photos, baptisms, christenings and graduations are all indicators to others of participation and 'integration' into the new society's processes and rituals, despite their existence at the margins as asylum seekers. Like the Langview Boys' creative use of street-space, these items are not only claims to a localised belonging but expressions of 'ownership' of a home space despite limited social, cultural and political resources.

Teresa's research explored the experiences of different asylum seeker and refugee groups, and the 'ordinariness' and typical nature of holding their monthly meetings in the NASS flats established a connection between members. Equally, the striking similarities between NASS accommodations create a very strong sense of familiarity within the unfamiliar context of the city and different neighbourhoods, consequently reinforcing the immediate sense of familiarity of this thirdspace. Thus belonging in these spaces takes on both 'real' and 'imagined' qualities: members are able to see that (most of them at least) live within similar surroundings and this in turns produces a sense of groupness and safety amongst members and from external categorisations of asylum seekers as undesirable others. This thirdspace is also unique and collectivising – illustrating 'home' here and 'home' elsewhere and providing both a 'real' and 'imagined' way to keep refreshing connections with 'home' left behind, either through socialising, visible symbols, or an intensive circulation of material culture (e.g. music, DVDs, books, and beauty products). This embodiment of belonging 'elsewhere' can be juxtaposed with a localised belonging expressed through photos and other symbols of 'settlement' in Glasgow.

Whilst the home site was primarily used for meetings mainly because of a lack of alternatives, using the private sphere in this way suggests a process by which *'non-settlement'* (Piacentini 2008), and its destabilising liminal effects, can be subverted and transformed into a thirdspace where collective identities can be reforged and resituated (Soja 1998). Although asylum seekers have no indication of how long they will stay in this temporary accommodation, they begin processes of 'home-making'.[14] Moreover, the act of opening the home space to others (both insiders, for example group members, co-nationals, or visiting friends, and outsiders such as community development workers, invited guest speakers, or group supporters) in a social way provides a degree of stability and certainty in this 'unstable' environment. It seems an important process for producing belonging for individuals and groups: this thirdspace of the NASS flat in the high rise block – where group life is largely experienced – becomes a place where liminality, marginality and the search for belonging in the context of structural constraints intersect and produce a sense of home-making that is safe and boundaried. In so doing, there is a clear intersection with Conquergood's (1994: 39) work on the creation of 'dwelling-place' within 'dominant space' for gangs in Chicago: 'Against a dominant world that displaces, stifles, and erases identity, the homeboys create ... a subterranean space of life-sustaining warmth, intimacy and protection' (Conquergood 1994: 47; see also Bauman 2012).

As Sandrine wrote in an online discussion about the future of her association (ASSECS):[15]

> ASSECS during these years has played a very crucial role by creating a platform where new English Speaking Cameroonians coming to Scotland can meet in our homes and speak pigin, and eat eru (*wild leaf vegetable*), achu (*pound cocoyam*) and fufu-corn (*cassava*) giving them that sense of home. ASSECS also has played some very important role to supporting members both emotionally, physically and psychologically.
>
> (Sandrine, Cameroonian woman, refugee, email, 25 June 2011)

Prior to the compulsory dispersal set out in the 1999 Immigration and Asylum Act, the majority of newly arrived refugees settled in areas where they had family, friends or where there were pre-existing communities (Bloch 2002), most commonly London or the South East of England. The specifically non-integrative norm of dispersal changed this. However, the process of living through dispersal reveals an interesting paradox: the development of territorial affinities which surface when refugees face being moved on from original dispersal areas to other parts of the city. Although asylum seekers are housed on a no-choice basis, as refugees, they must vacate dispersal accommodation, despite having 'rooted in' to dispersal neighbourhoods. The overall shortage of available housing stock in Glasgow has in many cases meant a second housing-led relocation to other parts of the city where housing is available. This poses different challenges for sustaining community (Ager and Strang 2008). Rather than stability and security, there is a second upheaval of both actual social ties and a sense of identification with others to a specific place, as Alice and Heloise explain:

> I want to move back to Red Road [Sighthill] (laughs) ... yes it true! I miss the area, I lived there for 5 years. I miss it. It's not because people said 'oh the high flats and they are for asylum seekers', I don't care about that, I just miss it, it's my neighbourhood, if I could move back I would. I wanted to stay but they said no. My neighbour here he doesn't know about asylum seekers or anything, so, it's like being new again you feel everyone is staring at you. I've put my name down for a house back there.
>
> (Alice, Ivorian woman, refugee)

> I have a house now, and a back door. But I really miss Sighthill, I miss it, it's where I belong I feel, it's my home. Pollok is good, but it's too far away. It's like ... Sighthill is where it all happened, and where I know people. If I could move my new house to there, that would be perfect.
>
> (Heloise, Congolese woman, refugee)

These interview excerpts reveal a sense of belonging and a form of neighbourhood nationalism that emerged for some as a result of the limitations of mobility placed upon dispersed asylum seekers. This raises an interesting question about whether neighbourhood nationalism has to have aggressive and masculine overtones as is the case with 'gangs'. The participants in this study were adult men and women (average age in their mid-thirties), and so processes of localised belonging are structured by a range of variables, including age.[16] Their exclusion as asylum seekers led them to assert a localised inclusion that extended beyond the NASS flat, either through taking part in local support groups, going to local colleges, worshipping locally or their children attending local schools. Moreover, these indicators of localised belonging were also used by external actors (e.g. Home Office) as evidence of integration to support outstanding asylum claims.[17]

Existing in this liminal thirdspace of the high rise flats has, for some, had very strong collectivising effects – many asylum seekers talk about feeling part of a local community, and of a local identity being forged (Scottish Refugee Council 2011). This enforced onward relocation as refugees then produces a renewed out-of-placeness when that mobility is, to all intents and purposes, reinstated. This mirrors the experiences of many when they were originally dispersed, discussed later in this chapter. Once more, participants spoke of experiencing racism, but this time from new neighbours and local people in predominantly 'white' neighbourhoods. In this sense, mobility, like immobility, can also be understood as destabilising, unsettling, and experienced with ambivalence, leading to the creation of new tyrannical spaces and processes of racialised othering.

As we have articulated, there are interesting and important points of intersection between the lived experiences of young people identifying with youth 'gangs' and that of individuals seeking asylum in Glasgow. Through an interlocking set of global, national and local forces, both groups are frequently co-located within areas of socio-spatial marginality and territorial stigma in the city. However, for both groups this experience is instilled with belonging, identification and the search for security. As Soja argues, the shared experience of thirdspace can give rise to the formation of new forms of intercultural and interstitial linkages. We do not, however, wish to present a false harmony in what are frequently fragmented and divided social terrains – it is important to note that the co-creation of space among these groups is achieved *separately*, and there is little evidence of *shared* identity in either study. There remain instances of conflict, discrimination, and othering at an everyday level within and between these communities. Moreover, while young people and asylum seekers may co-create identity in the midst of limiting social environments, these identities have a constraining effect – for young people, placing further limits on their mobility, and for asylum seekers providing what can for many only be an ephemeral sense of local belonging. In the following sections, we attempt to draw out some of these experiences.

## Young people, tyrannical spaces and (im)mobility

The bounding of the Langview community as a territorial 'gang' space, while fostering a degree of trust and solidarity amongst some young people in the area, also creates a parallel set of risks and insecurities both within and outwith these boundaries. Within the area, the 'microgeographies' of the Langview Boys frequently overlap and collide with other groups of young people who experience the Boys as inherently threatening and dangerous. As a result, certain spaces become 'no go' areas for groups of young people. Percy-Smith and Matthews (2001) describe these areas as 'tyrannical spaces':

> … some children, through their propinquity within neighbourhood spaces, clash and collide to such an extent that their experiences of a locality become severely blighted. For these unfortunate young people local environments are tyrannical spaces, defined in terms of 'no-go areas', danger and threat.
>
> (Percy-Smith and Matthews 2001: 49)

Like the young people in MacDonald and Shildrick's study in the north-east of England, it was clear that young people operated with 'subjective, mental maps of their area that sub-divided it into separate locales, each with their own reputations (i.e. greater or lesser associations with crime and risks to personal safety)' (MacDonald and Shildrick 2007: 345; see also Kintrea *et al.* 2008). These interlocking fears and insecurities indicate some of the reasons for the relative emptiness of the streets of Langview at certain points. During Alistair's street outreach work, for example, there would be long periods each night in which few contacts were made with groups of young people. In no small part, this related to the ubiquity of the Langview Boys in the public spaces of the area, and the local forms of 'tough', white masculinity that was layered into their group behaviour. Beneath the veneer of neighbourhood nationalism, therefore, there exist complex structures of age, gender, class and ethnicity that can result in further marginalisation of those deemed weak or vulnerable; reflecting broader social stigmatisations relating to hierarchies of 'whiteness' (Nayak 2007; Webster 2008). In the following fieldnote, Jay and Kris are taunting Bobby for being *too white*:

> Jay and Kris taunted Bobby for having very pale skin, saying he 'went on his holidays to Ayr' [a seaside town in Scotland]. During this, Bobby kept his head down and said nothing, kicking the ball against the wall on his own. Kris was clearly trying to make himself look good, by belittling a younger, weaker male. He used the talk of holidays to assert that he 'went on his hoalidays tae Spain every year'.
>
> (Fieldnote, 24th April 2007)

These configurations of domination and subordination, at a micro-level, demonstrate the ongoing salience of discrimination and difference in the lived experiences of young people. While there may be affinities based on residence, there remains a strong desire for distinction and domination.

These processes, moreover, interlock with a corresponding set of risks, fears and uncertainties *beyond* the Langview community. Rivers, canals, roads, and railways, engineered to facilitate greater mobility to and from the city centre, take on a different quality – they become immobile borders, no longer linking but separating. For some, the globalisation and development of transport has created new configurations of time and space; for others, these developments have placed further boundaries – economic, spatial, and social – on their lives. These cross-cutting boundaries, moreover, create a complex patchwork of security and danger, risk and uncertainty. These topographies of risk formulate spaces as 'tyrannical', infused with the threat of violence and othering. As Jock mentions:

> Certain buses, people won't go on. Like the Number 17 bus has got a big reputation, cos it goes through literally all the territories. So people don't feel comfortable going on that bus, cos they know it's got to go through somewhere that they know that they'll get attacked. So they avoid doing jobs in town, or far from where they live, cos they know it's going to be hard for them, or not worthwhile.

In a mapping exercise with the Langview Boys – in which the boys were asked to place stickers on a map of Langview illustrating their homes, their friends' homes, and the places where they spent time – it was notable how clustered the stickers were around the space of a few streets. Significantly, however, none of the stickers illustrating 'no-go' areas were in Langview, but were instead clustered around the areas immediately over the boundaries with Swigton, Oldtoun and Hillside. Thus, while the Langview Boys felt confident roaming within Langview, in fact they spent the majority of their time within this relatively small geographical area. This highlights the complex and scalar nature of (im)mobility for young people in Langview and beyond, and the configurations of 'territorial stigma' for young white men in Glasgow. In the following section, comparable 'tyrannical spaces' for asylum seeker, refugee and migrant groups are explored.

## Tyrannical spaces and othering amongst asylum seekers, refugees and migrants

During meetings and interviews with asylum seekers, refugees and migrants, many talked about dispersal sites as places of threat and fear, of being racially abused in their housing estates, at bus stops, in supermarkets, and on the streets.

> Ehm at the beginning it was a bit difficult because when I went out, I was often alone and it was a bit hard because I would often come across young people who are a bit ... who don't really like to see black people out and about ... so I often had quite a few problems with them. But after, you know, I got used to it and I would say to myself well it's normal you know ... when I got to know them and they got to see me more and more I saw they were decent people, we just didn't know each other you know, and also, we don't have the same skin, we don't have the same ways of seeing things ... I think it was because we didn't know each other, I think that over time ... well they are going to get used to seeing us.
>
> (Virginie, Ivorian woman, asylum seeker)

Virginie went on to explain she was reluctant to report racialised crime or victimisation because she didn't want to be seen as a 'trouble maker'. That Virginie did not want to raise this as a problem demonstrates that society operates within a racialised order and that social relations are indeed racialised (Miles 1993). But this also reveals how individuals have to find ways of negotiating their difference to help them cope with the experiences of heightened visibility as 'black' Africans, and their invisibility as marginalised and stigmatised asylum seekers with limited rights.

Virginie's assessment of the situation featured in the narratives of other research participants. When asylum seekers, refugees and migrants spoke about these experiences, they did so in equally pragmatic terms: they didn't want to '*cause trouble*'; they felt it more important to '*keep their head down*'; that 'white' Scottish people were simply '*not used to seeing black faces*' and over time this would improve as '*more "black" people settled in Glasgow*' (cf. Daniel 1968). Racism was indeed an everyday occurrence; nonetheless it impacted less on their daily lives than the effects of trying to survive their legal liminality. Of note however, is that these racist acts occurred in localities and contexts that cannot always be avoided, such as bus stops, shops, post offices and at entrances to high rise blocks (cf. Percy-Smith and Matthews 2001). Although asylum seekers found racism extremely unpleasant, one of the most frequently deployed risk-avoidance strategies was to avoid being outside the relative safety of the home space in the evening (Ager and Strang 2008; Wren 2007; Scottish Refugee Council 2011).

Despite then the development of local ties and belonging discussed earlier, the spatial concentration of asylum seekers resulting from dispersal can be understood as contributing to the creation of racialised tyrannical spaces (Percy-Smith and Matthews 2001) and territorial stigma (Wacquant 2007), not just for asylum seekers but other migrants living in these areas. As Adegoke a (non-asylum seeking) Cameroonian student pointed out during an interview:

> Ehm … personally I hate the bus just now … I really hate the bus. Because you just get on the bus and the way people look at you and things like that. I think one thing, when I came to Glasgow I didn't know anybody here, but I knew Rexon [ … ] I called him up and he told me he lived in Pinkston Drive so I lived with him for maybe a week or so and I got a flat in Pinkston Drive. Then I don't know, maybe after a couple of months of living in Glasgow I knew that Pinkston Drive was … a very bad place to live. It has a kind of stigma, asylum seekers and things like that. So one thing I've experienced is when you are going to tell people you live in Pinkston Drive and, you know, you are African, you are just associated with asylum … They think you are asylum seeker and people look at you like you are being a drain on the resources of Glasgow.
>
> (Adegoke, Cameroonian man, student)

In this excerpt we also see how the asylum seeker category has come to be a racialised and classed identity. Through the coincidence of being 'black' and living in an economically deprived dispersal area, Adegoke is constructed as a specific (and particularly undesirable) migrant other. He left Sighthill as soon as he could: his socioeconomic background and migrant status (a self-funding, international Masters Student at university), meant he was then able to move to a more affluent 'student' area in Glasgow: territorial stigma is thus attenuated through relocation (Wacquant 2007). Responses to this territorial stigma also vary: for migrants like Adegoke, mobility is a stigma avoidance strategy but not all immigrants enjoy this geographical-social mobility. This exposes the way in which (im)mobility is graded for immigrants and the ways in which this is tightly bound up in immigration status. Asylum seekers are not 'mobile' and so are 'contained' within dispersal sites, unless they are forced to relocate. The labelling processes at play also highlight that despite the Scottish Government's efforts to promote anti-racist messages about 'cohesive Scottish society', the everyday nature of racism and discrimination, the ways these can be both explicit and coded in wider debates around deservedness, belonging, entitlement (Sales 2002), as well as socioeconomic status and class.

## Concluding comments and further questions

This chapter has sought to establish novel sites of intersection between two contemporary folk-devils of youth 'gangs' and 'asylum seekers' by exploring the commonalities – and differences – between the two groups in the context of global (im)mobilities, space and identity. In Glasgow, both groups are located in areas of social and economic marginality, and experience spatial immobility, but create meaning in these environments through claims to space and the articulation of a desire for belonging, home-making and security. Through engaging with concepts drawn from human geography and the sociology of space and ethnicity – thirdspace and neighbourhood nationalism – we demonstrated the ways in which locality comes to be invested with meanings that can be contrasted with those projected from the outside (Back 1996). Evidence of the lived experience of thirdspace presented in this chapter reveals the complex ways in which global, national and local forces cohere in the construction of insider and outsider status; and the hierarchies of Otherness and difference that occur below the level of statistics. Crucially, too, we have attempted to demonstrate that the categories of youth 'gang' and 'asylum seeker' are not fixed or static identities, but subject to temporality and change. Collectivism stemming from the experience of thirdspace can be moved beyond and through – in what might be conceived as 'transitioning identities' – whether this relates to young people 'growing through gangs' or asylum seekers moving on to refugee status and/or asserting different identities; and receiving recognition for these.

The comparative framework we offer in this chapter is necessarily exploratory. We have sought to move beyond statistics that can only tell a partial picture of a very complex and multilayered social reality. But in doing so, we have raised further questions. These relate to the potential for more comparative research in order to identify whether the repositioning of current discourses of 'Scottish belonging' in terms of '*No Us, No Them, Just We*'[18] in the debate for Scottish independence may impact on ethnicity and difference. The lack of crime reporting reflects a wide range of social concerns with difference, othering and belonging that are both about 'race' and ethnicity but also the politicisation of asylum and the criminalisation of migration. This suggests that further work is needed on issues of 'race', ethnicity and crime in Scotland, but which also factors in immigration status and the construction of 'white others' as key variables. From a policy perspective, further questions relate to the potential impacts the continuing economic recession may have for newly establishing migrant populations and 'local white' working class populations in areas of social and economic decline. In moving towards a more inclusive politics, grounded accounts of the lived experiences of 'hidden communities' seem all the more vital.

## Notes

1 Whilst recognising the inherent mistrust and stigmatisation which has become implicit in the term 'asylum seeker', the authors believe the distinction between legal categorisations is important to illustrate that these different groups experience different scales of (im)mobility as it specifically relates to their immigration status. This also highlights ways in which immigration status is both situational and contingent. We use the following definitions: an 'asylum seeker' is someone who has left their country, has applied for asylum and is awaiting refugee status determination. 'Refugee' describes a person who has been recognised as a refugee as defined by the 1951 Geneva Convention relating to the Status of Refugees. 'Migrant' encompasses a broader category of students, workers, dependents and tourists who are not subject to asylum legislation. Distinguishing between asylum seekers, refugees and migrants in this way is intended to indicate the contingencies, contradictions and continuities involved in identification or categorisation as a member of one or other of these groups.

2 Wacquant suggests this stigma may be attenuated, or even be annulled through geographic mobility (Wacquant 2007: 67; see also Rogaly and Taylor 2011).

3 Robins and Cohen (1978) in fact hint at this form of inclusion and exclusion in their discussion of racial conflict between groups from different areas (1978: 115–18).

4 For a high-level summary of net migration in Scotland, 1951–2011, see: www.gro-scotland.gov.uk/files2/stats/high-level-summary/j11198/j1119806.htm (16 August 2012).

5 Statistics suggest that one-third of racially aggravated behaviour reported in Scotland in 2007/8 took place in the street, shops or dwelling places, underlining their everyday nature (Croall and Frondigoun 2010).

6 *The Guardian*, 24 November 2010, www.guardian.co.uk/society/2010/nov/24/asylum-seekers-glasgow-face-eviction. 2010 figures reveal that 2,300 asylum seekers were housed in Glasgow. By way of a comparison, in 2009, the three local authorities in England with the highest populations of asylum seekers in dispersed accommodation were Liverpool (1,375), Birmingham (1,345) and Manchester (950) (ICAR).

7 Around 10 per cent of the city's asylum seekers lived in the Petershill area in North Glasgow in 2008 (COSLAa 2011).

8 Territorial groups of young men, referred to as 'gangs', have been reported in Glasgow since the 1880s, and remain part of the social geography of the city in former working-class communities and peripheral housing estates. For more information, see Patrick (1973), Davies (1998), Deuchar (2009) and Bannister *et al.* (2010).

9 In both studies, the multiple roles adopted by Alistair and Teresa were highly beneficial, especially in establishing rapport and gaining access to participants. But role switching also raised different practical and ethical challenges, particularly in relation to managing 'new' roles, research participants' expectations and potential blurring of boundaries. For reflections on the 'backstage' of ethnographic research, see Ashe, Fraser and Piacentini (2009).

10 Information posted on COSLA website, www.asylumscotland.org.uk/theasylumprocess.php (accessed 10 July 2012).

11 Information posted on COSLA website, www.migrationscotland.org.uk/migration-info-centre/migration-statistics/asylum-seekers-scotland (accessed 10 July 2012).

12 *Cosla* website: www.asylumscotland.org.uk/theasylumprocess.php (accessed 10 August 2011). However, this changed quite radically from May 2011. A drop in numbers being supported by GCC housing below the agreed minimum triggered a contract review between GCC and UKBA. As a result, the contract has been transferred to Y-People (formerly YMCA) and Angel Housing.

13 Home Office/UKBA Quarterly Supported Asylum seekers by constituency September 2010 (unpublished), www.publications.parliament.uk/pa/cm201011/cmselect/cmscotaf/733/73303.htm (accessed 15 July 2012).

14 Although there is a lack of official published data published on the onward movements of asylum seekers following refugee status determination, one study conducted in Scotland suggests that half of all clients dispersed to Glasgow decided to stay in the city (Stewart 2009), although this research does not record the return of refugees back to Glasgow, of which there was much anecdotal evidence during the Glasgow study.

15 ASSECS is the Association of English Speaking Cameroonians in Scotland.

16 However, Deuchar (2011) does appear to suggest that there are masculine and aggressive overtones for young asylum seekers as is the case with gangs, and these are a response to both territorialism and local-level racism.

17 In November 2007, the UK Home Office announced and implemented its Case Resolution policy to review outstanding claims that predate the Asylum and Immigration Act of 2004. In most cases, a questionnaire was sent to asylum seekers asking for evidence of 'integration', usually provided in the form of letters of support from a range of 'community' sources (e.g. schools, churches, community associations, voluntary organisations, and support groups). Local level integration – and the belonging it implied – was then deemed an important criterion for a positive refugee status determination.

18 www.scotlandagainstracism.com/onescotland/CCC_FirstPage.html (accessed 25 July 2012).

# References

Aas, K. F. (2007) 'Analysing a world in motion: global flows meet criminology of the other', *Theoretical Criminology*, 11: 283–303.

——(2011) 'Visions of global control: cosmopolitan aspirations in a world of friction', in M. Bosworth and C. Hoyle (eds) *What is Criminology?* Oxford: Oxford University Press.

Ager, A. and Strang, A. (2008) 'Understanding integration: a conceptual framework', *Journal of Refugee Studies*, 21 (2): 166–91.

Alexander, C. (2008) *(Re)thinking Gangs*. London: Runnymede Trust.

Anie, A., Daniel, N., Tah, C. and Petruckevitch, A. (2005) *An Exploration of Factors Affecting the Successful Dispersal of Asylum Seekers*. Home Office Online Report 50/05. http://rds.homeoffice.gov.uk/rds/pdfs05/rdsolr5005.pdf (accessed 3 March 2011).

Ashe, S., Fraser, A. and Piacentini, T. (eds) (2009) *Critical Issues in Researching Hidden Communities*. Esharp: University of Glasgow. Available at www.gla.ac.uk/departments/esharp/otherpublications/specialissues/hiddencommunities/ (accessed 16 August 2012).

Back, L. (1996) *New Ethnicities and Urban Culture: Racisms and Multiculture in Young Lives*. London: UCL Press.

Bannister, J., Pickering, J., Batchelor, S., Burman, M. and Kintrea, K. (2010) *Troublesome Youth Groups, Gangs and Knife-Carrying in Scotland*. Edinburgh: Scottish Government.

Bauman, Z. (2000) *Globalization: The Human Consequences.* New York: Columbia University Press.

——(2002) 'In the lowly nowherevilles of liquid modernity: Comments on and around Agier', *Ethnography*, 3 (3): 343–49.

——(2004) *Wasted Lives: Modernity and its Outcasts.* Oxford: Polity Press.

——(2012) *On Education: Conversations with Richard Mazzeo.* Cambridge: Polity Press.

Blagg, H. (2008) *Crime, Aboriginality and the Decolonisation of Justice.* Sydney: Hawkins Press.

Bloch, A. (2002) *Refugee Migration and Settlement in Britain.* Basingstoke: Palgrave.

Brun, C. (2001) 'Reterritorializing the relationship between people and places in refugee studies', Theme Issue, Series B Human Geography, *Geografiska Annaler*, 83 (1): 15–25.

Burawoy, M. (ed.) (2000) *Global Ethnography: Forces, Connections, and Imaginations in a Postmodern World.* Berkeley: University of California Press.

Castells, M. (1996) *The Rise of the Network Society.* Oxford: Blackwell.

Childress, H. (2004) 'Teenagers, territory and the appropriate of space', *Childhood*, 11 (2): 195–205.

Cohen, S. (2002) *Folk Devils and Moral Panics.* London: Routledge.

Conquergood, D. (1994) 'Homeboys and hoods: gang communication and cultural space', in L. Frey (ed.) *Group Communication in Context: Studies of Natural Groups.* Hillsdale, New Jersey: Lawrence Erlbaum Associates, 23–56.

COSLAa. Convention of Scottish Local Authorities, Strategic Migration Partnership. www.migrationscotland.org.uk/migration-info-centre/migration-statistics/asylum-see kers-scotland (accessed 10 August 2011).

COSLAb. Convention of Scottish Local Authorities, Strategic Migration Partnership. www.asylumscotland.org.uk/theasylumprocess.php (accessed 10 August 2011).

Croall, H. and Frondigoun, L. (2010) 'Race, ethnicity, crime and justice in Scotland', in H. Croall, G. Mooney, and M. Munro, M. (eds) *Criminal Justice in Contemporary Scotland.* Cullompton: Willan Publishing, 111–31.

Damer, S. (1974) 'Wine alley: the sociology of a dreadful enclosure', *The Sociological Review*, 22 (2): 221–48.

Daniel, W. W. (1968) *Racial Discrimination in England.* Harmondsworth: Penguin Books.

Davies, A. (1998) 'Street gangs, crime and policing in Glasgow during the 1930s: the case of the Beehive Boys', *Journal of Social History*, 23 (3): 251–67.

de Lima, P. (2005) 'An inclusive Scotland? The Scottish executive and racial inequality', in G. Mooney and G. Scott (eds) *Exploring Social Policy in the 'New' Scotland.* Bristol: Policy Press, 135–56.

Deuchar, R. (2009) *Gangs: Marginalised Youth and Social Capital.* Stoke on Trent: Trentham.

——(2011) '"People look at us, the way we dress, and they think we're gangsters": bonds, bridges, gangs and refugees – a qualitative study of inter-cultural social capital in Glasgow', *Journal of Refugee Studies*, 24 (4): 72–689.

Elias, N. and Scotson, J. L. (1994) *The Established and the Outsiders: A Sociological Enquiry into Community Problems.* London: Sage.

Glasgow Anti-Racist Alliance (GARA) (2009) *The State of The Nation: Race and Racism in Scotland 2008.* Glasgow: GARA. Available online www.crer.org.uk/index. php?option=com_content&view=article&id=73:state-of-the-nation&catid=47&Itemi d=81 (accessed 16 July 2012).

Griffiths, D., Sigona, N. and Zetter, R. (2005) *Refugee Community Organisations and Dispersal: Networks, Resources and Social Capital*. Bristol: Policy Press.

Hagedorn, J. (2006) 'Race not space: a revisionist history of gangs in Chicago', *Journal of African American History*, 91 (2): 194–208.

——(2008) *A World of Gangs: Armed Young Men and Gangsta Culture*, Minneapolis: University of Minnesota Press.

Hanley, L. (2007) *Estates: An Intimate History*, London: Granta.

Hayward, K. and Yar, M. (2006) 'The 'chav' phenomenon: Consumption, media and the construction of a new underclass', *Crime Media Culture*, 2 (1): 9–28.

Held, D. (2000) 'Regulating globalization? The reinvention of politics', *International Sociology* 15 (2): 394–408.

Hynes, P. (2006) 'Dispersal of asylum seekers and processes of social exclusion in England', PhD Thesis. Middlesex University.

Joshi, H. E. and Wright, R. E. (2004) *Starting life in Scotland in the new millennium: population replacement and the reproduction of disadvantage* (Report). www.strath.ac.uk/media/departments/economics/fairse/media_140852_en.pdf (accessed 23 July 2011).

Kintrea, K., Bannister, J., Pickering, J., Reid, M. and Suzuki, N. (2008) *Young People and Territoriality in British Cities*. York: The Joseph Rowntree Foundation.

Law, A., Mooney, G. and Helms, G. (2010) 'Urban "disorders", "problem places" and criminal justice', in H. Croall, G. Mooney and M. Munro (eds) *Criminal Justice in Scotland*. Cullompton: Willan Publishing.

Leonard, M. (2006) 'Teens and territory in contested spaces: negotiating sectarian interfaces in Northern Ireland', *Children's Geographies*, 4 (2): 225–238.

Ley, D. and Cybriwsky, R. (1974) 'Urban graffiti as territorial markers', *Annals of the Association. of American Geographers*, 64: 491–505.

Macdonald, C. M. M. (2012) 'Imagining the Scottish diaspora: emigration and transnational literature in the late modern period', *Britain and the World*, 5 (1): 12–42.

MacDonald, R., and Shildrick, T. (2007) 'Street corner society: leisure careers, youth (sub)culture and social exclusion', *Leisure Studies*, 26 (3): 339–55.

Massey, D. (1994) *Space, Place and Gender*. Cambridge: Polity Press.

Matthews, H., Limb, M. and Percy-Smith, B. (1998) 'Changing worlds: the microgeographies of young teenagers', *Tijdschrift voor Economische en Sociale Geografie*, 89 (2): 193–202.

Matthews, H., Limb, M. and Taylor, M. (2000) 'The street as "thirdspace"', in S. Holloway and G. Valentine (eds) *Children's Geographies: Playing, Living, Learning*. London: Routledge, 63–79.

McCrone, D. (2001) *Understanding Scotland: The Sociology of a Nation*. London: Routledge.

Miles, R. (1993) *Racism after 'Race Relations'*. London: Routledge.

Miller, W. (2005) 'Adolescents on the edge: the sensual side of delinquency', in S. Lyng (ed.) *Edgework: The Sociology of Risk-taking*. London: Routledge.

Nayak, A. (2006) 'Displaced masculinities: chavs, youth and class in the post-industrial City', *Sociology*, 40: 813–31.

——(2007) 'Critical Whiteness Studies', *Sociology Compass*, 1 (2): 737–55.

——(2009) 'Beyond the pale: chavs, youth and social class', in K. P. Sveinsson (ed.) *Who Cares about the White Working Class?* London: Runnymede Trust, 28–35.

Office of National Statistics (2002) 'Social focus in brief: ethnicity', full report. Available at www.ons.gov.uk/ons/rel/ethnicity/social-focus-in-brief-ethnicity/full-report/index.html (accessed 16 August 2012).

Patrick, J. (1973) *A Glasgow Gang Observed*. London: Eyre-Methuen.

Pearson, G. (2011) 'Perpetual novelty: youth, modernity and historical amnesia', in B. Goldson (ed.) *Youth in Crisis? 'Gangs', Territoriality and Violence*. London: Routledge.

Percy-Smith, B. and Matthews, H. (2001) 'Tyrannical spaces: young people, bullying and urban neighbourhoods', *Local Environment*. 6 (1), pp 49–63.

Phillips, C. (2008) 'Negotiating identities: ethnicity and social relations in a young offenders' institution', *Theoretical Criminology*, 12 (3): 313–31.

Piacentini, T. (2008) 'Contesting identities in exile: an exploration of collective self-understanding and solidarity in refugee community organisations in Glasgow', *eSharp* Issue 11 (Spring 2008): Social engagement, empowerment and change. www.gla.ac.uk/departments/esharp/issues/11/ (accessed 20 June 2012).

Poole, L. and Adamson, K. (2008) Report on the situation of the Roma community in Govanhill, Glasgow. Glasgow: Oxfam. www.oxfam.org.uk/resources/ukpoverty/downloads/roma_report.pdf (accessed 4 July 2012).

Rhodes, J. (2012) 'Stigmatization, space and boundaries in de-industrial Burnley', *Ethnic and Racial Studies*, 35 (4): 684–703.

Robins, D. and Cohen, P. (1978) *Knuckle Sandwich: Growing Up in the Working-Class City*. Harmondsworth: Penguin.

Robinson, V. (2003) 'An evidence base for future policy: reviewing UK resettlement policy', in V. Gelsthorpe and L. Herlitz (eds) *Listening to the Evidence: The Future of UK Resettlement*, Home Office RDS Conference Proceedings. London: HMSO, 3–17.

Rogaly, B. and Taylor, B. (2011) *Moving Histories of Class and Community: Identity, Place and Belonging in Contemporary England*. London: Palgrave MacMillan.

Ross, N. J., Hill, M. and Shilton, A. (2008) '"One Scotland, Many Cultures": The views of young people from white ethnic backgrounds on multiculturalism in Scotland', *Scottish Affairs*, 64: 97–116.

Runnymede (2009) *Who Cares about the White Working Class?* London: Runnymede Trust.

Sales, R. (2002) 'The deserving and the undeserving? Refugees, asylum seekers and welfare in Britain', *Critical Social Policy*, 22 (3): 456–78.

Schuster, L. (2003) *The Use and Abuse of Political Asylum in Britain and Germany*. London: Frank Cass.

——(2005) 'A sledgehammer to crack a nut: deportation, detention and dispersal in Europe', *Social Policy & Administration*, 39 (6): 606–21.

Scottish Executive (2004) *Analysis of Ethnicity in the 2001 Census – Summary Report*. Edinburgh: Scottish Executive. Available at www.scotland.gov.uk/Publications/2004/02/18876/32937 (accessed 19 July 2012).

Scottish Refugee Council (2011) *Community and Neighbourhoods Briefing – Scottish Refugee Council Integration Study*. Glasgow: Scottish Refugee Council. Available at www.scottishrefugeecouncil.org.uk/policy_and_research/research_reports (accessed 19 July 2012).

Soja, E. W. (1998) *Thirdspace: Journeys to Los Angeles and Other Real and Imagined Places*. Cambridge, MA: Blackwell.

Stewart, E. (2009) 'The integration and onward migration of refugees in Scotland: a review of the evidence', *New Issues in Refugee Research*, Paper No. 174.

Stumpf, J. (2006) 'The crimmigration crisis: immigrants, crime, and sovereign power', *American University Law Review*, 56: 367–419.

Virdee, S., Kyriakides, C. and Modood, T. (2006) 'Codes of cultural belonging: racialised national identities in a multi-ethnic Scottish neighbourhood', *Sociological Research*

*Online*, 11 (4). Available at www.socresonline.org.uk/11/4/virdee.html (accessed 7 April 2012).

Wacquant, L. (2007) 'Territorial Sstigmatization in the age of advanced marginality', *Thesis Eleven*, 91: 66 – 77.

——(2008) *Urban Outcasts: A Comparative Sociology of Advanced Marginality*. Cambridge: Polity Press.

Webster, C. (1996) 'Local Heroes: violent racism, localism and spacism among white and Asian young people', *Youth & Policy*, 53: 15–27.

——(1998) 'Researching racial violence: a scientific-realist approach', in J. Vagg and T. Newborn (eds) *The British Criminology Conferences: Selected Proceedings*, Vol. 1: Emerging Themes in Criminology. London: British Society of Criminology.

——(2008) 'Marginalised white ethnicity, race and crime', *Theoretical Criminology*, 12 (3): 293–312.

Wren, K. (2007) 'Supporting asylum seekers and refugees in Glasgow: the role of multi-agency networks', *Journal of Refugee Studies*, 20 (3): 391–413.

Zetter, R. and Pearl, M. (2000) 'The minority within the minority: refugee community based organisations in the UK and the impact of restrictionism', *Journal of Ethnic and Migration Studies*, 26 (4): 675–98.

# 5 Citizenship and belonging in a women's immigration detention centre

*Mary Bosworth and Blerina Kellezi*

## Introduction

Under conditions of mass mobility, the relationship between citizenship and belonging has become increasingly interconnected, as neo-liberal states around the world have tightened border control, making it more difficult for large sections of the global population to enter legally or to remain in their countries. Such developments follow predictable, racialised, pathways in which citizens from the global 'south' have been particularly disadvantaged, despite long-standing chains of migration sustained by colonial and post-colonial relations with the economically developed North (see, *inter alia*, Balibar 2004, 2005; Guild 2009; Sassen 2007). Migrants from these Southern states are treated quite differently from citizens of the European Union who have benefited from shared rights to move and work throughout the European Community.

Globalisation and mass mobility have also had a profound impact on the nature of contemporary criminal justice and criminal law (Aas and Bosworth, 2013). Increasingly pressed into the service of border control, prisons (Kaufman 2012), police (Weber 2011; Bowling, Phillips and Sheptycki 2012) and the criminal law (Stumpf 2006; Aliverti 2012; Dauvergne 2008) have become global in outlook and effect. At the same time, Britain, along with other states pursuing neo-liberal policies, has introduced a slew of new immigration offences and constructed webs of immigration detention centres (Aliverti 2012; Bosworth 2012; Wilsher 2012; Brotherton and Barrios 2011; Kanstroom 2012). Such developments symbolically and in quite practical ways signify and enforce the boundaries of the nation state through legal and affective categories of belonging.

Border control, particularly in its intersections with criminal justice techniques, has recast citizenship as a form of governance (Rygiel 2010; Tyler 2010). Non-citizens are subject to increased scrutiny and intervention while citizens constantly must prove their eligibility for the enhanced protections their legal status now guarantees (Zedner 2010; Fekete and Weber 2010). Such developments have been particularly skewed towards black and minority ethnic communities who find themselves subject to new forms of policing in the search for suspected terrorists, asylum seekers, and undocumented workers (Parmar 2011). For these communities, longstanding and more recent fears about the 'enemy within' intersect with and amplify concerns about 'external threats' raising questions about belonging and entitlements even for long-term residents and UK citizens.

While a large immigration detention estate is relatively recent, its origins can be found in the Immigrants Appeals Act of 1969, which gave Commonwealth citizens the right to in-country appeal. Detention and immigration legislation is, thus, intimately connected to a racialised, post-colonial British national identity. Under these circumstances, it is surprising and somewhat disconcerting that so little of the burgeoning, interdisciplinary work concerned with migration control in criminology explicitly addresses race or ethnicity, while much of the criminological literature on race and ethnicity remains similarly uninterested in citizenship. Such oversights are all the more perplexing given the long historical connections between these matters.

Though the scale of mobility is new, much of the population on the move has been present in the UK for some generations (Hall 2001; Hall 2006). There have been prior moral panics about immigrants and crime and over assimilation and Britishness (Hall *et al.* 1978; Gilroy 1987). Critical race scholarship in criminology has productively focused on the role of the police in defining a racialised group membership (see, *inter alia*, Hall *et al.* 1978; Bowling 1999; Bowling, Parmar and Phillips 2008). Years of research demonstrate how black and ethnic minority men are subject to intrusive policing practices that implicitly and explicitly define them as not belonging, undeserving and potentially dangerous (Bowling, Parmar and Phillips 2008; Bowling, Phillips and Sheptycki 2012). These days, for foreigners, the Home Office plays a similar role. Those without UK citizenship, no matter what their legal status, simply do not have the same rights and protections as the rest of us (Zedner 2010; Dembour and Kelly 2011). Those in detention are particularly vulnerable, legally and symbolically denied recognition as subjects by their incarceration (Bosworth 2011b, 2012).

This article takes one particular site – the women's immigration removal centre Yarl's Wood – to consider the lived experiences of this kind of racialised 'precarity' (Di Giorgi 2010; De Genova 2008). Drawing on six months of observation and interviews that we conducted with over 130 women and 30 staff from June to December 2010, as part of the first national, academic study of life in detention, it explores women's views about identity, citizenship and belonging. In detailing women's testimonies, this chapter builds its analysis on the views and experiences of this otherwise silenced custodial population. Their stories enrich and challenge the dominant understanding of border control that characterises such places merely as 'zones of exclusion' both in the conflict they reveal within the detainee population and in their shared aspirations (for example, see Pratt 2005; Gill 2009; De Genova and Peultz 2010; though see also Rygiel 2012; Walters 2008). As such, they raise important questions about recognition and shared group membership

demonstrating the salience of detention centres – and migration – for criminological research on race/ethnicity. From a critical race perspective, these
institutions, where the state wields almost unimaginable amounts of power
against a dizzying array of nationalities, are both bewilderingly unfamiliar
and depressingly predictable. As Effa, a detainee from the Cameroon, bluntly
put it, 'In here don't see white people apart from those wearing uniforms.'

## Detaining women in Britain: the research context[1]

IRC Yarl's Wood is one of ten immigration removal centres scattered around
the country, which, together, hold 3,000 men and women under Immigration
Act powers. Others may be found in prison post-sentence, or in police lock-
up.[2] Detainees are not serving criminal sentences, and, therefore, have little
way of knowing how long they will be held. Although, legally, they should
only be detained if their deportation is 'imminent', in practice IRCs hold
some individuals for considerable periods.[3]

There is a national system of carceral institutions, yet detention centres
vary considerably. They are contracted out by the Home Office to private
companies and HM Prison Service and can feel (for detainees and staff alike)
quite localised. Notwithstanding national guidelines and detention service
orders, each institution operates under the terms of its confidential contract,
offering slightly different activities, conditions, and food.

Yarl's Wood opened in November 2001 and is currently run by Serco. It is
a secure custodial environment, situated behind razor wire at the back of a
former Ministry of Defence site in Clapham, Bedfordshire. Surrounded by
green rolling hills and quaint villages, Yarl's Wood is not easily accessible
without a car, since it is situated nearly 20 minutes drive from the nearest
train station.[4] It was originally twice the size and designed to hold as many
men as women, but, within months of its opening, the male detainees
destroyed their section, burning it to the ground.

The current building holds over 400 detainees in four residential wings and
a segregation unit, all of which, given the women's ultimate enforced 'flight',
are somewhat ironically named after birds: Dove, Avocet, Crane, Bunting and
Kingfisher. Until January 2011, when they were relocated to Tinsley House
and then to the so-called 'pre-departure accommodation' Cedars Unit near
Gatwick airport, the Crane wing held families with young children. These
days it contains married couples, families with adult children and, since
March 2012, a small number of single men as well. Bunting is an induction
unit, where women are placed for their first few nights, while Kingfisher is the
segregation unit.[5]

In the two regular housing units of Yarl's Wood, women are grouped in
pairs in small rooms that include a separate shower and toilet area. On
Bunting, the rooms are single occupancy, whereas on Crane families of four
may be placed in adjacent rooms with interlocking doors. Most of the rooms,
other than those in Kingfisher, look over grassy outdoor association areas.

They include a small wardrobe, a desk and a notice board. A small television set with an integrated VCR player is bolted to the wall. With their brightly coloured curtains and shabby furniture they resemble student halls of residence as much as prison wings. Yet, each housing unit is connected to the main part of the institution by an iron gate, which can only be opened by a staff member carrying keys.

For much of the day detainees are free to wander around the building, carrying the key to their room with them. However, they are never allowed into any other residential unit than their own. They are locked in their unit for lunch and dinner, and, following an evening period of general association, must remain there from 9pm–9am. Each unit has its own dining room and a number of small lounge areas containing sofas from Ikea, a television and some books.

Those who leave the units during association time can mingle with others in the main area of the institution where there is a large indoor gym, a doctor's surgery, a library, a hairdressing salon, a small indoor cinema, a 'cultural kitchen', and a number of designated religious areas including a Christian church, a mosque and a Hindu/Sikh temple. Some detainees congregate on the 'activities corridor' that includes an art and craft area and an IT room equipped with computers from which they may email friends and family outside the centre.[6] Others sit in small 'association' rooms, chatting to one another or calling friends and relatives on their mobile phones.

The 'cultural kitchen' can be booked for a whole day by six women at a time. They are provided with raw ingredients and are allowed to cook lunch and dinner under the supervision of a Detention custody officer (DCO).[7] The room is decorated to resemble a middle-class British family house, complete with dining table, sofa, large screen television and a CD player. The Ikea tableware is brightly coloured and the kitchen implements and electric goods homely; these are not institutional items, but ones picked out at the local superstore, including a mid-range quality kettle, microwave, oven, and blender. The women are allowed to bring in their own DVDs and CDs and quite often everyone ends up dancing after the meal is finished. They are not allowed to share the food they make with any women other than those in the room, although custodial staff members routinely drop by to sample it.

Notwithstanding its range of activity areas, there is a minimally structured regime in Yarl's Wood. The centre offers scant paid work other than 'servery' and cleaning, while education, at least when we were present, was limited to a few hours of art and craft on weekdays. Whereas most of the men's institutions we visited as part of the wider study offered IT training and ESOL classes, Yarl's Wood IT officer did not seem to provide any lessons, and the centre deployed their trained ESOL teacher as the librarian. She helped individual women who asked for assistance with learning how to read and write. However, she did not teach formal classes. Instead, she had the women read out the words of a dictionary. One day, as a member of the research team (MB) was hanging around in the library, a Chinese woman, Bao-Yu, asked her to help her in this task. In one of the ironies of fieldwork, that day, Bao-Yu had reached the letter 'R': 'resist, revolt, revolution'.

Together then, Yarl's Wood offers carefully choreographed levels of freedom within constraints. The women are allowed to wander, but not everywhere. They are free to cook, but not to share their meal. They are encouraged to speak English, but not to learn it. In these and many other ways, the institution includes while simultaneously excluding the detainees from a range of everyday expectations and practices. Not quite prisoners, yet certainly not free, the 'residents'[8] (not citizens), in detention exist literally and symbolically in a liminal space. Under these conditions, questions of identity become important mechanisms for sorting, coping and understanding, at the same time as matters of identity remain also always the basis and justification for detention itself.

## Identity matters: diversity in detention

The residents of Yarl's Wood are a mixed population, united primarily by their lack of British citizenship. Some are ex-prisoners, others failed asylum seekers, and still others visa over-stayers. Most have lived in the UK for many years. Nearly all are awaiting deportation or removal.[9] The centre holds an additional population of asylum seekers who have been designated eligible for a 'fast track' decision. These women, whose cases have been flagged as unlikely to succeed, attend the Yarl's Wood Asylum and Immigration Tribunal that is accessible via a locked door from within the removal centre.[10]

Though detainees in principle can hale from any part of the world, their nationalities reflect broader historical and contemporary migration trends. Like many of the migrants in the broader British community, detainees tend to be from former British colonies. Unlike the wider population, however, removal centres hold very few Australians, New Zealanders or Canadians. Rather, their inhabitants originate in the so-called 'New Commonwealth', with particular concentrations from Nigeria, Jamaica and Pakistan. Yarl's Wood, in common with other 'removal' centres, also houses a number of Chinese and Vietnamese nationals.

At the time of our fieldwork, Yarl's Wood counted 63 different nationalities among its population (Serco 2011). Only the top ten – Nigeria, China, Jamaica, India, Sri Lanka, Vietnam, Ghana, Pakistan, Brazil and Uganda – corresponded to groups of ten or more women. The rest of the national groups were much smaller, with the majority accounting for only one or two women in the institution. In addition to their range of citizenship, women also differed from one another in terms of their religion, their length of stay in the UK, their prison record and their marital status. While the predominant religious groups were Christian, Muslim, and Hindu, there were many kinds of denominations of each, as well as other belief systems and those who were not religious at all.

This diversity encouraged many types of social exchanges. Some women enjoyed getting to know people from other countries and cultures. Although upset about the length of her incarceration, Pam, an elderly woman from Nigeria who had worked in the UK for many years as carer before being imprisoned for document offences, typified this view of detention:

> When I came here, sometimes I think is the wish of God that I should come to a place like this. But I never wanted it to be too long. So as we've seen so many people from different backgrounds. If I'd not come here I wouldn't have known. If I see them maybe on television or on the streets, I would just walk past them. But now that I'm here ... It's a wonderful thing.
>
> (Pam, Nigeria)

Pam found that the experience of detention enabled cultural sharing and communication. Other detainees, however, were not so open-minded, preferring the company of their co-nationals, turning to them for friendship and support. 'In here,' Ania claimed, 'people just tend to straight away go for their own nationality. It doesn't really matter if it's the type of person they hate, because it's from their nationality, it's like this weird bond that's instant' (Poland). For still others, however, the problem was intractable and the sheer range of people disorienting. 'I don't really have friends like close friends,' Isa admitted sadly, 'Because to me, you know, we have different styles, different nature, different spirit' (Nigeria).

Indeed, in contrast to Pam's appreciative stance, 'difference' was often the source of considerable tension and conflict in Yarl's Wood. To a far greater extent than in the men's facilities we visited, there were frequent disputes between Chinese nationals, Jamaicans and Nigerians. Racist comments in English, Mandarin and other local dialects were common currency between these three groups. Jamaican and Nigerian women often mimicked Chinese accents and made up speech patterns, referring to them as 'chin chow min'. For their part, Chinese nationals maligned black women as overly sexual, promiscuous, and aggressive, referring to them by the highly pejorative appellation of 'black ghosts'. At times the hostility between these groups erupted into violence:

> In the past, black ghosts always jumped the queue and the officers would not stop them. There is only once that a Chinese girl jumped the queue and was disciplined by the officer. On that day, I spotted a black woman jumped queues again, without any interference by the officer, who is white. I felt angry and I thought it was unfair, getting into argument with the officer. The black ghosts heard it and insulted me. They then smashed a glass bottle on the corner of my forehead. You can still see the scar here ... They locked me up after I was hurt and hardly gave me any medical treatment. Then when I finally got the chance to be examined by the doctor, he found that I have slight concussion. The officer didn't apologize to me, nor did she say anything to me so far. I am not asking

them to do anything. I just hope that they won't be partial to the black ghosts all the time. It is unfair that there are certain things here that the black ghosts can do, but we as Chinese cannot do.

(Kyla, China)

What was most dispiriting about these interactions was the familiar racist tropes both groups deployed against the other, a strategy recognised by a Taiwanese detainee Ada[11] as she defused a conversation with a Nigerian woman in the art and craft room that was rapidly becoming antagonistic. As the topic turned to food, Ada claimed laughingly that, when she next used the 'cultural kitchen', she would 'eat dog! Dog keeps you warm!' (Ada, Taiwan). In this instance, the (white) custody officer Leah joined in the 'joke' urging Ada not to eat her pet 'Staffy'.[12]

Further problems arose between different religions. Non-Christians complained about the noisy midnight services of their Evangelical neighbours. Even those who were themselves devout expressed concerns about other ways of praying.

If I want to go to church it's always full with Africans or Chinese, but I don't get time to even sit quietly and pray. I use the garden for my pray. And I don't like to pray so loudly and disturb everybody ... But I have seen faith in African people, honestly. They literally pray, pray, pray from morning to night they are praying. I hope it has some meaning. Means the matter of praying is very important. I was telling some of them, because shouting and you know, playing the drums loudly or just lying on the floor and offering yourself to Jesus, I don't think it's the right way to go about.

(Gena, India)

Additional factors divided the population as well, from banal everyday complaints over food to more serious ones of discrimination. Many African and Chinese women blamed the [entire] Asian population, at least in part, for the food, claiming that it was too spicy and 'Indian' for them. They also suggested that Asian detainees received preferential treatment from the small number of Asian staff. Others spoke of pressure to hide their sexual orientation. Nia, from Malawi, for instance, who was claiming asylum as a lesbian kept her story secret in Yarl's Wood: 'I can't tell them about who I am because they are African and they will judge me. So I just am alone' (Nia, Malawi).

Mental illness was also, for some, highly stigmatised. 'I am on antidepressants now since I had the shock ... ', Cora (from Zimbabwe) told us, 'In my country it is taboo to take medication. We don't take anything about depression or stress. I am so embarrassed to tell the other women. They will think I am crazy.' Finally, some were ashamed about their criminal conviction. Pam from Nigeria, who otherwise emphasised the positive aspects of her detention experience, was concerned about the impact of her criminal sentence in detention and when she was returned:

> You know the other African women they look at me and say, you are criminal. They say that other person was working with fake documents, why did they bring me in here? They did not bring other people in here. They said that they were taken from work too and with fake documents but don't understand why they took you to prison and not me. All my African sisters look at me as a criminal. Why did they choose me for this? Why did they bring me in here? When the time in prison finished I thought they were going to let me out or send me back home, but they did not. Why did they choose me? Why don't they take me home? What have I done to deserve this? I will be labeled for life.
>
> (Nigeria)

As Effa explained it:

> There is a lot of tribalism in here … Jamaicans think the Africans are very primitive, so they're very nasty towards us. And we think some other cultures are primitive too. So we say things about them behind their backs … so you have this whole mix up … We're quite nasty to each other to be honest, which is sad, we are. Even among the Africans. No, even among the Africans, they're quite rude. And Nigerian will talk to this one [a woman from Malawi] like she's some kind of – you know …
>
> (Cameroon)

Such divisions among the detainees reveal a population, however uneasily, marked out by its 'hyper-diversity' (former IRC Manager, HMIP). As in the community, cultural overlap coexists in such places with cultural conflict. Yet, inside the detention centre both are intensified by the conditions of confinement. As one staff member at Yarl's Wood put it rather clumsily, 'diversity is where we are here' (DCO, Troy).

It is ironic, then, that in their emphasis on citizenship and nationality, the logic of immigration detention explicitly denies the relevance of diversity. In legal terms, detainees are simply not British. They are foreigners and non-citizens. They do not belong in Britain, so their particular perspectives on culture and national belonging are easily discounted. According to immigration law their nationality is all.

The binary logic justifying detention centres sits in stark contrast to their detained population. The dissonance between these factors is often disorienting for staff and detainees alike. In response, detainees expend considerable energy attempting to claim an equivalent form of citizenship that might overrule their legal status, while staff members frequently differentiate between detainees, viewing some as deserving and others as undeserving of deportation. In these kinds of discussions, which one of us has covered in more detail elsewhere (Bosworth 2011b, 2012), staff and detainees debate the grounds for recognition. One long-term British resident raged against her situation, comparing herself to the prime minister, David Cameron, her hyperbolic tone revealing the extent of her frustration with finding a legitimate identity from which to appeal her predicament. Drawing on a familiar moral hierarchy she casts herself first as a worker and then as a mother, yet, as she recognises both subject-positions, usually revered, are reduced to nothing by her lack of citizenship.

> I have paid taxes in this country. I have worked. My children are outside. My son has been suspended from school. He is 10 and my daughter is 17. And they tell me I don't have enough family ties? What is the relationship of a mother with her children? Is that not strong enough? You see Cameron rushing to be by the side of his father and he rushed there before he died as there are ties between father and son. He has his own family and children and he still has ties to his 70-year-old father. And my children are not tied to me? And they are so young and need me but they tell me there are not strong ties. Cameron is tied to his young daughter, and I am not. Whose children are these? Do they know how tied a mother is to her children? But God punished him. His son died and his father died.
>
> (May, Jamaica)

In accounts like this detainees seek legitimate subject position from which to be recognised. Staff, too, search for answers, finding the treatment of some detainees more troubling than others.

These matters are painful and, as such, are not ones that many staff voluntarily explore. Members of the senior management team explicitly discouraged emotional engagement with the detainees, a view that was reiterated to us by staff as a requirement that they exhibit 'empathy not sympathy'. Whereas detainees who seek to resist their removal have little choice but to try to make themselves heard, staff learn to shut down and to generalise; saving their emotional energy for a small selection of individuals. As Todd said, 'when I first started, it weren't easy. But now, I would say, probably say I was a bit blasé, but I just deal with it' (DCO).

If recognition calls matters of citizenship into question, lack of recognition, in day-to-day life in detention was often facilitated by ideas about nationality. Just as the citizenship detainees sought to assert was not a legal one (Bosworth 2012), nor is the staff's understanding of nationality. Rather, citizenship is elided by staff into 'nationality' – a series of 'others' all too easily synonymous with racialised stereotypes.

Although they were always careful not to be overtly racist with us, staff commonly differentiated between 'polite', 'aggressive', and untrustworthy national groups. As one male officer literally stuttered in his bid to explain what he meant while avoiding saying anything too pejorative:

each nationality has certain ... I'll use the word, 'traits' but it sounds a bit of a negative word. Certain characteristics about, about them. For instance a, a Nigerian lady is not like a Chinese lady in, in behaviour or, or, or anything like that ... some, some nationalities are much more volatile than others but I'll, I'll, I'll say Sri Lankan people are the most calm and, and easygoing and passive people you could meet, whereas it could be said that some of the African nationalities are quite volatile ...

(DCO Sean)

Reflecting (and presumably shaping) the institutional relationships, many staff members in formal interviews and in passing conversation explicitly contrasted Chinese and Jamaican women. Their views, however, were inconsistent. For one female DCO who worked on the activities corridor, 'the Chinese nationality' was 'extremely intelligent' and 'very educated', unlike the 'Jamaican ladies' whom, she claimed, were not (DCO, Leah). In contrast, Sean negatively compared the hygiene of Chinese women to the 'Jamaican ladies' who were 'absolutely fastidious about cleanliness'. While most commonly, a nurse in healthcare complained about the difficulty of communicating with the Chinese women and criticised the Jamaican population for being aggressive. 'Culturally', Alys said, 'they're very, they're quite loud, they're quite shouty. ... That can be quite difficult.'

Even those who appeared not to favour one group over the other characterised them in starkly different terms. Troy, for instance, first appeared to emphasise their similarities, asserting that, 'the Jamaicans and Nigerians and the Chinese are loud by nature. Or by culture, whatever you want to call it' (DCO, Troy). The reason for their behaviour, however, he attributed to quite different causes:

Chinese are easier to control, yeah, because I think they've been used to authority more in their life. The Nigerians and Jamaicans are much more difficult to control ... Why? I don't know the answer ... Maybe because they've had to fight for things from day one, you know. Fourteen children at the table, scrabbling for whatever's there, I don't know. I'm guessing, you know, speculating. But they're much more difficult to control than the Chinese. Chinese respect authority. Nigerians and Jamaicans don't. Not the authority that they see me as, you know.

(DCO, Troy)

These staff views are intimately linked to the purpose and justification of detention centres. As sites designed to exclude on the basis of nationality, removal centres present subjectivity purely as a matter of legal citizenship. Other aspects of people's lives cease to matter and detainees are rendered effectively 'unrecognisable'. Matters are compounded by the material similarities between these institutions and prisons (high walls, segregation blocks, keys, razor wire) that impute a level of dangerousness and culpability to those confined within. National stereotypes, particularly racialised ones, further these institutional effects, denying the familiarity of much of the population along with their goals and aspirations. In so doing, they ease the conscience of (some) line staff and assist in repudiating individual claims. Together, the binary logic of citizenship and the racialised national categories delegitimise the women's claims and aspirations while also redirecting attention away from their gendered effect. It is this final issue, of gender, to which we turn in the next section.

## Longing and belonging in a global world

Soon after we arrived in Yarl's Wood, a senior member of the onsite UKBA (now Home Office)[13] team at Yarl's Wood proudly asserted that, 'There is a fantastic community spirit here. You can see it in how the ladies sit around doing clothes, hair and nails. They are always smiling' (Abby, UKBA). This heavily feminised view of cosy companionship denied the evident fractures and tensions that subsequent interviews with women revealed. It also glossed over the more troubling gendered aspects of many of these women's lives, a number of whom had survived considerable levels of domestic violence, often at the hands of husbands, fathers and brothers. For these women Britain had offered a gendered sanctuary that Yarl's Wood and UKBA were working to deny.

For Arah, the link between gender, safety and economics was direct. Her sense of security depended on her material situation. 'In UK, as a woman, I felt, you know, safe and, you know, okay, you know, like food, you know, you don't have to struggle to buy food, you know. ... Back home you have to struggle' (Jamaica). For Evie, the dangers lay closer to home. Her mother had given her money to leave, but the British state would not allow her to stay. 'My problem is my father and that's it. Hitting ... all the time hitting, all the time like you're a bitch, in my country, what my father does is normal, the police won't help ... ' (Evie, Turkmenistan).

Safety, the women pointed out in a variety of ways, was intimately connected to their capacity for agency and autonomy. Without it, they could not truly be themselves. 'In Africa the men dominate. Women just have to do what they say. There I am subdued, I cover my hair. Here I can express myself' (Ena, Gambia). As the basis for their immigration case, however, such claims were weak. In an account alluding to, but not fully articulating sexual violence, Nya from Uganda wept, as she said, 'I was told I didn't have proper ties here, because I have no children, because I am not married. But there are some things I cannot do because of what happened to me.'

Others were more recognisably political, using the language of equal rights familiar to most liberal feminists. Kela, from Nigeria, for instance, believed that, 'In UK whatever man can do, I think woman can do it. ... Back home is a bit, it's not that the same. Because sometimes our men, they don't give chance to a woman.' Struggling to articulate herself in a language in which she was not fluent, Kela worried that her capacity to be herself would be compromised upon return:

Sometimes the men ... back home ... will say 'No. You are a mother, you need to take care of the house'. ... in white system, they used to give that opportunity to people like you can use your brain. You can make use of your brain. But back home, most of the time they don't really give that chance. ..: Feel well here because in this country, I don't know how to put it. In this country they give you that more chance to do something. More than back home.

(Kela, Nigeria)

For these women, their banishment from Britain, made possible by their citizenship status, would deny them the capacity for agency and self-determination, locking them into traditional gender roles which they longed to transcend.

Not all the stories were equally bleak. Some women were happy to leave. Others had always intended on going, though perhaps at a later point in the future. So, too, in many interviews, detainees (and staff) resisted the exclusionary logic of detention and deportation. Hali, who had spent 15 years working in UK, insisted her time had not been wasted:

Oh, the best part, the best part of my life which I will never forget, even if I'm deported, the best part of my life is UK. Yes! Because at least I achieved my dream – I want to be a nurse. I'm so happy. Even if I go to Nigeria and die, I don't regret my stay in the UK. Yes, I don't regret it.

(Nigeria)

Likewise, Bao-Yu, a former factory worked from China, retained a dogged admiration for England itself, despite her current predicament. Bao-Yu, who had come to England because, as she said, 'I want to change my life. So have a better life, was in China very hard. So, and also can give more education my daughter, yeah.' Until the UKBA came to her door one morning with an arrest warrant, England had borne out her hopes. She had made new friends and formed a romantic relationship with a man who wanted to marry her. Notwithstanding her looming administrative removal, she continued to speak approvingly of all things British from the food to the landscape, sighing:

Oh, England. I love the English culture, like, I like the English garden and then the ... people have a very private life. And I like English National Trust. ... Beautiful place. Yeah. I couldn't find that sort of place in China.

(Bao-Yu, China)

It was not just detainees who refused to accept the oppositional discourse of belonging and exclusion. Staff, too, played a role. Though for the most part, they referred to detainees unquestioningly as 'foreigners' and outsiders, all sought, at times, to be compassionate and understanding, sometimes breaking detention centre rules in the process to mail a letter outside for a detainee or to bring in a particular item for them. Less controversially, a Welfare officer established a scheme by which the women could transfer funds from their inaccessible UK bank accounts into a local credit union that would then hand over the cash. In his view, they had earned the money and so should be allowed to take it with them.[14] 'We have some real gifted people that come through these places', the Christian pastor asserted, 'Doctors and people with PhDs and, you know, Masters and all sorts.'

## Conclusion: diversity, detention and exclusion

With their high walls and razor wire, as well as metal doors, locks and keys, immigration centres are clearly modelled on prisons, harnessing the power of the state to exclude. Compounding matters, even before deportation or removal has occurred, their restricted regimes make clear the logic and inevitability of exclusion; the population is evidently not considered worth investing (much) time or energy in occupying. In Zygmunt Bauman's (2004) terms, such examples paint detainees as merely the 'waste product' of globalisation, a precarious labour force (Di Giorgi 2010) subject to 'the deportation regime' (De Genova and Peultz 2010).

Yet, as this chapter has argued, these centres are more than simply symbolic zones of exclusion, peopled with 'non-citizens'. Rather they are filled with people each of whom has a life story, and most of whom are busy making claims, building relationships, quarrelling with one another and the staff. In order to understand these places better, far more attention needs to be paid to life inside them.

As the women's accounts in this chapter movingly demonstrate, contemporary practices of detention and deportation that are justified by citizenship and facilitated by long-standing racialised tropes about dangerous and undeserving 'Others', have a highly gendered effect. As such, they remind us that questions of citizenship and nationality – which both define life in the detention centres and legitimate it – are related at fundamental levels to beliefs about what it means to be a woman and to have an opportunity at being a self in the world. For what these women fear most is the loss of subject-hood itself, and with it, the capacity of experiencing and shaping life in their own terms. In their fears we hear an echo of Judith Butler's (2010: 31) warning that 'Part of the very problem of contemporary political life is that not everyone counts as a subject'. Non-subjects, she asserts, in typically opaque terms, are particularly precarious, existing outside our usual ethical and normative frames and expectations, as well as sometimes outside the law. They are 'ungrievable', expendable, unrecognisable (Kaufman and Bosworth 2013).

By segregating foreign citizens behind bars, detention centres materially, and metaphorically, excise those within them from the wider British community, erasing their subjectivity and refusing them the benefits of shared group membership. In so doing, they deny the reality, that a DCO casually noted one day, in a wide-ranging discussion about her local town, Bedford, 'you sit next to these people on the bus every day. They are part of the community' (DCO, Leah). Strangers in a strange world though some of them are, detainees express remarkably familiar aspirations to citizens: a desire for safety, autonomy and agency. When viewed through this lens of recognition, rather than exclusion, the costs and contradictions of immigration detention become clearer. It is not just that they foster an exclusionary notion of British national identity, but also that they deny shared bonds of humanity.

## Notes

1 This research was funded by a British Academy Research Award and by the OUP John Fell Fund at the University of Oxford. We would like to thank the Home Office and the Centre Manager at Yarl's Wood for allowing us research access and to all the staff and detainees who spoke with us and shared their stories. All respondents have been anonymised appearing with a pseudonym and their nationality, or, in the case of staff, their officer grade. We would also like to thank Colin Webster, Hindpal Bhui, Richard and Michal Bosworth and Emma Kaufman for their comments on an earlier draft.

2 Whereas the numbers in police cells are never published, the Prison Service and other organisations periodically report the numbers of ex-foreign national prisoners. In 2011 a report by the Chief Inspector of the UK Border Agency, John Vine (2011), counted 800 ex-prisoners held this way. By January 2012, a report released in response to a Freedom of Information Request from the Charity Detention Advice Services, showed that total had fallen to 595 (www.detentionadvice.org.uk/uploads/1/0/4/1/10410823/foi_21786_response.pdf, thanks to Hindpal Singh Bhui for providing me this reference).

3 In the month of November 2010, for example, the average length of stay in Yarl's Wood was two months. Around one in five women, however, had been there for 100–500 days (Serco, 2011).

4 The centre runs a free coach service to and from Bedford train station most afternoons to help those making social visits. Lawyers or other advocates who can visit in the morning have to make their own way there.

5 In IRCs detainees may be held for a short period (usually only up to 24 hours) in segregation on either R40 or R42. Those on R42 are usually held only briefly. In either case their segregation must be signed off by the in-house Immigration contract manager.

6 Many of these spaces are duplicated on the family unit, reflecting the historical segregation of the two populations. When Yarl's Wood still held children they were always kept wholly apart from the single women other than in the visiting hall.

7 When we began our research the DCO would collect cash from the women and buy specialist ingredients for them from local shops. This practice, however, was soon abandoned due to questions over parity and the staff member's time. From that point detainees were able to select from items used in the institution's own kitchen.

8 This was the preferred term used by staff to refer to the women, rather than 'detainee'.

9 Though in practical terms these processes have the same outcome: exclusion from British soil, legally they are distinct and follow separate administrative processes. While former offenders are usually deported, visa over-stayers may be removed. In both cases their exclusion from Britain prevents them from entering other EU countries as well. This nature of state power is referred to as elsewhere as the 'Ban-opticon' (Bigo 2008; Aas 2011).

10 On gender and asylum more generally see Baillot, Cowan and Munro 2012 and Querton 2012. On asylum and the law see Thomas 2011.
11 Ada, who had lived legally in the UK for over two decades with her English husband and children was deported to Taiwan following a criminal conviction. While in Yarl's Wood she acted as an unpaid interpreter for many of the Chinese women. She found this role emotionally demanding and exhausting.
12 Staffordshire terrier.
13 In March 2013 the UK Border Agency (UKBA) was returned to the direct oversight of the Home Office.
14 Many undocumented workers either share bank accounts or use savings accounts from which they can only withdraw in person upon presenting their pass book. Once in detention these people effectively lose access to their savings. The system established at Yarl's Wood enabled women to instruct their bank to transfer their funds into the local credit union who would then hold regular surgeries in the IRC to enable them to withdraw their cash.

# References

Aas, K. (2013) 'The ordered and the bordered society: Migration control, citizenship and the Northern penal state', in K. Aas and M. Bosworth (eds) *Migration and Punishment: Citizenship, Crime Control, and Social Exclusion*. Oxford: Oxford University Press.

Aas, K. F. (2011) '"Crimmigrant" bodies and bona fide travelers: survillance, citizenship and global governance', *Theoretical Criminology*, 15 (3): 331–46.

Aas, K. and Bosworth, M. (eds) (2013) *Migration and Punishment: Citizenship, Crime Control, and Social Exclusion*. Oxford: Oxford University Press.

Aliverti, A. (2012) 'Making people criminal: The role of the criminal law in immigration enforcement', *Theoretical Criminology*, 21 (4): 417–434.

Baillot, H., Cowan, S. and Munro, V. (2012) '"Hearing the right gaps": enabling and Responding to disclosures of sexual violence within the UK asylum process', *Social & Legal Studies*, 21 (3): 269–296.

Balibar, E. (2004) *We, the People of Europe? Reflections on Transnational Citizenship*. Oxford: Princeton University Press.

——(2005) 'Difference, otherness, exclusion', *Parallax*, 11 (1): 19–34.

Bauman, Z. (2004) *Wasted Lives: Modernity and its Outcasts*. Cambridge: Polity Press.

Bigo, D. (2008) 'Globalized (In)Security: The field and the Ban-Opticon', in D. Bigo and A. Tsoukala (eds) *Terror, Insecurity and Liberty: Illiberal Practices of Liberal Regimes after 9/11*. London: Routledge.

Bosworth, M. (2011a) 'Deporting foreign national prisoners in England and Wales', *Citizenship Studies*, 15 (5): 583–595.

——(2011b) 'Human Rights and Immigration Detention', in M.-B. Dembour and T. Kelly (eds) *Are Human Rights for Migrants? Critical Reflections on the Status of Irregular Migrants in Europe and the United States*. Abingdon: Routledge, 165–183.

——(2012) 'Subjectivity and identity in detention: Punishment and society in a Global Age,' *Theoretical Criminology*, 16 (3): 123–140.

——(2013) 'Can immigration detention be legitimate?', in K. Aas and M. Bosworth (eds) *Migration and Punishment: Citizenship, Crime Control, and Social Exclusion*. Oxford: Oxford University Press.

——(forthcoming, 2014) *Inside Immigration Detention: Foreigners in a Carceral Age*. Oxford: Oxford University Press.

Bosworth, M. and Kellezi, B. (2012) 'Quality of life in detention: results from the MQLD questionnaire data collected in IRC Yarl's Wood', IRC Tinsley House and IRC Brook House, August 2010–June 2011. Oxford: Centre for Criminology.

——(2013) 'Developing a measure of the quality of life in detention', *Prison Service Journal*, 205: 10–15.

Bowling, B. (1999) *Violent Racism: Victimisation Policing and Social Context*. Oxford: Oxford University Press.

Bowling, B., Phillips, C. and Sheptycki, J. (2012) 'Race, political economy and the coercive state', in J. Peay and T. Newburn (eds) *Policing, Politics and Control*. Oxford: Hart.

Bowling, B., Parmar, A. and Phillips, C. (2008) 'Policing ethnic minority communities', in T. Newburn (ed.) *The Handbook of Policing*, 2nd edn. Cullompton: Willan.

Brotherton, D. and Barrios, L. (2011) *Banished to the Homeland: Dominican Deportees and Their Stories of Exile*. New York: Columbia University Press.

Butler, J. (2010) *Frames of War: When is Life Grievable?* London: Verso.

Dauvergne, C. (2008) *Making People Illegal: What Globalization Means for Migration and Law*. Cambridge: Cambridge University Press.

Dembour, M.-B. and Kelly, T. (eds) (2011) *Are Human Rights for Migrants? Critical Reflections on the Status of Irregular Migrants in Europe and the United States*. Abingdon: Routledge.

Fekete, L. and Weber, F. (2010) 'Foreign nationals, enemy penology and the criminal justice system', *Race & Class*, 51 (4): 1–25.

De Genova, N. (2008) '"American" Abjection "Chicanos," gangs, and Mexican/migrant transnationality in Chicago', in *Aztlán: A Journal of Chicano Studies*, 33 (2): 141–173.

——(2010) 'The deportation regime: sovereignty, space and the freedom of movement', in N. De Genova and N. Peultz (eds) *The Deportation Regime: Sovereignty, Space, and the Freedom of Movement*. Durham, NC: Duke University Press.

De Genova, N. and Peultz, N. (eds). (2010) *The Deportation Regime: Sovereignty, Space, and the Freedom of Movement*. Durham, NC: Duke University Press.

Gill, N. (2009) 'Governmental mobility: the power effects of the movement of detained asylum seekers around Britain's detention estate', *Political Geography*, 28 (3): 186–196.

Gilroy, P. (1987) *There Ain't no Black in the Union Jack*. London: Routledge.

Di Giorgi, A. (2010) 'Immigration control, post-Fordism, and less eligibility: A materialist critique of the criminalization of immigration across Europe', *Punishment & Society*, 12 (2): 147–67.

Guild, E. (2009) *Security and Migration in the 21st Century*. Cambridge: Polity Press.

Hall, C. (2006) *At Home with the Empire: Metropolitan Culture and the Imperial World*. Cambridge: Cambridge University Press.

Hall, S. (2001) 'Conclusion: the multicultural question', in Hesse, B. (ed.) *Un/Settled Multiculturalisms: Diasporas, Entanglement, Transruptions*. London: Zed Books.

Hall, S., Critcher, C., Jefferson, T., Clarke, J. and Roberts, R. (1978) *Policing the Crisis: Mugging, the State, and Law and Order*. London: Macmillan.

Kanstroom, D. (2012) *Aftermath: Deportation and the New American Diaspora*. New York: Oxford University Press.

Kaufman, E. (2012) 'Finding foreigners: race and the politics of memory in British prisons', *Population, Space and Place*. 18 (6): 701–714.

Kaufman, E. and Bosworth, M. (2013) 'The prison and national identity: citizenship, punishment and the sovereign state', in D. Scott. (ed.) *Why Prison*. Cambridge: Cambridge University Press.

Parmar, A. (2011) 'Stop and search in London: counter-terrorist or counter-productive?', *Policing & Society*, 21 (4): 369–382.

Pratt, A. (2005) *Securing Borders: Detention and Deportation in Canada*. Vancouver: University of British Columbia Press.

Querton, C. (2012) '"I feel like as a woman I'm not welcome": a gender analysis of UK asylum law, policy and practice'. London, Asylum Aid.

Rygiel, K. (2010) *Globalizing Citizenship*. Vancouver: University of British Columbia Press.

——(2012) 'Politicising camps: forging transgressive citizenships in and through transit', *Citizenship Studies*, 16 (5–6): 87–825.

Sassen, S. (2007) *The Sociology of Globalization*. New York: Norton.

Serco, (2011) 'November 2011. Monthly Statistics, IRC Yarls' Wood'. Yarl's Wood: Serco.

Stumpf, J. (2006) 'The crimmigration crisis: immigrants, crime and sovereign power', *American University Law Review*, 56 (367).

Thomas, R. (2011) *Administrative Justice and Asylum Appeals: A Study of Tribunal Adjudication*. Oxford: Hart Publishing.

Tyler, I. (2010) 'Designed to fail: a biopolitics of British citizenship', *Citizenship Studies*, 14 (1): 61–74.

Vine, J. (2011) *A Thematic Inspection of How the UK Border Agency Manages Foreign National Prisoners*. London: Independent Chief Inspector of the UK Border Agency.

Walters, W. (2008) 'Acts of demonstration: mapping the territory of (non-)citizenship', in E. Isin and G. Neilsen (eds) *Acts of Citizenship*. London: Zed Books.

Weber, L. (2011) '"It sounds like you shouldn't be here": immigration checks on the streets of Sydney', *Policing & Society*, 21 (4): 456–467.

Wilsher, D. (2012) *Immigration Detention: Law, History, Politics*. Cambridge: Cambridge University Press.

Zedner, L. (2010) 'Security, the state and the citizen: the changing architecture of crime control', *New Criminal Law Review*, 13 (2): 379–403.

points to its failure to recognise the multiple layers of oppression that Black people experience and in some instances, it can be accused of playing experiences of racial oppression down. Left-realist thinking has been particularly instrumental in this regard. Advancing the idea that Black people choose to commit crime in response to their disadvantaged socio-economic position, consequentially, the role of class takes precedence over race (Kalunta-Crumpton 2004). For example, whilst it was widely accepted that African Caribbean boys were disproportionately underachieving in education, the revelation that White working class males were also disproportionately underachieving (Cassen and Kingdon 2007) has been used to forward the argument that 'class trumps race' (Hill 2009), and to suggest that in terms of oppression, some White working class groups are oppressed too. Race then tends to be seen as a secondary or less significant factor. In his article for *The Telegraph* titled 'Poverty, not colour, is the real dividing line in modern Britain', Nelson (2012) cites the educational underachievement of White boys as an example of where class oppression supersedes racial oppression, because, he argues, 'British whites have it just as bad'. Whilst attempting to portray a contemporary and (an almost) 'post-racial' image of Britain, Nelson also argues that particular forms of crime can be explained solely in terms of class, thus, he states:

> Unlike America, gangs in Britain have no ethnic dimension: they reflect the communities from which they are drawn. Unlike America, our underclass is an equal opportunities employer.

Putting aside the question of whether there is in fact no 'ethnic' dimension to gangs in Britain, in these discourses, any racial discrimination in and outside of the criminal justice system, (or indeed the education system) and its effects, and a real understanding of racial dynamics, becomes submerged under issues of class. Furthermore, whilst the two are often closely interlinked, ignoring the distinctions in these identities and experiences suggests or perpetuates indifference to these identities and experiences (Potter 2006).

### UK Criminology – White by default?

This lack of scholarship in British Criminology on the experiences of racial oppression and its relationship to Black people's experiences of crime and criminalisation can, in part, be understood by examining discourses on 'Whiteness'. An interest in Whiteness studies within mainstream sociology (particularly in the US) has led to a growing recognition amongst sociologists of 'Whiteness' as a body of knowledge, ideologies, norms and 'system of privilege' (Garner 2007). A few academics, within social work and cultural studies in particular, have identified the ways in which 'Whiteness' reinforces and perpetuates systems of racial inequality (Yang 2000; Bush 2004; MacMullan 2009). Whiteness studies, according to Shohat and Stam (2003: 3), is a movement that:

... responds to the call by intellectuals of color for an analysis of the impact of racism not only on its victims but also on its perpetrators. It was also a response to the multiculturalist questioning of the quiet yet overpowering normativity of whiteness, the process by which race and ethnicity were attributed to others while whites were tacitly positioned as invisible norm.

Whiteness studies is based on the notion that a person's self-identity and world view is informed or affected by historical factors as well as their understanding of their 'ethnic group history'. This definition can become particularly problematic when confronted with the reality that a deeper analysis of what it means to be White reveals that White ethnicity is composed of both ethnically privileged groups and relatively powerless, stigmatised and oppressed groups; for example, White working class immigrant groups and those referred to as the underclass (Webster 2008). Acknowledging this however, does not delegitimise the need for a critical reflection on how Whiteness in a broader sense, has shaped knowledge, ideologies and norms within criminological discourses (particularly discourses around race, crime and criminalisation) and the impact that this has on non-White populations.

## Contextualising Black experience

In contrast, within mainstream sociology, explorations and reflections on Blackness (what it means to be Black in Britain) have been considered to a much greater degree and have been instrumental in mainstream criminological discourse (Hebdige 1979; Pryce 1979; Gilroy 1982; and Perry and John-Baptiste 2008). My contention however, is that despite this broad knowledge base, research on the 'Black experience' in criminological discourses on race and crime tends to be either outdated or limited in its scope. Existing studies that attempt to capture or reflect the experiences of Black people as a means of explaining their involvement in crime or with the criminal justice system have essentially failed to contextualise these experiences adequately, resulting in a superficial account of what it is like to be Black in Britain. Agyeman (2008: 269) explains that to contextualise individual (Black) experiences researchers need to go *'beyond current day economic, social and cultural contexts'* and *'extend this into political and historical contexts'*, thereby acknowledging that discourses on the *Other* (Black) are 'embedded in historical conditions of slavery, colonialism and racism'.

## My research

In acknowledgment of this, I embarked on a study of the changing nature of Black youth crime in Britain that would elicit a more *multidimensional* explanation of Black young males' experiences of offending, victimisation and criminal justice processing (Phillips and Bowling 2003) and move beyond the boundaries of the usual structural and cultural explanations offered by mainstream academia. In doing so, the study examined and sought to explain Black youth crime in relation to the complex social, economic, political, cultural and historical contexts in which it occurred.

The research, which was a cross-generational study, explored the impact of racism and discrimination on three successive generations of Black Britons (young males in particular) in terms of their experiences in education, in employment, in housing, in healthcare, in the criminal justice system and on the street. The participants were all Black and largely made up of African Caribbean residents from the same inner-city neighbourhood in London. Data was collected through field observations and 40 face to face interviews with 20 males and five females aged 16–24 years. The older cohorts consisted of 12 males and three females and ages ranged from 35 to 55. Whilst access to some participants was possible because they were people I already knew, most of the respondents were accessed through snowball sampling.

As well as the impact of racism, the research also explored the way that these experiences have been understood and made sense of over time and by different groups[3] within the Black community. In doing so, it sought to discover whether and to what extent these experiences have led to their involvement in criminal behaviour and particular forms of crime.

## The significance of group histories

How individuals make sense of their world however, is also defined to some extent by their social, economic, political and cultural environment and their group history. The historical background of Black Caribbeans and Africans in Britain was deemed important for my research as many of the (Black) respondents that I engaged with in the early stages of my study indicated that it was key to understanding much of the violence that Black young males are involved in today. They believed that the injustices that they were experiencing were linked to racist ideologies rooted in slavery,[4] although the extent to which they believed this impacted on their lives varied. For social scientists, through exploring how slavery and colonialism are understood and interpreted by both White and Black Britons, and impact on the present, particularly through Western Enlightenment philosophies (Bush 1999; Sivanandan 2004 and Garner 2007) of innate 'White superiority' and 'Black inferiority' we can begin to make sense of its relevance.

Whilst there was an appreciation of some of the socio-economic causes of crime, and individual choice, many of my respondents across the three generations had observed the relationship between Black young males and crime in a broader historical context and tended to view their criminality, particularly intra-racial violence, as a result of racial oppression over many generations. As one of the respondents in my study articulates:

> Slavery was abolished physically but not mentally so that mental inferiority passed down to generations who never experienced mental freedom can cause a young black man to resort to a life of crime because they think their life's worthless. Slavery came with stripping away identities and once you strip a man off his identity you've altered his destiny ... unless they break away from this.
>
> (Jennifer, aged 21)

The belief that the transatlantic slave trade and the subsequent colonisation of African and African Caribbean people feeds into notions of 'Black' inferiority and self hate is at the centre of much of the discourses amongst Black residents in the neighbourhood, on intra-racial violence. As one of the older respondents argues, 'Since slavery, oppression is very well settled in society and in our minds. This leads to a hopeless view of our own lives; if there is no respect and value for our own lives how can we have respect and value for other people's?' (Francis). For Phillip, aged 19, the violent youth crime that we are currently witnessing represented the 'psychological downfall' of Black people, brought about by ' ... mimicking the ways of our so called "colonial masters", pillaging, raping and thriving on even the unnecessary'.

Regardless of whether there is there is any validity in this, Pitts and I (Palmer and Pitts 2006) have argued elsewhere that in terms of the violence that young males in the neighbourhood were involved in, the people that were most likely to be victimised were, more often than not, members of their own local community and race. This contrasted with the experiences of the elder cohort who grew up in a culture where ' ... you wouldn't steal from your mate ... from your own Black person'.

The respondents clearly suggest that there are psychological effects associated with slavery which continue to impact on Black people in Britain today. One respondent however, also made mention of the economic effects, in contextualising the relationship between Black males and crime. According to Marcus', aged 24, analysis:

> Slavery was a mass kidnapping and a crime in itself which yielded great economic profitability for the criminals and a great loss for the victims. Today those who were victims yesterday have turned to their kidnappers' ways and seek to eat from the same criminality pie.

The widely held belief was that as a result of the ongoing experiences of contemporary racism which began with the enslavement of Africans, Black young people have lost their sense of who they are. Respondents believed that through mediums such as the media, the British schooling system and the police, they have learnt to despise who they are and have adopted an identity created for them by White power structures to ensure their continued oppression.

Mullard (1973) for example, provides a disturbing account of how some of the racist ideologies that he encountered in school portraying Black people as inferior and inadequate, had the effect of making him want to distance himself from the 'wild' and 'backward' image of Africans that he was presented with. According to Daye (1994) the negative portrayal of Black people as inferior, backward and animal-like had become internalised by some members of the Black immigrant population who arrived in Britain during the 1950s and the children of immigrants, and they came to believe that 'White was right' and 'Black was wrong' (Daye 1994). Consequently, they began to despise their Blackness (Mullard (1973) and some sought to emulate Whites and assimilate into White hegemonic culture. As Tatum (1992) suggests, they had begun to identify with their oppressors.

In terms of the younger generations, the internalisation of these ideas may have a very different effect. In Britain, analysis of the race and crime debate in its broader historical context is rarely considered within mainstream criminology today, thus little is known about the legacy of slavery and colonialism and their possible impact on Black communities in contemporary times. In contrast to this, scholars (mostly Black) in the US have suggested that there is a clear link between Black offending (violent crime in particular) and the historical legacies of slavery and racial oppression that has afflicted successive generations of Black people in the US and elsewhere in the Black Diaspora (Crawford *et al.* 2003; Pinderhughes 2004 and Leary 2005).

For these Black scholars, it is impossible to unyoke many of the current experiences of Black people from their ancestors' experiences of racism and slavery. They view the oppression of people of African descent as a form of 'trauma' and by doing so, they not only highlight the magnitude of this 'assault' but they also create a framework for making sense of many of the symptoms of that trauma within Black communities today, in particular, low self esteem, grief, rage, and violence (Pinderhughes 2004 and Leary 2005).

Researching the impact of slavery on Blacks in America, Leary (2005) suggests that the legacy of slavery has had a profound effect on the consciousness of Black people in North America which to some extent can help to explain particular types of offending by young Black males. According to Leary, hundreds of years of unpaid labour, subjugation and oppression under slavery have ensured that successive generations of White Americans would inherit wealth, privilege and power. The descendants of Africans however, have inherited debt and suffering. For Leary, the emotional and psychological scars of slavery not only on slaves, but also their descendents need to be taken into consideration, demonstrating an appreciation that over time racism and racist ideologies that underpin it have been internalised by White and Black populations alike. Thus, for Black people, the displacement of Blacks from their homeland and their culture, the internalisation of ideas around Black inferiority, along with their experiences of contemporary racism have contributed to low self esteem and a sense of hopelessness which Leary argues have resulted in some of the current issues around identity, masculinities and 'respect' amongst young Black males. Furthermore, as Aird (2008: 9) explains:

A growing body of evidence suggests that the lie of black inferiority negatively affects black people's sense of self-worth and efficacy, undermines relationships between black men and women and between parents and children, limits black children's possibilities, and contributes to destructive behaviors in the black community.

Taking into account the ideas of scholars concerned with the psycho-social impact of slavery such as Leary (2005) and Poussaint and Alexander (2000), Aird goes on to suggest that growing rates of suicide, depression, stress-related illnesses and (intra-racial) homicides among Black people in the US can be attributed to a communal self-hatred, anger, self-loathing, and a sense of hopelessness that leads to a devaluation of their own lives and the lives of other Blacks.

Recognising the importance of the historical context of racism and the impact that the experience of slavery has on contemporary Black African Caribbean communities in the UK, Sharpe and O'Donnell (2000) point out that Black youth cultures in Britain today include strong elements of macho resistance which are:

> ... generated out of displacement, trauma and subjection ... Just as the contradictions of industrial labour experienced by the working class male provoked sometimes embattled and uncompromising collective resistance, so the experience of slavery generated a culture of injured pride, anger and resistance among many black men.
>
> (Sharpe and O'Donnell, 2000: 64, 66)

Whilst assimilation was deemed a necessary response to the legacy of slavery and its racist ideologies by some, others chose to resist. Revolts and black-led resistance against slavery in the Caribbean and North America and (African) colonialism have been well documented. Pan Africanism, a movement which since the early Nineteenth Century sought to unify and as a consequence empower Black people around the globe, was as Bush (1999: 14) succinctly describes 'a direct response to the imperialist annexation of Africa and Eurocentricism', and represented 'an exercise in consciousness and resistance'. As an ideology, it was instrumental in the fight for independence amongst some colonised African countries and continues to influence many Black political, social, and religious organisations today.[5]

For successive generations of young Black Britons, group and individual experiences of racial oppression and other forms of disadvantage, and awareness of their group history,[6] have had an influence on their identity formation. According to Brake (1985) the multiple disadvantages that young Black males were subjected to in the 1970s and early 1980s for example, had created the social and symbolic contexts for the development and reinforcement of a collective (Black) identity and individual self-esteem. Hence the emergence of Black youth sub-cultures during that period that united on the basis that they shared a destiny, an identity, and a common enemy that was the State (Pryce 1979 and Cashmore and Troyna 1982). These identities adopted were thus 'oppositional' identities based on notions of resistance to the racism and oppressive conditions that they were understood to be living under (Castells 2004). A number of minority scholars have also argued that some acts of 'criminality' such as the 'riots' of the 1950s and the 1980s represented a form of resistance to the multiplicity of shared injustices experienced by the Black community (Gilroy 1982; Sivanandan 1982; Hall 1982; Howe 1988; Chigwada 1991 and Howson 2007). More recently, there appears to be less consideration of the extent to which crime committed by Black young males today can be explained with reference to political resistance, a possibly unintended consequence of left realist ideology which emphasises the reality of crime and its impact on poor working class people.

## The dilemmas of researching Black issues whilst Black

There is an apparent tendency for Black scholars to display an interest in ideas and an engagement in research on issues that affect Black people, and in particular, research that examines the impact of slavery and racism on individuals and on society. When researching 'their own' communities, Black researchers can often benefit from an 'insider status' where a familiarity (sometimes through first-hand experience) with the research participants' experiences and lives and the issues that affect them, can be an advantage. For example, access to participants and gaining their trust may be easier, and familiarity with the groups being studied can lead to more accurate interpretations of data.

This familiarity and close identification with the groups being studied however can also be counterproductive, most notably, by clouding the researcher's objectivity. Rather than engaging in a more general discussion on the advantages and disadvantages of being a Black researcher researching 'their own' (Black) community (which has been covered extensively elsewhere; see Agar 1980; Andersen 1993; Mirza 1995; Serrant-Green 2002 and Aldridge 2003), in this section I will draw on my own research to reflect on some of the key methodological issues and dilemmas encountered by myself and other Black researchers specifically involved in research in the area of race and crime.

A key aim of my research, which had been framed as a case study, was to explore and account for any differences in the way that different generations (and different groups) of Black Britons in one neighbourhood, experience and understand issues around race, crime and justice and to explore any significant changes in local attitudes. Using a purposive sampling technique, participants were chosen on the basis that they were deemed the most appropriate people to elicit the required information. As an ex-resident of the neighbourhood, many of the participants were known to me as childhood friends or acquaintances. While the benefits of this familiarity where I felt more of an 'insider' than an 'outsider' include access to participants and prior knowledge and greater insight into their lived experiences, this approach can be seen as open to researcher bias where the research design and interpretation of the results, for example, are informed by the personal values of the researcher.

As Bromley and Carter (2001) have argued, by taking an 'insider' status researchers can benefit from the insight that can be gained into the phenomena they are studying, however to explore the objective meaning of who they are and what they have studied, they must 'step outside' of that status. Thus, by 'shifting roles' and adopting a reflexive approach researchers can try to bring balance and objectivity to the research.

One of the dilemmas that I faced was how to take advantage of my 'insider status' whilst remaining objective. By virtue of being Black, sharing the same class status and (local) cultural background, and my past experiences of offending and associating with offenders, I had more than a tacit understanding of some of the groups that I studied and I wanted to make the most of this. It is through these experiences and insights that I have been able to analyse criteria developed from what can be referred to as a 'Black perspective', a perspective which advances the representation, knowledge production, and historical contextualisation of minority experiences in areas such as theory development and in which criminological data can be reconciled with the 'lived experiences' and subjectivities of minorities (Phillips and Bowling (2003). As well as being constantly reflexive about my approach and the possible impacts of my own subjectivities on the research, I found myself regularly checking with (mainly) 'White' colleagues, because of their academic seniority and objective standpoint, to validate my ideas.

Other Black researchers have reflected on this dilemma. Glynn (2012) also found it difficult to find a balance between his familiarity with the subject matter and remaining objective. While conducting his research on Black men's desistance from crime, which he saw as an attempt to give voice to Black men who need to 'tell' and 'own' their own stories, he found that:

> As a black researcher operating within a racialised context I was constantly questioning my own reality as a black man in academia. The dominant research paradigms can at times marginalise a black researcher, when having to defend your 'blackness' in relation to the community you come from.

According to Glynn (2012) the 'colour blind' position of current mainstream criminology which is perceived as scientific and therefore objective, '*renders the black contribution to criminology invisible*', which, he argues '*means that the expression of my "blackness" is seen at times as lacking in objectivity*'. Yet, he argues, '*Seldom have I experienced a questioning about white male researchers researching white men*'. The question that therefore remains for Black researchers who see much value in this type of research for both the groups they want to give voice to and for advancing academic debates, theory and practice, is, as Glynn succinctly puts it:

So how does a black researcher's expression of their 'blackness' gain or reduce the possibility of academic validation, when constantly having to confront 'whiteness' in both the research environment and the academy?

For Black (and also for some White) criminologists, a key issue within the wider race and crime debate that they often have to contend with is whether they accept that Black people (particularly young males) are more likely to offend,[7] and then they also have to contend with the consequent fall-out from this. The dilemma they face is that if their research and contributions indicate that Black groups are more likely to engage in crime, however unintentional, this may serve to reify what Gilroy (1987) referred to as the 'myth of Black criminality' and could potentially present Black groups as having a cultural predisposition to crime and as a 'social problem' that needs to be controlled. As Gunter (2008) has found more recently, Black scholars who undertake empirical research that 'gives voice' to Black subjects, are particularly sensitive to the need to avoid the creation of 'false pathologies' that uphold stereotypes of Black people as a criminal 'other'.

Whilst it is fair to say that research on this issue is often guilty of painting 'an academic gloss' over the major problems of racism in the criminal justice system and in a 'racist society' (Keith 1991), I acknowledge that some young Black men *do* become involved in crime and rather than enter the circular debate about how much crime they commit, I am more concerned with understanding why those that commit crime do so (Hallsworth 2005; Gunter 2008).

As a Black academic, I am also acutely aware of the importance of 'giving voice' to 'minority' populations (Phillips and Bowling 2003) whose views and perspectives have remained to a great extent unheard, and in the tradition of many other Black scholars, I attempted to do that through my research.

### *Giving voice or reinforcing stereotypes?*

One particularly interesting observation about the race and crime debate is the significant number of contributions by Black commentators. Yet although the views of Black scholars (Hall *et al.* 1978; Pryce 1979; Gilroy 1987; Bowling and Phillips 2002; West 1993 and Wilson 1987) have featured prominently in these debates, the views of the Black working classes, and more specifically, the young Black males whose lives and behaviours are under scrutiny are rarely included. Pryce's (1979) ethnographic study of Black residents in a community in Bristol was one of the earliest studies to consider the attitudes and perceptions of different sections of Black communities towards Black youth crime. More recently, Gunter's (2008) ethnographic study of Black youth sub-cultures and youth transitions in an East London neighbourhood, explored young people's attitudes to and reasons for engaging in various forms of crime. To some extent, both these studies could be accused of reinforcing negative stereotypes (Ratcliffe 2004).

Gunter (2008), acknowledging this, states that even in their well-meaning attempts to conduct research that is culturally sensitive and more representative of minority populations, researchers run the risk of pathologising the populations that they are scrutinising. He accepts that by highlighting the specific cultural contexts to crime and victimisation of its Black Caribbean male participants, his study may only contribute further to the stereotyping and stigmatisation of Black young males. Nevertheless, it is also possible that the new information and understanding that can be gleaned from studies such as these, which contribute to a more multidimensional approach to understanding their world views and their experiences, render such ventures as still worthwhile. Thus, Black academics should not shy away from doing research on the basis that it may be misapplied or misinterpreted.

Indeed, this appreciative stance (Matza 1969) together with Becker's (1967) injunction that the researcher must decide 'whose side they are on', places the researcher in the position of advocate, an often uncomfortable position but one which offers a unique vantage point from which to glimpse the power relations at work in the debates about Black young males and crime within the Black community. However, it also provides rich data for understanding the complex origins of crime amongst Black young people, and one which may well pose a challenge to more conventional explanations.

## What can Black perspectives tell us about race and crime?

One of the key themes that has emerged from the study is that amongst participants of all three generations, there was a strong desire for a sense of community and racial (Black) solidarity. As successive studies on the Black experience have shown, since the 1970s, Black people have continued to be affected by various forms of discrimination, and as John Pitts and I have demonstrated elsewhere, in some of the poorest neighbourhoods this appears to have worsened (Palmer and Pitts 2006). We have also outlined and demonstrated in some detail, how and why Black political protest against discrimination and injustices (which was at its height during the 1970s and 1980s) in all its forms, and for a number of reasons, seems to have been somewhat suppressed.[8] One of the key explanations for this was that many Black activists were absorbed into the political mainstream during the 1980s, and grew increasingly reluctant to represent concerns that were specific to the Black communities (Gilroy 1987; Daye 1994; Shukra 1998; Palmer and Pitts 2006 and Palmer 2012).

For the young people growing up today, in neighbourhoods similar to the one that my study was set in, with no political voice or support from their own communities (Shukra 1998) which were becoming increasingly weak and fragmented (Palmer and Pitts 2006), there is a sense that they are essentially 'on their own'. Unlike their parents, for the younger respondents, the concept of a 'Black community', despite living in a predominantly Black neighbourhood, was one that they did not recognise (Palmer and Pitts 2006). One of the young respondents in my study, Marcus, was very descriptive about what that lack of community felt like:

> Ever since I've been growing up, I've seen my Black community divided; I've never seen us together as one community. ... I share skin complexion with them, but as far as the Black community is in my eyes, we're just a sea of lost, confused and insecure people and everything we do is dictated to us sublimely through the media and through the lack of education. Our understanding ... of who we are is so low that we're just lost. We have little pieces of what we're about, but we don't really know what we're about ... about we just follow whatever we see, which is why we are so disorganized and un-united.

Interestingly, this did not lessen their desire for such a community, and for some of the respondents, again across all cohorts, a 'united' Black community would also reduce the violence that was occurring, particularly the intra-racial violence between young Black males (Palmer and Pitts 2006). Janet, one of the younger participants who was particularly passionate about the need for a sense of community, spoke about wanting to:

> ... make a change to our lives and what we've all experienced, and get us to be working together so we can all accomplish something. So I would like us to all be communal and for people to come together to do something about it. That's where my mind is set, for us to be together.

Making reference to the American Rapper 'Tupac', Mark also shares a desire to bring about a sense of community. Thus he suggests:

> He (Tupac) was about speaking his mind. I don't focus on the violence associated with him; I focus on the power of his words. Black power. Cos we will have that one day. Right now, I don't see no Black power nowhere. I've been here for 20 years and I'm still looking for it. It's only a few of us who have had the bottle to get together and say yeah, we're not having that no more.

What is particularly apparent here is that the younger cohort felt that they have in a sense been failed by their elders. Indeed, this desire to make a change and bring about a degree of unity within the Black communities implies that the older generation have in some ways failed to 'put one in place'. Some of the young people indicated that poor parenting was a significant problem for some families within these communities, although acknowledging that poor parenting was merely a symptom of the structural pressures that their communities were up against. Thus rather than seeing Black families as pathological, they believed that the real pathologies lay in the state and its institutions, in particular, schools and the criminal justice system. As indicated by Robert, also one of the younger respondents:

In my area there is a lot of high crime, but as I said to you earlier before we began this interview, we got children with parents who are suffering from the system, the system transforms them from what they was, to something that nobody should have to go through in one lifetime, you know what I mean?

He goes on to acknowledge that as a result of this 'poor' parenting, the children consequently receive little or nothing in terms of discipline, adopting 'positive' values and general guidance when navigating their way through what he sees as an oppressive system.

But at the same time while the children are getting so much freedom, they wonder why. When you watch that, all you see is materialistic things, you get me? 'I got a girl, I got a car, I got this, I got that' and nobody is not sharing. That's what they teach you on TV, nobody ain't sharing. If it's yours, it's yours and if it's not then boy, then maybe one day, you know? Eventually though, it worked for most of the children either end up in jumping through somebody's window, or turning to drugs to either hustle or take because your life's that bad. If you're a child that was hanging around a crowd of Black youths when you was growing up, then normally you'll get into just hustling of drugs and try and obtain that image.

Robert also goes on to suggest that as well as feeling depressed and helpless, some parents have 'given up fighting' or 'trying to find some sort of hope' in a hopeless situation, by way of an improvement in their material conditions and in their dealings with the education system, the criminal justice system and other state agencies. Whilst most respondents stopped short of saying that they felt let down by their own parents due to their inability to help them, a few young people who I interacted with during this research did make clear statements about feeling let down by the older generation more generally. Adopting a general view of Black (working class) culture and Black parenting as pathological and Black people as victims however, ignores the resilience of these families in the face of multiple disadvantages and, just as importantly, the majority of Black parents who parent well despite the socio-structural pressures and discrimination that they and their families may experience.

In terms of the key aim of this research then, respondents across the board, tended to believe that given the difficulties that young Black males faced and continue to face, such as their underachievement in education, the high rates of school exclusion and stop and search (House of Commons Home Affairs Committee 2007), it is not difficult to understand why young Black males would become involved in crime, particularly acquisitive crime such as selling drugs or committing robberies to gain an income. Although material deprivation may be a factor, these crimes were also, to a great extent, attributed to the widely held beliefs amongst the participants that 'unnecessary injustices' were occurring (Lea and Young 1984). It is difficult to know the extent to which this sense of injustice contributes to an *actual* increase in particular forms of criminal activity, but what this study does suggest is that there may be a relationship. Likewise, the research suggests a possible relationship between the psycho-social impact of slavery on African-Caribbean young people, and intra-racial crime.

Armed with the belief that they have little or no support from their own communities to address the challenges they face, some young Black males appear thus to be responding to these pressures in ways that are not conducive. The community leaders, who are essentially the new Black middle class 'whose expansion' Wacquant (2001: 106) argues 'hinges, not on its capacity to service its community, but on its willingness to assume the vexing role of custodian of the black urban sub proletariat on behalf of white society', compound their exclusion by 'othering' them (Palmer and Pitts 2006). Added to this, many of the young people feel they have been let down by their parents and their 'community' who as a result of their own pressures, feel helpless.

In an attempt to make sense of who they are, or more precisely, who they can *be*, it seems that some young people have adopted a response and even a lifestyle which allows them to vent their frustrations, yet, when we look at the disturbing incidents of intra-racial violence, is simultaneously self destructive. Although other ethnic groups may face similar challenges, this research indicates that their trajectories are, to some extent, also shaped by their specific group histories, so the low sense of self-worth which undermines Black relationships (Aird 2008) may be a factor that needs to be considered in current debates on the involvement of young Black males in violent crime.

## Pretending the elephant is not in the room

This chapter began with the following quote:

> A society which can enslave without compunction cannot escape responsibility; a society which, today, still depends on the black world for much of its wealth cannot afford to free itself of a racist ideology.
>
> (Mullard 1973: 45)

The slavery that Mullard refers to may have been a long time ago, but as has been demonstrated here, its legacy and its benefits are still with us and as Mullard rightly implies, the past benefits of slavery and current benefits of its legacy are hard to give up. Whilst racism may not be a direct cause of crime, the way it is internalised and its impact on how young Black males see themselves and other Black people, do appear to be relevant. Because of the multiplicity of disadvantages they face, it will be premature to assume that Black people who commit crime do so for exactly the same reasons as White people as 'race' and 'racism' have to be taken into account. Thus, to ignore their experiences as Black as well as British is to ignore the impact of racism in today's society.

In my attempts to 'give voice' to particular groups and views that are not often heard or listened to, I have tried to show how some of the discourses within Black communities, or 'Black perspectives' on the relationship between Black young people and crime, may offer greater insight into why they offend. Thus, further research on the historical legacy of slavery and colonialism, which as the evidence strongly suggests, has an impact on the material conditions and the self and world view of both Black and White populations, may offer insight into the relationship between Black[9] young people and crime and provide possible explanations for offending patterns. The imprint of slavery and colonialism on the psyche of criminologists and those working in criminal justice also needs to be explored further. Reflections on Whiteness and how it impacts on the discipline in terms of how it views and represents Black experiences, and an exploration of the concepts of Blackness and Whiteness within the context of mainstream criminology are necessary, particularly in terms of understanding the causes and possible solutions to racism within the criminal justice system.

Research on the extent to which notions of Whiteness and Blackness inform the relationship between Black young males and the criminal justice system in terms of policing practices or sentencing for example, may help to explain the differences in outcomes. I have also indicated that studies that focus on race are at risk of unfairly pathologising particular groups whether that is the author's intention or not. However, *not* taking into account the relevant differences in experiences, cultural practices and world views of different groups can be equally problematic. For example, Rowe (2012) suggests that whilst the 'racialisation' of gun crime at the turn of this century, in which gun crime was presented by the media and the police as a specific problem for 'Black' communities and portrayed Black young males as the key perpetrators and victims does not mean that gun crime was not a real problem within some Black communities. If, as I argue throughout this piece, a more complete understanding of the relationship between Black males and crime can be useful to help reduce the increasingly disproportionate number of Black males in the criminal justice system or the number of young Black male perpetrators and victims of peer violence, then discussions about race, ethnicity and culture are crucial.

In terms of reducing crime and the implications for policy, my research suggests that a more empowered and self-supporting Black community which is somewhat in line with the current Government's notion of the 'Big Society' may be useful for reconciling the class and generational differences, for understanding and challenging racism and reducing intra-racial violence. In light of the Coalition government's economic policies however, the 'hopeless' condition that some Black families find themselves in is likely to deteriorate and so based on the findings of my study, a significant challenge for Black communities seems to be how to rebuild a sense of community and help its most vulnerable members with very little resources.

## Notes

1 I use the term 'Black' is used to refer to people of Sub-Saharan African ancestral origins. Historically in the UK, the term 'Black' has been used in a political sense to refer to all non-white groups of people including South Asian populations and as Baldwin (2004: 70) suggests 'those who have a shared history of European colonialism, neo-colonialism, imperialism, ethnocentrism and racism'. However there is an on-going debate about the appropriateness of this term as a blanket definition to describe multiple 'racial' and 'ethnic' groups, the main criticism being that conflating ethnic groups in this way masks the many differences between and within each of the groups (Solomos and Back 1996). My use of the term 'Black' is thus largely restricted to those of African and Black Caribbean populations in the UK, and although I acknowledge that there are differences between and within each of these groups, this paper is more concerned with the similarities in their experiences. Where differences are deemed as significant, I have tried to acknowledge and account for these. The more generic term 'Black', has been used when describing the experiences and events that are, to a significant extent, shared by both Black Caribbean and Black African populations in the UK and when referring to these groups in the plural, the term 'Black communities' has been used in acknowledgment of the variety that exists within the group(s).
2 Thus, the unchecked biases of White Western culture are used by criminologists in Britain to analyse and develop theories on other cultural groups (Karstedt 2011).
3 Commentators such as Sivanandan (1990), Daye (1994), Robins (1992) and in particular Pryce (1979) have identified some of the differences in respect to age, gender, class, cultural values, political and religious ideologies within the Black communities and it would therefore be inaccurate to describe the 'Black community' as an entirely homogenous group. However useful, categories based on factors such as class, political and religious ideologies or behaviour should not be viewed as either exhaustive or rigid (Henry 2005).
4 Respondents are referring to the 'Transatlantic slave trade' which began during the sixteenth century.
5 Rastafarianism, The Nation of Islam, The Uhuru Movement, The Nuwapian Movement and even some Christian churches are just a few examples.
6 As I found when doing my fieldwork, young people have an awareness and knowledge of the enslavement of their ancestors and/or 'people who look like them'. Children are also taught about the Atlantic slave trade in some schools.
7 Or more likely to commit particular offences.
8 Recent demonstrations against Black deaths in police custody occurred after my research findings were completed so have not been taken into account here. Furthermore, these relatively large demonstrations followed the death of the well known reggae artist David Emmanuel, also known as Smiley Culture and were well attended by his fans and supporters, so it would be premature to suggest that this represents a significant change in political activity.
9 Particularly African Caribbean young people.

## References

Agar, M. (1980) *The Professional Stranger: An Informal Introduction to Ethnography.* New York: Academic Press.

Agyeman, G. (2008) 'White Researcher–Black Subjects: Exploring the Challenges of Researching the Marginalised and "Invisible"', *The Electronic Journal of Business Research Methods*, 6 (1): 77–84. Available at www.ejbrm.com/issue/download.html?idArticle=186 (accessed 2 September).

Aird, E. G. (2008) 'Toward a Renaissance for the African-American Family: Confronting the Lie of Black Inferiority', *Emory Law Journal*, 58: 7–21.

Aldridge, D. P. (2003) 'The Dilemmas, Challenges, and Duality of an African American Educational Historian', *Educational Researcher*, 32 (9): 25–34.

Andersen, M. (1993) 'Studying Across Difference: Race, Class and Gender in Qualitative Research', in D. J. Stanfield (ed.) *Race and Ethnicity in Research Methods*. London: Sage Publications.

Baldwin, E. (2004) *Introducing Cultural Studies*. New York: Pearson.

Becker, H. (1967) 'Whose Side Are We On', *Social Problems*, 14 (3): 239–47.

Bowling, B. and Phillips, C. (2002) *Racism, Crime and Justice*. Harlow: Pearson Education Limited.

Brake, M. (1985) *Comparative Youth Culture: The Sociology of Youth Cultures and Youth Subcultures in America, Britain and Canada*. London: Routledge and Kegan Paul.

Bromley, D. G. and Carter, L. F. (2001) *Toward Reflexive Ethnography: Participating, Observing, Narrating*. New York: JAI.

Brown, J. (1977) *Shades of Grey*. Cranfield: Cranfield Institute of Technology.

Bush, B. (1999) *Imperialism, Race and Resistance: Africa and Britain 1919–45*. London: Routledge.

Bush, M. (2004) *Breaking the Code of Good Intentions: Everyday Forms of Whiteness*. Lanham, MD: Rowman and Littlefield Publishers.

Cashmore, E. and McLaughlin, E. (1991) *Out of Order? Policing Black People*. London: Routledge.

Cashmore, E. and Troyna, B. (1982) *Black Youth in Crisis*. London: George Allen and Unwin.

Cassen, R. and Kingdon, G. (2007) *Tackling Low Educational Achievement*. York: Joseph Rowntree Foundation.

Castells, M. (2004) *The Power of Identity, the Information Age: Economy, Society and Culture*, Vol. 2, 2nd edition. Oxford: Blackwell.

Chigwada, R. (1991) 'The Policing of Black Women', in E. Cashmore and E. McLaughlin (eds) *Out of Order? Policing Black People*. London: Routledge.

Crawford, J., Nobles, W. and Leary, J. (2003) 'Reparations and Health Care for African Americans: Repairing the Damage from the Legacy of Slavery', in R. Winbush (ed.) *Should America Pay?: Slavery and the Raging Debate on Reparations*. New York: Amistad.

Daye, S. (1994) *Middle-Class Blacks in Britain*. London: Macmillan.

Garner, S. (2007) *Whiteness: An Introduction*. London: Routledge.

Gilroy, P. (1982) 'Stepping Out of Babylon: Race, Class and Autonomy', in University of Birmingham Centre for Contemporary Cultural Studies (ed.) *The Empire Strikes Back: Race and Racism in 70s Britain*. London: Hutchinson.

Gilroy, P. (1987) *There Ain't no Black in the Union Jack*. London: Routledge.

Glynn, M. (2012) *Researching Black Men's Desistance: Researcher Positionality*. Available at http://blogs.iriss.org.uk/discoveringdesistance/2012/03/10/researching-black-mens-desistance-researcher-positionally/ (accessed 22 September 2012).

Goodey, J. (1998) 'Understanding Racism and Masculinity: Drawing on Research With Boys Aged Eight to Sixteen', *International Journal of the Sociology of Law*, 26 (4): 393–418.

Gunter, A. (2008) 'Growing up Bad: Black Youth, Road Culture and Badness in an East London Neighbourhood', *Crime Media Culture*, 4 (3): 349–65.

Hadley, M. (2001) *The Spiritual Roots of Restorative Justice*. Albany: State University of New York Press.

Hall, S. (1982) 'The Lessons of Lord Scarman', *Critical Social Policy*, 2 (2): 66–72.

Hall, S., Critcher, C., Jefferson, T., Clarke, J. and Roberts, B. (1978) *Policing The Crisis: Mugging, the State and Law and Order*. London: Macmillan.

Hallsworth, S. (2005) *Street Crime*. Cullompton: Willan.

Hebdige, D. (1979) *Subculture: The Meaning of Style*. London: Methuen.

Henry, W. A. (2005) 'Projecting the Natural: Language, Citizenship and Representation in Outernational Culture', in J. Besson and K. F. Olwig (eds) *Caribbean Narratives of Belonging*. London: Macmillan Press Ltd.

Hill, D. (2009) 'Does "Race" Really "Trump" Social Class in Educational (Under) achievement? Statistical Skullduggery in the Case for Critical Race Theory?', in *Theory and Evidence in European Educational Research*, EERA Conference, 28–30 September 2009, Vienna (Unpublished).

Howe, D. (1988) *From Bobby to Babylon: Blacks and the British Police*. London: Race Today Publications.

Howson, C. (2007) 'Development of Black Consciousness in an Oppressive Climate,' in M. Sallah and C. Howson (eds) *Working with Black Young People*. Lyme Regis: Russell House.

House of Commons Home Affairs Committee (2007) *Young Black People and the Criminal Justice System*, Second Report of Session 2006–7. London: House of Commons.

Kalunta-Crumpton, A. (2004) 'Criminology and Orientalism', in A. Kalunta-Crumpton and B. Agozino (eds) *Pan-African Issues in Crime and Justice*. Aldershot: Ashgate.

Karstedt, S. (2011) 'Comparing Justice and Crime Across Cultures', in D. Gadd, S. Karstedt and S. F. Messner (eds) *Sage Handbook of Criminological Research Methods*. London: Sage.

Keith, M. (1991) 'Policing a Perplexed Society? No-go Areas and the Mystification of Police-Black Conflict', in E. Cashmore and E. McLaughlin (eds) *Out of Order? Policing Black People*. London: Routledge.

Kitossa, T. (2012) 'Criminology and Colonialism: Counter Colonial Criminology and the Canadian Context', *The Journal of Pan African Studies*, 4 (10): 204–26.

Lea, J. and Young, J. (1984) *What is to be Done About Law and Order?*. London: Pluto Press.

——(1993) *What is to be Done About Law and Order?* 2nd edition. Harmondsworth: Penguin.

Leary, J. (2005) *Post Traumatic Slave Syndrome: America's Legacy of Enduring Injury and Healing*. Milwaukie, OR: Uptone Press.

Matza, D. (1969) *Becoming Deviant*. New York: Prentice-Hall.

MacMullan, T. (2009) *Habits of Whiteness: A Pragmatist Reconstruction*. Indianapolis: Indiana University Press.

Mirza, M. (1995) 'Some Ethical Dilemmas in Fieldwork: Feminist and Antiracist Methodologies', in M. Griffiths and B. Troyna (eds) *Antiracism, Culture and Social Justice in Education*. Stoke-on-Trent: Trentham Books.

MORI (2004) *Youth Survey 2004*. London: Ofsted.

Mullard, C. (1973) *Black in Britain*. London: Allen and Unwin.

Murji, K. (2007) 'Sociological Engagements: Institutional Racism and Beyond', *Sociology*, 41 (5): 843–55.

Murray, C. (1994) *The Crisis deepens*. London: IEA.

——(1996) 'The emerging British Underclass', in R. Lister (ed.) *Charles Murray and the Underclass: The Developing Debate*. London: IEA.

Nelson, F. (2012) 'Poverty, not Colour, is the Real Dividing Line in Modern Britain', *The Telegraph* (Online), 5th January. Available at www.telegraph.co.uk/news/uknew s/law-and-order/8995295/Poverty-not-colour-is-the-real-dividing-line-in-modern-Brit ain.html (accessed 20 October 2012).

Palmer, S. (2012) '"Dutty Babylon": Policing Black Communities and the Politics of Resistance', *Criminal Justice Matters*, 87: (1): 26–27.

Palmer, S. and Pitts, J. (2006) 'Othering the Brothers', *Youth and Policy*, 91: 5–22.

Perry, B. and John-Baptiste, C. (2008) 'Identity Crisis? Negotiating Blackness in the British Police Service: A Regional Perspective', *Internet Journal of Criminology* (Online). Available at www.internetjournalofcriminology.com/Perry%20and%20John -Baptiste%20-%20Identity%20Crisis.pdf (accessed 22 September 2012).

Phillips, C. and Bowling, B. (2003) 'Racism, Ethnicity and Criminology – Developing Minority Perspectives in Criminology', *British Journal of Criminology* (2003), 43: 269–90.

Phillips, C. and Bowling, B. (2007) 'Ethnicities, racism, crime, and criminal justice', in Maguire, Mike, Morgan, Rod and Reiner, Robert (eds) *Handbook of Criminology*. Oxford: Oxford University Press.

Pinderhughes, E. (2004) 'The Multigenerational Transmission of Loss and Trauma: The African-American Experience', in F. Walsh and M. McGoldrick (eds) *Living beyond Loss*. 2nd edition. New York: Norton.

Potter, H. (2006) 'An Argument for Black Feminist Criminology Understanding African American Women's Experiences with Intimate Partner Abuse Using an Integrated Approach', *Feminist Criminology*, 1 (2): 106–24.

Poussaint, A. F. and Alexander, A. (2000) *Lay My Burden Down: Unraveling Suicide and the Mental Health Crisis among African Americans*. Boston, MA: Beacon Press.

Pryce, K. (1979) *Endless Pressure: A Study of West-Indian Lifestyles in Britain*. Bristol: Bristol Classical Press.

Ratcliffe, P. (2004) *'Race', Ethnicity and Difference: Imagining the Inclusive Society*. Buckingham: Open University Press/McGraw Hill.

Robins, D. (1992) *Tarnished Vision – Crime and Conflict in the Inner Cities*. Oxford: Oxford University Press.

Rowe, M. (2012) *Race and Crime*. London: Sage.

Serrant-Green, L. (2002) 'Black on Black: Methodological Issues for Black Researchers Working in Minority Ethnic Communities', *Nurse Researcher*, 9 (4): 30–44.

Sewell, T. (1997) *Black Masculinities and Schooling*. London: Trentham Books.

Sharpe, S. and O'Donnell, M. (2000) *Uncertain Masculinities: Youth, Ethnicity and Class in Contemporary Britain*. London: Routledge.

Shohat, E. and Stam, R. (2003) *Multiculturalism, Postcolonialism, and Transnational Media*. New Brunswick, NJ: Rutgers University Press.

Shukra, K. (1998) *The Changing Pattern of Black Politics in Britain*. London: Pluto Press.

Sivanandan, A. (1982) *A Different Hunger*. London: Pluto Press.

——(1990) *Communities of Resistance – Writings on Black Struggles for Socialism*. London: Verso.

——(2004) 'Racism in the Age of Globalisation', speech given at The Third Claudia Jones Memorial Lecture, National Union of Journalists Black Members Council, 24 October.

Solomos, J. and Back, L. (1996) *Racism and Society*. London: Macmillan.

Tatum, B. (1992) 'Talking about Race, Learning about Racism: The Application of Racial Identity Development Theory in the Classroom', *Harvard Educational Review*, 62: 1–24.

Wacquant, L. (2001) 'Deadly Symbiosis: Rethinking Race and Imprisonment in 21st Century America', *Boston Review* (Online). Available at www.bostonreview.net/BR27.2/wacquant.html (accessed 10 September 2012).

Webster, C. (2008) 'Marginalized White Ethnicity, Race and Crime', *Theoretical Criminology*, 12 (3): 293–312.

West, C. (1993) *Race Matters*. Boston, MA: Beacon Press.

Wilson, W. J. (1987) *The Truly Disadvantaged. The Inner City, The Underclass and Public Policy*. Chicago, IL: Chicago University Press.

Yang, P. (2000) *Ethnic Studies: Issues and Approaches*. Albany, NY: State University of New York Press.

# 7 Configuring ethnic identities

## Resistance as a response to counter-terrorist policy

*Alpa Parmar*

Identity is not in the past to be found, but in the future to be constructed.

(Hall 1995: 13)

The more that people like the police see me as a Muslim, the more I want to show them that I'm not what they think I am.

(Casim, 25 years)

### Introduction: ethnic identities, race and criminal justice

The formation and construction of ethnic group identity is increasingly important in the diverse, globalised world in which we live. The way in which people perceive and present their ethnic identities is volatile and influenced by their diasporic pasts and presents. The salience of ethnic identity in reference to, and in contrast and conjunction with religious, cultural, class, gender or geographical identities has been discussed in the context of the impact it may have on a person's self-perception since the 1960s onwards (Erikson 1968; Tajfel 1978). Ethnic identity has been carefully examined across social science disciplines, including sociology, anthropology, philosophy, ethnic, racial and post-colonial studies. However, the most significant shift in knowledge, was introduced by Stuart Hall's conception that ethnic identities are fluid, constantly re-negotiated and subject to experiences in the present and central to a person's affirmation of their sense of self (Hall 1995). Scholars have argued that the *process* whereby identities become configured is more important and meaningful than identity *per se* and that identity does not exist as an essence in and of itself (Martin 1995). Concomitantly, the relational aspects of ethnic identity are crucial to its understanding particularly because alteration and change is inextricably linked to the construction of identities. Culture and identity are constructions which 'are always subject to the continuous interpretation and reinterpretation' (Said 1995: 332). Processes of identity construction are also contextual, which underlines the notion of identities as mutable and fluctuating, as subject to various changes during an individual's lifetime and inherently ambivalent. The influences on identity and its construction are complex and varied (Hall 1996). This chapter focuses on how interactions with criminal justice agents (and specifically the police) influenced the identity processes of a group of citizens in the UK.

The relationship between race, ethnicity and criminal justice has been long-standing and police discrimination, police racist cultures and disproportionate outcomes for minorities at various stages of the criminal justice system have all received important scholarly attention (Holdaway 1983; Bowling and Phillips 2002). Hitherto, criminological discussion about minority ethnic groups has tended to focus either on the elevated rates of offending or the forms of discrimination in the criminal justice process. For example, Black groups have been consistently shown to be more likely to be stopped and searched by the police and more likely to be arrested for certain types of crime (Ministry of Justice 2011). Debates about the rate of disproportionality in stop and search have shown that minority groups may be more available to be stopped and searched (Waddington *et al.* 2004), however, as Bowling and Phillips argue, the over-use of police stop and search powers, without genuine suspicion being held by officers, may have normalised speculative intrusions and discriminatory policing practice (Bowling and Phillips 2007). However, understanding whether, and if so how, experiences of racism or perceived injustices within the criminal justice system impact upon the actual formation of ethnic identity has received little empirical attention in criminological literatures. Furthermore, studies within criminology have tended not to venture further than establishing the connections between ethnicity and crime, and in doing so ethnicity has been reified, essentialised and given a hermetic permanence. The processes by which ethnic identity is formed have remained unexplored and in this respect, criminological analyses have remained static and unable to respond to changes presented by the increased interaction of some minority ethnic groups in offending figures and in the criminal justice system. The fluidity of ethnic identity and associated changes as reported in sociological studies of ethnicity and race have not been integrated into criminological literatures and do not sit well with analyses which primarily map levels and types of crime over time across different ethnic groups. Notable exceptions within criminology include Phillips' (2012) study of prisons, Maher's (2000) study of female drug users in Brooklyn and Bosworth's (2011) work on foreign national prisoners. Intersectionality in frameworks of research and analysis, though addressed by these studies, has generally been neglected within mainstream criminology – and the interplay between race, gender and religion in the context of criminal justice has hardly been addressed, despite the need for sustained conceptual and empirical work to excavate these crossovers (Bulmer and Solomos 2009).

Notwithstanding the importance of the scholarship describing police cultures in advancing our understanding of how police stereotypes of ethnic groups can shape their interactions with such groups and vice versa (Waddington and Braddock 1991; Holdaway and O'Neill 2006; Loftus 2009), there remains a lacuna in the literature regarding the impact of racism and stereotypes on citizens and their perceptions of authority and criminal justice agents. The comparison of more recent studies has revealed a disjuncture in the literature because on the one hand large-scale surveys indicate that on the whole, Black and Asian people are satisfied with the police (Jansson *et al.* 2007; Myhill and Beak 2008; Jackson and Bradford 2009), yet studies of direct observation of interactions between the police and citizens and levels of complaints made against the police suggest (e.g. after stop and search encounters) that minority groups' levels of dissatisfaction with the police are high (Havis and Best 2004; Sims and Myhill 2001; Trust 1990). Relatedly, studies show that experience of direct contact with criminal justice agents and the nature of this experience are important for influencing perceptions (Van de Walle 2009). Despite the capacity of these studies to provide insight into the complexity of the factors for understanding citizen perceptions of the police, less is understood about *how* and to what extent experiences of racism and perceptions of profiling in the context of policing (where expectations for the standards of procedural fairness and legitimacy are perhaps high – see Myhill and Quinton 2010) impact on an individual's self perception and the construction and assertion of their ethnic identity.

## Asians and crime: from victims to terrorists

The criminalisation of Asian people has been researched and reported by scholars over recent years (Webster 1997; Alexander 2000; Goodey 2001). Prior to this and bound by the structures of research agendas and perceived priorities, there was less concern and investigation into Asian people's levels of crime and deviance. The few early studies conducted tended to confirm (and perpetuate) the stereotype of Asians as inherently subservient, law-abiding and controlled by the tight-knit communities to which they belonged and which were thought to have intrinsically protective mechanisms that diverted them from deviance and criminality (Mawby *et al.* 1979). Police stereotypes of Asians framed them as being involved in crimes of fraud, tax evasion or contravening their immigration rights (Jefferson 1992). Asian people were often only perceived as victims rather than suspects and in a study by Waddington and Braddock (1991), Asian youth were found to perceive the police as 'guardians' as opposed to bullies – the latter view was dominant amongst Black Caribbean youth.

Later analysis has reflected on the shift in perceptions of Asian criminality and identified the processes of criminalisation they have been subject to. Asians and particularly Asian Muslims were perceived as increasingly involved in drug use (Webster 1997; Goodey 2001), gangs and violence (Alexander 2000) and riotous behaviour (Bagguley and Hussain 2008). However, rather than suggestive of an actual rise in criminality amongst this demographic group, scholarship has pointed to the increased policing and framing of British Muslims in the media and social policy responses as key in generating this perception. Asian male identities have been essentialised and represented as being 'in crisis' – discussions of Asian masculinities have remained obscured by the hyper-visibility of black masculinities and concerns with violence and criminality (Alexander 2000). The 2005 terrorist attacks in London and the knowledge that the acts were perpetrated by British Muslims prompted concerns about 'home-grown terror' and exacerbated the perception of British Muslims as 'the enemy within'. All Muslims were homogeneously perceived as fundamentalists and as representing a terrorist threat (Hudson 2007).

The research reported in this chapter discusses the way in which Asian males' experiences of racism and perceptions of being profiled as potential terrorists (because they were stopped and searched) influenced the construction of their ethnic identities and notions of belonging and citizenship. Against the backdrop of a counter-terrorist policy agenda which purported to build confidence and trust amongst minority and particularly Asian communities, the interviews explain how, in reality, the implementation of counter-terrorist strategies marginalised those very groups of people. Rather than being passive subjects to the processes of criminalisation, racism and profiling, participants were instead active agents in their responses and resisted the homogenisation they felt categorised by. Asian males' narratives of opposition and frameworks of interpretation demonstrated that they developed their own notions of fairness and justice. In following Alexander's (2000) analytical strategy the aim of the present study was to develop a nuanced, local and historically situated account of identity formation, which captured the resistant and agentic aspects of the oppositional narratives developed by the participants themselves. Counter-terrorist policing encounters prompted the reassessment and renegotiation of ethnic identity amongst Asian males in the UK and in some cases influenced their understanding of the ethnic group boundaries between themselves and other Asian groups belonging to the same broad category.

## The research

This chapter draws on interview findings that were collected as part of a wider study to examine the practice and impacts of counter-terrorist policing in London between 2007 and 2010. Observations of stop and search operations and in police stations in London were conducted by myself and qualitative interviews were conducted with 23 Asian males who had been stopped and searched under Section 44 of the Terrorism Act 2000. These interviews were augmented with follow-up interviews with the same individuals, six months after the initial stop and search encounter. The aim was to explore whether the interaction and in many cases perception of injustice, anger, or questions about 'why' they had been stopped had remained or impacted upon the participants beyond the initial interview that was conducted immediately or soon after the stop. Including the follow-up interviews, a total of 41 in-depth interviews were conducted and all of the participants were male and under the age of 35 years. The self-defined ethnic profile, of those interviewed was as follows: 19 Asian, three Other Asian, ten Black, seven White and one Mixed.

Of the Asian group, 11 described themselves as Muslim, four Sikh and four Hindu. The person of Mixed background specified that he was White and Asian and defined himself as a British Muslim. The discussion in this chapter draws on the interviews with the Asian/Asian Muslim (23) males.[1] The interviews were transcribed and underwent thematic analysis (Braun and Clarke 2006) and the excerpts from the participants' narratives were selected according to the relevance to the salient themes (Hammersley 1990). Some of the themes broached in the interviews included asking participants about whether they felt as though they belonged to a particular ethnic group, asking why they thought they had been stopped by the police, the effect that the stop and search encounter may have had on them and their understandings of fairness in the context of why they had been stopped. All of the interviews were conducted by myself, and though I was not matched with many of my participants in terms of gender or ethnic background, I was able to establish a rapport with the participants as we met on more than one occasion and the continuity between interviews encouraged a sense of openness.

## Ethnic groups, boundaries and identities

This section explores the theoretical framework that will inform the interpretation of the interviews which are presented later in the chapter. The way in which ethnic group distinctions have developed throughout history and how they are enacted in the present, is complex and contested. Barth (1969) was the first notable theorist to discuss the formation of ethnic group boundaries and highlighted that the interconnectedness of ethnic identities was key to understanding the boundaries between them. Ethnic distinctions were perceived as entailing social processes of exclusion and incorporation and suggested that through this, discrete categories were maintained despite changing participation and membership in the course of individual life histories. Stable, persisting and often vitally important social relations are maintained across such boundaries and are frequently based precisely upon the dichotomised ethnic statuses. This perspective highlights the relational aspect of ethnicity and the process of inclusion and exclusion as central to the way in which ethnic identities are understood, created and perceived.

In making sense of why they had been stopped and searched under counter-terrorist legislation by the police participants made reference to the specific ethnic group they felt they belonged to, and in doing so, emphasised the boundaries between themselves and other groups as a way of reaffirming who they were and how they were perceived by the outside world. Echoing some of the assertions made by Barth (ibid.) about boundaries as central to the formation of ethnic group identities, participants emphasised that they were upset because they felt they were targeted for who they were not, rather than who they were. As one Sikh male told me:

I am tired of people looking at me like I'm a threat. I'm insulted that I was stopped because the police obviously thought I was a Muslim.

(Harpal, 19)

Cultural or religious differences were used as strategies by the men in the study to assert the perceived ethnic group differences between them and the counter-terrorist stop and search experience was often referenced as emphasising and justifying the need to do this more vigorously. Active efforts were made by some participants to signal to people that they were not Muslim, nor practising Muslims. As one British Asian Hindu explained:

When I go out, I will drink alcohol – not always because I want to, but because it tells people that I am not Muslim. I used to wear an aum [Hindu religious symbol] round my neck, but I noticed people would look at it funny and then I made the connection – people don't understand the difference between Hindu and Islamic symbols, and why would they? We are all the same to them since the London bombings.

(Chetan, 24)

In a critical discussion against the idea of ethnic groupism (or using the notion of bounded groups as units of analysis), Brubaker (2004) suggested that the accurate analysis of ethnicity should accommodate dynamic concepts of group formation. The interviews raised the importance not only of the fluidity of the constitution of groups but also about how identities are often defined by experiences. Tilly characterised identity as 'an actor's experience of a category, tie, role, network' (1996: 7). The public representation of that experience was important, according to Tilly, and would often take the form of a shared story or a narrative. The shared narrative amongst participants in the current study indicated that the feeling of injustice, or being unfairly labelled and singled out, had a significant impact and had the potential to affect participants' sense of ethnic identity and group belonging.

The interviews supported the need to suspend ideas of ethnic groups as bounded or fixed and that collective action did not necessarily stem from a person's collective designation. Rather there were examples of the desire to divert from common understandings of the ethnic group to which people belonged. Much in line with Brubaker's suggestion that discursive frames or political affiliation may be more meaningful and representative of people's group connections, the interviews suggested that broader affiliations such as those based on language, or geographical place were at times more relevant to the formation of groups. The following quote from a British Asian Hindu highlights the point:

Faizal and me, religion never was mentioned. We started to hang out together because we both could speak Punjabi and so could communicate in class without the teachers knowing and we lived one street away from each other. Then since I was stopped by the police because they thought I might be a terrorist, it made me think that they see us all the same – all of us are brown. And then when I was asking why that happened to me it made me think about the differences I had with Faizal, you know you start to notice things more.

(Sanjay, 28)

Sanjay's experience shows how his own understandings of his group identity and notions of belonging to the broader Asian ethnic group underwent a process of reassessment. Although previous friendships and affiliations had not been bounded within the ethnic group, police attention had heightened awareness of cultural and religious differences within the group. More specifically, the experience of being stopped and searched under the Terrorism Act 2000 and the associated notions of religious profiling, served to draw out the differences between friends. This represents a reversal of findings from recent analyses, which have underlined that friendships between people in multicultural spaces are contextual, circumstantial and reflective of the multiple impacts on identity such as national and local (postcode) alliances, religion and solidarity (Phillips 2008). According to Phillips' analysis of a prison environment, religious identities and masculinities enmeshed and structured the everyday reality of social interactions and friendships (Phillips 2012). Inter-ethnic diversity (i.e. between Asian groups – Indians and Muslims for example) was valued and not thought to be divisive prior to anti-Muslim sentiment, according to my participants. However, boundaries were reaffirmed following the London underground attacks and media reports showed support of the lines of division solidifying – some Asians were reported as wearing t-shirts with the slogan 'don't freak I'm a Sikh' to allay concerns that they may appear to be Muslims (Parmar 2011).

## Assuming labels

The discussion in the preceding section has been suggestive of the process driven nature and fluidity of ethnic identities. The suggestion by Stuart Hall that identities are continually constructed and shaped resounded in the narratives of the participants in this study (Hall 1996). A number expressed that the external perception that they envisaged of themselves had changed over time, and in following this they referenced the central importance of external recognition for the configuration of their self-identity. As Casim (a British Asian Muslim) exemplifies:

It didn't used to be like this. But since people are now scared that all Muslims are terrorists or that we might secretly support them people expect us to be something. Expect us to believe something. And in the end, you wind up going that way ... you get me? ... like people and the politicians label you as a particular type of person and in the end you give in and give them what they expected. I dunno who ends up being happy, but that's the outcome.

(Casim, 25 years)

Casim explained that since feeling that he was only perceived as a Muslim, he had resigned himself to the label he was given. He described that his cultural style was previously framed by a hybrid of Punjabi and Muslim influences, and that he would identify with Black friends and role models and would listen to a range of different music and engaged in multiple cultures which embraced and expressed this hybridity. However, Casim went on to explain that over the past year and particularly over the last six months he had felt the need to 'focus on being a Muslim' and that the transition was difficult and did not represent what he wanted but the thought that he had no other option. As he went on to say:

People see me and they think Muslim terrorist, in the same thought. So I might as well be what they think I am.

(Casim, 25 years)

In accordance with Casim's expression, Stuart Hall (1995) has argued that identity is always part of a narrative and that external experiences are important for allowing us to understand who we are and the changes to our notions of self-identity:

… identity is not only a story, a narrative which we tell ourselves about ourselves, it is stories which change with historical circumstances. And identity shifts with the way in which we think and hear them and experience them. Far from only coming from the still small point of truth inside us, identities actually come from outside, they are the way in which we are recognized and then come to step into the place of the recognitions which others give us. Without the others there is no self, there is no self-recognition.

(Hall 1995: 8)

Scholars have noted the volatility and creativity inherent in the process of identity formation, referring to it as a verb rather than a noun (Bauman 1996) and the intersection of cultures and influences from music and arts has been particularly noted in reference to South Asian identities (Banerjea 2000). Amongst the celebratory aspects of the lived realities of diversity, energy and creativity, which moved beyond outmoded essentialist categorisations, concerns were raised about the place of racism and whether the relevance of structure and discrimination would disappear from the political agenda. For example, Alexander and Knowles (2005) called for the importance of engaging with notions of identity and difference in ways that locate theoretical issues in the grounded contexts of everyday life. In the present study however, discrimination, criminalisation and structural racism were evidently alive, as the participant's narratives enunciated. Examples of direct racism were often recounted and participants saw little merit in reporting racism to the police:

> I've been called a jihadist to my face and I've heard people wind their windows down while driving past and shouting terrorist … and worse. But I wouldn't bother reporting it to the police. There's no point. They think the same they just can't say it to your face, so they get their way by stopping you, cos that's something they can do. They think we deserve it.
>
> (Mustaq, 28)

The research presented here was a clear reminder of the need for analyses of identity to allow for an understanding of the potential for racist experiences and perceptions of being stereotyped to shape the process of identity formation amongst Asians. As the quote above shows, the police were understood to be constituent components of a racist and Islamophobic society and were thought to afford little understanding about or protection from racist attacks. As Mustaq's quote above indicates, police racism was perceived as influencing increased police attention towards Muslims, although its expression was understood to operate in a covert way and generated by resentment towards Muslims and more broadly towards the diversity agenda implemented following the recommendations from the Macpherson report (Loftus 2009). Furthermore, narratives from the participants tended to include references to the historically acrimonious relationship between the police and minority ethnic groups:

> When I was stopped, it was a reminder, that I am British, but only up to a point. I was talking with my mates about it, some of who are Black and they were understanding, but also said that it's about time the police looked somewhere else … We all know that the police are racist, with all the riots in the 80s and that … and up north … it happens for a reason. I think differently about myself now. I see that there are real differences between myself and my mates. People don't seem to remember that how you look – your colour isn't something that you can change.
>
> (Ebrahim, 19)

Another participant suggested that the experience of being stopped and feeling as though he was treated in a racist manner, had brought him closer into a circle of friends that had experienced the same. Shafiq, an Asian-Muslim, explained that he had felt 'different' since the underground attacks and that people would stare at him as he walked along the street. He felt trapped as he had lost his job and so would try and go out each day to keep his spirits up, however the verbal racial abuse he experienced made him want to withdraw from society: 'I was told to go back to where I'm from' and 'I've been called a scrounging bomb-maker while I was waiting in the queue to sign on at the job centre.' Initially Shafiq did not share the stop and search experience with his friends, but later, when he did he found that a number of them had also been stopped:

> In the end when I mentioned it to a few of the lads we all got talking about how angry we were. That even if you try your best, you will never be accepted. In the end the experience and talking about how we'd all been called names and looked at differently and hassled by the police ... it brought us closer. We started to chill together more.
>
> (Shafiq, 24)

This search for support and acknowledgement of the sense of injustice was a common theme amongst a number of the participants. The majority of Asians had not mentioned to their parents or other family members that they were stopped and searched. Most felt as though their parents wouldn't understand, or that they would be blamed for being stopped and searched. The sense of solidarity through struggle was clearly a source of strength for the group described here, however, it is in juxtaposition to the ways in which Asian Sikhs and Asian Hindus felt, rather, they experienced the need to separate themselves from being associated with Asian Muslims, as described earlier.

## Spaces to belong

Notions of belonging were raised in the participant's narratives, and this has received attention in recent political debates in Britain which have suggested that British Muslim communities were less well integrated into 'British' society (Cantle 2001). Scholarship examining British Muslims' experiences since the 2005 London terrorist attacks has indicated that despite feeling that they were perceived differently by people in society, Muslims were proud to be British and were hostile to Islamic extremism (Hussain and Bagguley 2013; Maxwell 2006). In the present study references were made to the catalytic nature of the stop and search encounter for some participants in relation to their 'Britishness'. Ishtaq who had been stopped three times previously, told me:

> It's just like been told to your face that life's not fair for you if you are Muslim and you just have to suck it up. Obviously it's not just bad luck or random that I am targeted. It's because of how I look, who I am. I've lived here all my life, but feel like an outsider. I said to the police that my race is British Muslim, not British or Muslim.
>
> (Ishtaq, 20)

Another participant told of how the stop and search encounter provided confirmation that wider society was racist and anti-Muslim and the police were simply reflecting this generalised view. Others expressed disappointment, anger and resentment towards the officers that stopped them, and many expressed a sense of residual anger about being stopped in their follow-up interviews. For others, the stop and search encounter was a watershed moment as they truly felt as though 'the police were not on their side' or that 'if push came to shove, in the eyes of the police you're just another Paki'. Another young Sikh lamented the progress that he felt had been lost and felt resentful towards Muslims for 'bringing down the reputation of Asians'. He went on to explain:

> I was so proud of being Asian, and there was a chance to do new things, bring in new styles. But by one act of stupidity by four people – it's all lost ... and what for? We all lose out in the end ... this is where I grew up and where I am from, so I don't know anything different.

The public nature of stop and searches and the embarrassment it produces has been shown in studies of police practice (Stone and Pettigrew 2000). This sense of public humiliation was echoed in my interviews and seemed to be further compounded because of the wider perceptions that they felt people held of British Asian Muslims. As Ebrahim stated 'people were looking at me while the police were patting me down and you could tell they thought – he's a terrorist, or he's a [drug] dealer'. Others felt aggrieved that they were stopped nearby to where they lived and suggested that this underlined the fact that they didn't really belong. Local identities were important in the lives of the participants and many had spent most of their lives in London and the borough in which they were stopped. Many reported feeling 'less comfortable' in walking home and as though the place where they had grown up was 'not the way it used to be'. As the data shows, identities and affiliations formed and negotiated through the geography of different local contexts allow a better basis for understanding multicultural society (Amin 2002; Parker and Karner 2010). The present study underlines the importance of reputational geographies for multi-ethnic locales and the way in which these can be disrupted. The modes of governance that were employed through the Terrorism Act 2000, resulted in subverting the sense of belonging that participants had and led to the anticipation that they would be treated unjustly by criminal justice agents. The logic of spatial choices for acts of disorder has been highlighted by analyses which showed that the patterns where the summer 2011 riots occurred were shaped by rational, planned choices as opposed to spontaneous events (Baudains, Braithwaite and Johnson 2012).

## Counter-terrorism, criminalisation and securitisation

The findings reported in this chapter are important to contextualise within the UK government strategy for counter-terrorism. Official government policy for counter-terrorism was revised in 2009 to respond to the 'evolving threat of terrorism', entitled the 'Contest Strategy'. Contest was organised around four principal work streams labelled 'pursue', 'prevent', 'protect' and 'prepare'. Pursue described the aim to stop terrorist attacks, Protect aimed to strengthen the UK from terrorist attacks and Prepare aimed to mitigate against the effects of attacks which might take place. The Prevent strand of the Contest strategy is of most relevance for the discussion in this chapter, as it held direct implications for policing and interaction between citizens and the police.[2] The aim of Prevent in 2009 (the strategy in place whilst the fieldwork was conducted) was to identify and take action against individuals who were deemed intent on promoting violence and who were planning to recruit young vulnerable individuals. Policing efforts were aimed at promoting resilience amongst communities and at providing support to community organisations. Since being implemented, the Prevent strategy has been criticised for galvanising perceptions of Muslims as representing a 'suspect community' (Kundnani 2009; McGhee 2008; Pantazis and Pemberton 2009; Nickels *et al.* 2010) and the strategy's failure to separate community cohesion work from intelligence gathering functions has resulted in its reputation as a legitimate guise to spy on Muslims (Walker and Rehman 2011). The subtext for the Prevent and wider counter-terrorism strategy intimated a binary framework according to which all Muslims were assumed to be struggling between extremist fundamentalism and a moderate and integrated attitude that was commensurate with the aims of British society.

The contradictions of the Prevent strategy were exemplified by the participants' narratives reported in this chapter. In contrast to the aim to build trust, confidence and resilience amongst Muslim communities in the UK, Asian Muslims expressed that they were labelled, stigmatised and criminalised by police actions towards them. Some participants were aware that section 44 of the Terrorism Act 2000[3] was under scrutiny because it did not have the requirement for reasonable suspicion (which would ordinarily act as safeguard against arbitrary stops) and were well versed with the argument against the use of section 44:

> Stop and search under the Terrorism Act goes against my human rights. There has to be a real reason why people are stopped, but thinking someone is a terrorist is not enough. I know loads of people who have complained, but they are only made to listen when white people are stopped and then they are able to take them to court.
>
> (Casim, 25 years)

This quote is indicative of the sense of injustice evoked by the stop and search practices that Asians were subjected to and the resulting resentment, which was in stark contrast to the strategy's aims of creating 'resilience' and 'trust' at the local level. The interaction with the police tended to create the very alienation and disaffection that the strategy was purporting to prevent and counteract. Casim also alludes to his wider perception of racism in society and amongst criminal justice institutions. In expanding on this point Casim talked of how the *Gillan and Quinton*[4] case made him angry because it provided confirmation to him that for complaints or actions about racism to be taken seriously, white people had to be the complainants. This sense of inferiority was echoed by others:

There's no point someone like me making a fuss – I ain't got any power or influence. Even though I thought I was treated badly and I tried to take it further, nothing came of it. After I complained they called me in a week later to meet with some other higher ranking police officer and a community police officer who explained that I wasn't targeted because of my colour or religion. But the guy wouldn't look me in the eye, and I just felt fobbed off.

(Waqas, 29 years)

## Criminalisation

Early sociological research focussed on the criminalisation of Black youth through moral panics about mugging and violence (Hall *et al.* 1978). Some have suggested that British Muslim youth have been the focus of a moral panic and that they represent the 'new folk devils' of society (Alexander 2000). As discussed in the introduction, Asian youth were largely omitted from these debates as they were stereotyped as law-abiding and victims rather than perpetrators of crime. Asians and particularly Asian Muslims fell within the criminalising gaze during the Rushdie affair and following the moral panics around their perceived involvement in gangs and violence (Webster 1997; Alexander 2000). The 2001 northern England riots were also important in reframing the image of Muslim young men as violent, militant and aggressive (Archer 2001) and the ensuing policies on community cohesion forced a re-examination of the place of Muslims in British society. Following the terrorist attacks in London, Muslims have been reported as inherently suspect (Pantazis and Pemberton 2009), demonised as terrorist or extremist (Virdee *et al.* 2006) and reports of increased racism and religious hatred have been documented (Poynting and Mason 2006; Ramamurthy 2006). The actual processes and experience of criminalisation and its consequences have been less well understood and it is here that this chapter claims its significance. Rather than being passive towards the criminalising process, the Asian youth were active agents, analysing and questioning the treatment they were receiving and created an oppositional narrative of fairness and justice. For example, there was a resistance to the sense of racist homogenisation and reification of Asian groups as being the same. The following quote by a Sikh male makes the point:

I was angry for being stopped and for them thinking that I was going to be a threat to national security. I mean, it was just obvious, why they decided to choose to stop me. I suppose as well, and you know I shouldn't say this, but it's like they thought I was Muslim, just cos I had a beard. I'm a proud Sikh and it just made me want to go round telling everyone that I'm not Muslim.

(Jags, 21)

The criminalising experience that Asian participants felt subject to was reported as a wider sentiment, often unspoken and encapsulated in a 'funny look' (Hussain and Bagguley 2013) or by staring:

It's strange. People either stare, or look straight through you. It's like they don't want to see you as a friend, a passenger or someone that might have similarity to them. This definitely was not the case before ... [the London terrorist attacks] and it makes me react by making sure that I try to strike up a conversation, or I act more outgoing than I normally would, so that people start to think I am normal. I try my best to make sure that people see me as British as well, rather than a stereotyped Muslim.

(Ali, 28)

In discussing the complexities of the criminalising process of British Asians since the London underground attacks and the ways in which the implementation of counter-terrorist policy has advanced this process in a dynamic way, the research described here is able to add to the extant discussion of the criminalisation of Asian males first described by Webster (1997), Alexander (2000) and Goodey (2001). Webster (1997) found that racial stereotypes had changed in his study in Northern England because young Asians were challenging rather than accepting racist violence from white people in the area. The informal vigilantism or acts of resistance were reframed as representing violent racism on the part of Asians. In congruence with this Desai (1999) found that hyper-masculine representations of self, by Bangladeshi males in North London were misinterpreted as racist violence towards white youth. These new spaces of identity tended to reinforce the existing boundaries between the two ethnic groups. Similarly, in the present study, the experiences of criminalisation were resisted and perceived by the police as arrogance or 'difficult behaviour' from the Asian men when they asked questions or complained.

## Securitisation

Securitisation analyses aim to excavate the process by which an issue or groups are defined as a security threat in order that governmental and societal resources can be galvanised in the aim to counter or prevent it (Buzan *et al.* 1998). The securitisation process ensures that a group or issue is automatically perceived as a threat. A similar process was described by Keith (1993) who explained that when criminalisation and racialisation work together, the couplet 'Black youth' can be employed in racist discourse to signify criminality. Descriptive concepts can change over time if they are securitised or criminalised. Body-Gendrot (2010) has discussed this process in reference to the term *banlieu*, which has been transformed through its use in the media and popular discourse to refer to urban deprivation, illiteracy, segregation, poverty, drugs and crime – the subtext being that large immigrant families concentrated in public housing estates are inherently the source of problems.

Perceptions of Muslims since the London underground attacks have shifted and anti-Muslim sentiment is said to have increased (Bleich 2009; Kundnani 2009). The media is thought to have played a central role in this process and in particular Muslims are constructed as a threat to Britishness on the grounds of representing a homogenised religious identity (Nickels *et al.* 2010). There has been little empirical research, which has unpacked the process of criminalisation and the racialisation of Muslim people over recent years although a recent study by Hussain and Bagguley (2012) provides a notable exception. In examining views of Muslims and non Muslims following the 7/7 London terrorist attacks, they propose that the concept of securitisation allows for a more accurate understanding of the way in which Islamophobia, racialisation and racism interact in specific historical circumstances. Through their contention that securitisation, Islamophobia and racialisation are analytically distinct, Hussain and Bagguley (2012) were able to tease out the ways in which the two processes came together in the anti-Muslim identifications amongst some of the non-Muslims they interviewed. Furthermore, in consonance with the findings of the present study, Hussain and Bagguley (2012) revealed the various impacts of securitising processes on local Muslims in Leeds – a city in Northern England. Importantly, in their study, although Muslim participants identified with a global Muslim community, this did not straightforwardly result in identification with the use of violence or terrorism. In the present study, the participants tended to regard the media as the main sources of securitisation and there was little suggestion of the support for extremism or the potential for the young men to be radicalised.

## Resistance and identity configuration

Notwithstanding the powerful influence of processes of criminalisation and securitisation described above, the findings in this chapter detail the ways in which young Asian men resisted, disrupted (and at times transformed) the categories of identity into which they felt placed. The ascription of group identities by authorities in relation to ethnicity or race is and always has been a political and contentious project. Ethnic cartographies were imposed through slavery and the rigidifying of borders instituted by colonial processes served to ossify groups and their assumed characteristics and boundaries. The ascription of identities in the past has met with acceptance and rejection – for example, the rejection of the term 'coloured' and ethnic mobilisation resulted in the alternative use of the term 'Black' and galvanised (and was galvanised by) the Black liberation movement. The dangers of applying limited definitions of identity to groups can lead to violence, according to Maalouf (1996), who regards identity and its assertion to be inextricably linked to protest and fighting. The awareness of the fluid, multiple and often contradictory aspects of identity was most comprehensively addressed by Hall. For Hall, the human subject is:

> Conceptualized as having no fixed, essential or permanent identity. Identity becomes a 'moveable feast'; formed and transformed continuously in

relation to the ways we are represented or addressed in the cultural systems which surround us. It is historically, not biologically defined.

(Hall 1992: 277)

In attempting to understand the processes and negotiation of identity config-uration and its changes this chapter has discussed the ways in which interac-tions between groups of citizens and authority (in this instance the police) can have important consequences at both societal and individual levels. The present research has therefore been able to engage with the interaction of social structure (criminal justice) and human agency (reinterpretation and resistance from participants). This has resulted in a textured analysis of the responses to criminalisation and reactions to being over policed. Participants were often keen to reject and resist the identities they felt ascribed and inscribed by, through their interpretation of why the police had stopped them. Other respondents adopted the label they felt ascribed, but not in a straightforward way. Rather, there was evidence of individuals feeling as though they may as well arrogate aspects of Islam or provide signals of their religion outwardly, because they were labelled as Muslims and as a threat. A minority of parti-cipants accepted that they had been criminalised and sympathised with the focus on Muslims and discourses of terrorism surrounding Islam:

> To some extents I can see why I was stopped. I mean the lads who carried out the attacks, they were British Muslims and so that's gonna make people suspicious towards us. But they need to understand that not all Muslims are evil and that what they [the bombers] did is not religion, it's not Islamic, it's not even an interpretation of Islam. I blame the news – they're always making out that all Muslims are fundamentalists … sometimes it's real subtle like, but if you look carefully it's there. No wonder the police act on that and then stop people that look like me.
>
> (Hamid, 24)

The participant's quote above also demonstrates his resistance to the homo-genisation of all Muslim people as the same. As discussed above, the media were often referred to as catalytic to the processes of criminalisation and anti-Muslim portrayal (see also Hussain and Bagguley 2012). Police processes were vindicated within this broader socio-political context and the enforce-ment of legislation was regarded as an extension of this sentiment rather than its cause.

The misrecognition of minority ethnic groups by agencies of criminal jus-tice has been shown to have lasting and negative consequences and the indignity of being repeatedly labelled as something you are not, promotes an entrenched sense of resentment (Parmar 2007). Muslim people who were stopped felt a sense of injustice and humiliation at having been singled out. This concurs with the findings from Blackwood *et al.*'s study in which Muslim people felt unfairly scrutinised when they were stopped at airports for further security screening. Passengers in Blackwood *et al.*'s study felt as though they were denied their sense of identity which ordinarily afforded them pride and respectability from others (because they were Muslim). The misrecognition and humiliation felt has been reported to promote a sense of self-policing of one's own outward and internal religious and cultural practices. In the present study, some thought it necessary to actively disguise their religious backgrounds, or not to draw attention to it. Muslim men talked of advising their wives and partners to give up wearing the hijab, as it may provoke racist attacks or draw attention from the police. Interestingly, it was the policing of Muslim women's appearances and bodies that was referred to the most, implying that they were regarded to be symbolic bearers of religion and culture, thereby highlighting the importance for gender to be included in future analyses of the impacts of securitisation and criminalisation. The present study for example is only able to report on findings related to British Asian males.

## Concluding remarks

This chapter has discussed the ways in which ethnic identities and people's constructions of their identities were influenced by the criminalised labels that they were ascribed (or thought to have been ascribed) by the police. Identity is acquired and self-constructed and can therefore be framed as being in juxtaposition to processes which assign 'common sense' identities to groups of people or which stereotype, and impose categories. The reality is that ethnic identities are more likely to be a complex interplay of these two aspects – an unstable balance between self-construction and ascription by outsiders (Martin 2013). Identities are never simply our own and rather are embedded with relations with others, our visions of ourselves necessarily include the conceptions that we believe other people have of us (Ricoeur 1992). The research discussed in this chapter affirms these understandings of identity configuration processes but also directs us to looking to the contemporary influences (both positive and negative) on such practices. It has also shown how people are active agents in deciding how to respond to the various (structural) influences on their ethnic identities and that they play an active role in deciding and negotiating how these influences are able to shape and inform a person's self-perception. Significantly, the research indicates that experiences of racism and the process by which ethnic and religious groups are framed as suspicious or as representing a violent threat can impact on the ethnic identities of individuals, the formation of group identities and multicultural relations in society.

In keeping with the theme of this volume, this chapter has presented a new direction for thinking about the consequences of counter-terrorist policies – which arguably represent a 'new generation' in aiming to ensure the security of citizens. In this context, stop and search practices and police actions are perhaps better understood as processes rather than as discrete encounters. As this chapter has highlighted, the reach of counter-terrorist policies and securitisation goes beyond the aims for which they were crafted and the reality of the unintended consequences is that they may engender the very forms of disenfranchisement and marginalisation they purport to prevent.

## Notes

1 All of the initial participants were interviewed twice, except two participants who were unreachable.
2 It is notable that the policing role in the 2011 review of the Prevent strategy was played down.
3 Section 44 of the Terrorism Act 2000 was in use at the time of the study and subsequently withdrawn in 2011.
4 Section 44 of the Terrorism Act 2000, which allowed a police officer to stop and search an individual or a vehicle without the need for reasonable suspicion, was ruled as unlawful by the European Court of Human Rights, in January 2011. It was held that the use of Section 44 violated Article 8 of the European Convention on Human Rights (the right to respect for private and family life). In the landmark ruling it was stated that Section 44 powers were 'not sufficiently circumscribed' and lacked 'adequate legal safeguards against abuse' (Gillan and Quinton v. The United Kingdom, the European Court of Human Rights).

## References

Alexander, C. (2000) *The Asian Gang: Ethnicity, Identity and Masculinity*. Oxford: Berg.

Alexander, C. and Knowles, C. (eds) (2005) *Making Race Matter: Bodies, Space and Identity*. Basingstoke: Palgrave Macmillan.

Amin, A. (2002) 'Ethnicity and the multicultural city: living with diversity', *Environment and Planning A*, 34 (6): 959–80.

Archer, L. (2001) 'Muslim brothers, black lads, traditional Asians: British Muslim young men's constructions of race, religion and masculinity', *Feminism Psychology* 11: 79–105.

Bagguley, P. and Hussain, Y. (2008) *Riotous Citizens: Ethnic Conflict in Multicultural Britain*. Aldershot: Ashgate.

Banerjea, K. (2000) 'Sounds of whose underground? The fine tuning of diaspora in an age of mechanical reproduction', *Theory, Culture & Society*, 17 (3): 64–79.

Barth, F. (ed.) (1969) *Ethnic Groups and Boundaries: The Social Organization of Cultural Difference*. London: Allen and Unwin.

Baudains, P., Braithwaite, A. and Johnson, S. D. (2012) 'Spatial patterns in the 2011 riots', *Policing*, 7 (1): 21–31.

Bauman, Z. (1996) 'From pilgrim to tourist – or a short history of identity', in S. Hall and P. du Guy (eds) *Questions of Cultural Identity*. London: Sage.

Blackwood, L., Hopkins, N. and Reicher, S. (2012) 'I know who I am, but who do they think I am? Muslim perspectives on encounters with airport authorities', *Ethnic and Racial Studies* (Online). Available at www.tandfonline.com/doi/pdf/10.1080/0141987 0.2011 (accessed October 2012).

Bleich, E., (2009) 'Where do Muslims stand on ethno-racial hierarchies in Britain and France? Evidence from public opinion surveys, 1988–2008', *Patterns of Prejudice*, 43 (3–4): 379–400.

Body-Gendrot, S. (2010) 'Police marginality, racial logics and discrimination in the banlieues of France', *Ethnic and Racial Studies*, 33 (4): 656–74.

Bosworth, M. (2011) 'Deportation, detention and foreign-national prisoners in England and Wales', *Citizenship Studies*, 15 (2): 583–95.

Bowling, B. and Phillips, C. (2002) *Racism, Crime and Criminal Justice.* Harlow: Longman.

——(2007) 'Disproportionate and discriminatory: reviewing the evidence on police stop and search', *The Modern Law Review*, 70 (6): 936–61.

Braun, V. and Clarke, V. (2006) 'Using thematic analysis in psychology', *Qualitative Research in Psychology*, 3 (2): 77–101.

Brubaker, R. (2004) *Ethnicity Without Groups.* Cambridge, MA: Harvard University Press.

Bulmer, M. and Solomos, J. (2009) 'Gender, race and religion: intersections and challenges', *Ethnic and Racial Studies*, 32 (2): 215–17.

Buzan, B., Waever, O. and de Wilde, J. (1998) *Security: A New Framework for Analysis.* London: Lynne Reinner.

Cantle, T. (2001) *Community Cohesion: A Report of the Independent Review Team.* London: Home Office.

Desai, P. (1999) 'Spaces of identity, cultures of conflict: the development of new British Asian masculinities', unpublished thesis, University of London, Goldsmiths College.

Dodd, V. (2010) 'Police demand new powers to stop and search terror suspects', *Guardian Online*, 29 December. Available at www.guardian.co.uk/uk/2010/dec/29/police-stop-and-search-powers (accessed 29 December 2010).

Erikson, E. H. (1968) *Identity and Youth Crisis.* New York: W.W. Norton Company.

Goodey, J. (2001) 'The criminalization of British Asian youth: research from Bradford and Sheffield', *Journal of Youth Studies*, 4 (4): 429–50.

Hall, S., Critcher, C., Jefferson, T., Clarke, J. and Roberts, B. (1978) *Policing the Crisis: Mugging, the State and Law and Order.* London: Macmillan Education.

Hall, S. (1992) 'The question of cultural identity', in S. Hall, D. Held and T. McGrew (eds) *Modernity and its Futures.* Cambridge: Polity Press.

——(1995) 'Negotiating Caribbean identities', *New Left Review*, 209: 3–14.

——(1996) 'Introduction: who needs identity?', in S. Hall and P. du Gay (eds) *Questions of Cultural Identity.* London: Sage.

Hammersley, M. (1990) *Reading Ethnographic Research: A Critical Guide.* London: Longman.

Havis, S. and Best, D. (2004) *Stop and Search Complaints 2000–2001: A Police Complaints Authority Study.* London: Police Complaints Authority.

Holdaway, S. (1983) *Inside the British Police: A Force at Work.* Oxford: Blackwell.

Holdaway, S. and O'Neill, M. (2006) 'Ethnicity and culture: thinking about "police ethnicity"', *British Journal of Sociology*, 57 (3): 483–502.

Hudson, B. (2007) 'Diversity, crime and criminal justice', in M. Maguire, R. Morgan and R. Reiner (eds) *The Oxford Handbook of Criminology*, 4th edn. Oxford: Oxford University Press.

Hussain, Y. and Bagguley, P. (2012) 'Securitized citizens: islamophobia, racism and the 7/7 London bombings', *The Sociological Review*, 60: 715–34.

——(2013) 'Funny looks: British Pakistanis experiences after 7 July 2005', *Ethnic and Racial Studies*, 36 (1): 28–46.

Jackson, J. and Bradford, B. (2009) 'Crime, policing and social order: on the expressive nature of public confidence in policing', *British Journal of Sociology*, 60 (3): 493–521.

Jansson, K., Budd, S., Lovbakke, J., Moley, S. and Thorpe, K. (2007) 'Attitudes, perceptions and risks of crime: Supplementary Volume 1 to Crime in England and Wales 2006/07', 2nd edn. London: Home Office.

Jefferson, T. (1992) 'The racism of criminalization: policing and the reproduction of the criminal other', in L. Gelsthorpe (ed.) *Minority Groups in the Criminal Justice System*, Conference Proceedings of the 21st Cropwood Roundtable Conference. Cambridge: Institute of Criminology.

Keith, M. (1993) *Race, Riots and Policing: Lore and Disorder in a Multi-racist Society*. London: UCL Press.

Kundnani, A. (2009) *Spooked: How not to Prevent Violent Terrorism*. London: Institute of Race Relations.

Loftus, B. (2009) *Police Culture in a Changing World*. Oxford: Oxford University Press.

Maalouf, A. (1996) *In the Name of Identity: Violence and the Nneed to Belong*, Trans B. Bray (2003). New York: Penguin Books.

Maher, L. (2000) *Sexed Work: Gender, Race, and Resistance in a Brooklyn Drug Market*. Oxford: Oxford University Press.

McGhee, D. (2008) *The End of Multiculturalism? Terrorism, Integration and Human Rights*. Maidenhead: Open University Press.

Martin, D. (1995) 'The choices of identity', *Social Identities*, 1 (1): 5–16.

——'The political configuration of identities', paper presented at Cambridge University, Centre for Arts, Social Sciences and Humanities, January 2013.

Mawby, R., McCulloch, J. and Batta, I. (1979) 'Crime amongst Asian juveniles in Bradford', *International Journal of the Sociology of Law*, 7: 297–306.

Maxwell, R. (2006) 'Muslims, South Asians and the British mainstream: a national identity crisis?', *West European Politics*, 29 (4): 736–56.

Ministry of Justice (2011) 'Statistics on race and the criminal justice system. A Ministry of Justice publication under Section 95 of the Criminal Justice Act 1991'. London: Crown Copyright.

Myhill, A. and Beak, K. (2008) *Public Confidence in the Police*. London: National Policing Improvement Agency.

Myhill, A. and Quinton, P. (2010) 'Confidence, Neighbourhood Policing, and Contact: Drawing together the evidence', *Policing* 4 (3): 273–81.

Nickels, H., Thomas, L., Hickman, M. and Silvestri, S. (2010) 'A comparative study of the representations of "suspect" communities in multi-ethnic Britain and their impact on Irish communities and Muslim communities – Mapping newspaper content'. London: City University.

Pantazis, C. and Pemberton, S. (2009) 'From the "old" to the "new" suspect community: examining the impacts of recent UK counter-terrorist legislation', *British Journal of Criminology*, 49 (5): 646–66.

Parker, D. and Karner, C. (2010) 'Reputational geographies and urban social cohesion', *Ethnic and Racial Studies*, 33 (8): 1451–70.

Parmar, A. (2007) 'Crime and the Asian community: disentangling perceptions and reality', unpublished thesis, University of Cambridge.

——(2011) 'Stop and search in London: Counter-terrorist or counter-productive?', *Policing and Society*, 21 (4): 369–82.

Phillips, C. (2008) 'Negotiating Identities: ethnicity and social relations in a young offenders' institution', *Theoretical Criminology*, 12 (3): 313–31.

——(2012) *The Multicultural Prison: Ethnicity, Masculinity and Social Relations among Prisoners*. Oxford: Oxford University Press.

Poynting, S. and Mason, V. (2006) 'Tolerance, freedom, justice and peace? Britain, Australia and anti-Muslim racism since 11th September 2001', *Journal of Intercultural Studies*, 27 (4): 365–92.

Ramamurthy, A. (2006) 'The politics of Britain's Asian youth movements', *Race & Class*, 48 (2): 38–60.

Ricoeur, P. (1992) *Oneself as Another*. Chicago, IL: University of Chicago Press.

Said, E. (1995) *Orientalism: Western Conceptions of the Orient*. London: Penguin Books.

Sims, L. and Myhill, A. (2001) *Policing and the Public: Findings from the 2000 British Crime Survey*, Home Office Research Findings 136. London: Home Office.

Stone, V. and Pettigrew, N. (2000) *The Views of the Public on Stop and Searches*, Police Research Series Paper 129. London: Home Office.

Tajfel, H. (ed.) (1978) *Differentiation between Social Groups: Studies in the Social Psychology of Intergroup Relations*. London: Academic Press.

Tilly, C. (1996) 'Citizenship, identity and social history', in C. Tilly (ed.) *Citizenship, Identity and Social History*. Cambridge: Cambridge University Press.

Travis, A. (2009) Stop and search disproportionately targets black and Asian people. *Guardian Online*, 1 May. Available at www.guardian.co.uk/uk/audio/2009/may/01/stop-and-search-black-asian (accessed 2 May 2009).

Trust (1990) S*top and Search: The Views and Experiences of Black Communities on Complaining to the Police*. London: Metropolitan Police Authority.

Van de Walle, S. (2009) 'Confidence in the criminal justice system: does experience count?', *British Journal of Criminology*, 49 (3): 384–98.

Virdee, S., Kyriakidesk, C. and Modood, T. (2006) 'Codes of cultural belonging: racialised national identities in a multi-ethnic Scottish neighbourhood', *Sociological Research Online*. 11.

Waddington, P. A. and Braddock, Q. (1991) 'Guardians or bullies? Perceptions of the police amongst adolescent black, white, and Asian boys', *Policing in Society*, 2: 31–45.

Waddington, P., Stenson, K. and Don, D. (2004) 'In proportion: race and police stop and search', *British Journal of Criminology*, 44 (6): 889–914.

Walker, C. and Rehman, J. (2011) 'Prevent responses to Jihadi extremism', in V. Ramraj, M. Hor, K. Roach and G. Williams (eds) *Global Anti-terrorism Law and Policy*, 2nd edn. Cambridge: Cambridge University Press.

Webster, C. (1997) 'The construction of "Asian" criminality', *International Journal of the Sociology of Law*, 25: 65–86.

# 8   Offenders or victims?

## An exploration of Gypsies and Travellers as a policing paradox

### Zoë James

Gypsies and Travellers in England have historically been policed as a 'problem' to settled communities. Because of the lack of space provided to accommodate them their most likely sort of contact with statutory agencies has been in the context of their eviction from land deemed unsuitable for them to stay on or develop. At the same time however, there has been some recent recognition that Gypsies and Travellers are victims of hate crime. This has meant that statutory agencies have been increasingly required to engage with Gypsies and Travellers to provide support and guide them about their victimisation. This chapter considers how Gypsies and Travellers have experienced this dual approach by statutory agencies, particularly in relation to their encounters with the police. Thereby, the chapter addresses the extent to which it is possible for policing to ensure Gypsies and Travellers are supported as victims of crime while being dealt with as illegal campers and thus offenders themselves. In order to understand better the tension between the conflicting demands on the police in their management of Gypsies and Travellers as offenders and victims, the chapter addresses the underpinning factors that determine these experiences. These factors are their accommodation status and their perceived identity, coterminous factors that inform each other and create spatial boundaries between settled communities and Gypsies and Travellers.

The chapter initially sets out the research completed in order to present the discussion herein. It then goes on to reflect on the position of Gypsies and Travellers as offenders. It does so by outlining legislation and policy that determine accommodation provision for Gypsies and Travellers, Gypsy and Traveller accommodation requirements and the consequent extent of illegal encampment. Further, it considers the policing experiences of Gypsies and Travellers as illegal campers. The chapter then goes on to consider the hate victimisation of Gypsies and Travellers, their reporting of such problems, or lack thereof, and their experiences of support and guidance from the police in this area.

### The research

In order to carry out an analysis of Gypsies' and Travellers' policing experiences this chapter draws on a range of sources. Firstly an extensive review of

literature was carried out to inform discussion here. Most research and publication in this area has been completed within a disciplinary gaze, as part of
health studies (Hawes 1997; Hajioff and Mckee 2000; Parry *et al.* 2004) or
education (OFSTED 1996, 1999; Bhopal 2011) for example. I have likewise
published work regarding Gypsies and Travellers within the context of my
own discipline, as a criminologist (James 2005, 2006, 2007, 2011). However, I
have followed here and in other more recent research (James 2014, forthcoming), a different approach more akin to colleagues in this area who have
successfully addressed disciplinary divides (Clark and Greenfields 2006;
Bhopal and Myers 2008). I have been particularly drawn more recently to
analysis of Gypsies and Travellers within human geography. The work of
Peter Kabachnik (2009, 2010, 2012) has been influential in this regard and his
consideration of mobilities, that is, the study of the movement of people,
ideas, information and objects in society and the implication thereof, informs
the discussion below.

   Following the literature review, empirical research was carried out to
pursue the problem of a dual approach to policing Gypsies and Travellers.
That research involved analysis of a comprehensive, randomly selected
sample of all the Gypsy and Traveller Accommodation Assessments (GTAAs)
completed between 2006 and 2008 under the auspices of the Housing Act
2004. That Act required every local authority in England and Wales to assess
the specific accommodation needs of Gypsies and Travellers alongside such
assessments of the settled community. Local authorities across England and
Wales commissioned researchers to carry out GTAAs under the guidance of
the then Office of the Deputy Prime Minister (ODPM) (now Department for
Communities and Local Government) and following the good practice of
initial GTAAs (Home and Greenfields 2006). These commissions led to a raft
of reports and despite the guidance provided these reports varied extensively
in their scope, depth and quality. Niner (2007) suggests that the variability of
the GTAAs resulted in them failing to fulfil their remit as comparable measures of accommodation need. Indeed, their utility in providing an informed
basis on which to provide accommodation to Gypsies and Travellers has been
questioned (Brown and Niner 2009), particularly since the abandonment of
Regional Spatial Strategies by the Coalition government in 2010, into which
the GTAAs fed to inform provision. However, the GTAAs provide a raft of
information on the lived experiences of Gypsies and Travellers that has not
been gathered previously. Despite the varied methodologies used by the commissioned researchers, the GTAAs commonly contain information on the
types of accommodation inhabited by Gypsies and Travellers and its legal
status, their previous accommodation and reasons for moving on from it,
their experiences of eviction and mobility, as well as their experiences of service provision, including policing and security. Most importantly, the large
majority of GTAAs gathered this information from Gypsies and Travellers
themselves and those that followed best practice did so by using a sensitive
approach which recognised the 'hard to reach' nature of Gypsy and Traveller

communities living on illegal encampments (Home and Greenfields 2006; Southern and James 2006).

The GTAAs therefore represent an important resource for those of us interested in understanding the experiences of Gypsies and Travellers better. Furthermore, the publically available nature of the reports, as required by the process of their local authority funding, means that they allow a window into the lives of Gypsies and Travellers without requiring further field research; this is a welcome relief for Gypsy and Traveller communities who express 'research fatigue' (Robinson 2002). The GTAAs were sampled randomly from local authority web sites, resulting in 19 GTAAs being selected for analysis. The requirement to limit analysis to a random sample was due to researcher time and resource constraints. Once selected all of the GTAAs were scrutinised for their methodological authenticity, credibility, representativeness and meaning (Macdonald 1993).

Analysis of the GTAAs was carried out for this chapter using a simple process of thematic enquiry within the context of the chapter aims. It therefore involved a trawl through each sampled GTAA for information on illegal camping, victimisation and policing. These areas were then broken down further to consider: types of illegal camping, how such camping was policed, how Gypsies and Travellers experienced policing, how Gypsies and Travellers experienced victimisation, who victimised them, whether they reported such victimisation and to whom, the reasons for not reporting victimisation, and how their victimisation was policed. Due to the incomparable nature of the statistical data contained in the GTAAs, the analysis here utilised a qualitative approach and as such does not report the statistics cited in the GTAAs.

## Gypsies and Travellers as offenders

Gypsies and Travellers have posed a problem to settled society in that they have a predisposition to mobility that is commonly referred to as their 'nomadism', which places their lifestyles in direct contrast to the bounded, sedentary lifestyles of the rest of society. Gypsies and Travellers comprise multiple communities, whose mobility is determined by a number of factors, including their economic needs, their cultural expectations and the lack of space provided to them. Overall it has been estimated that Gypsies and Travellers constitute 0.6 per cent of the national population (ODPM 2006), though such an estimate has been contested for its reliance on annual 'caravan counts' carried out by local authorities (Niner 2004). Annual caravan counts generally measure numbers of caravan dwellings that are fixed or on 'sites' in local authority areas and therefore do not take into account Gypsies and Travellers living in more hidden locations (James 2005), those on the move or those living in 'bricks and mortar' accommodation (i.e. housing) (Greenfields 2006). Additionally, caravan counts often do not record Gypsies and Travellers living on their own land nor do they record numbers of people, but rather, they record numbers of 'caravans'. The completion of GTAAs by local authorities, aimed to resolve the lack of information on Gypsy and Traveller numbers and in doing so intended to provide comprehensive information on the accommodation needs of Gypsies and Travellers. Numerous studies had shown that Gypsies and Travellers were suffering a crisis of accommodation (for example see, Niner 2003, 2004; Morris and Clements 1999, 2002; Kenrick and Clark 1999) and were consequently living illegally and arguably thus placed within a discourse of punishment, rather than provision (Bancroft 2000).

In 1968 the Caravan Sites Act had required local authorities to provide sites for Gypsies and Travellers to stop and stay in their areas, following the closure of the commons in 1960 that had traditionally functioned as Gypsies and Travellers stopping places. Local authorities failed to fulfil their requirements under the Caravan Sites Act however because councillors were unwilling to support site provision that would risk their likelihood of electoral success amidst popular prejudice against Gypsies and Travellers (Casciani 2004). Gypsies and Travellers therefore increasingly resorted to stopping places that were not formally recognised by local authorities. Tensions between Gypsies and Travellers and the settled community consequently increased in the post-1968 period, as Gypsies and Travellers found themselves relying on places to stop and stay that encroached on settled communities lifestyles (Murdoch and Johnson 2004). So, for example, Gypsies and Travellers stopped and stayed in public spaces such as parks, community fields and car parks that caused disruption and confusion to the settled population. Settled communities were subsequently unable to use those spaces and they were considered a 'mess' because local authorities refused to provide services such as rubbish collection. Gypsies and Travellers were therefore increasingly feared by settled communities who perceived them as 'dirty' (Sibley 1994) strangers (Simmel 1971) who were 'invading' their places (Kabachnik 2010). Halfacree (1996) usefully identifies this process of othering Gypsies and Travellers as grounded in their conception of spaces as 'smooth', whereas sedentarists 'striate' the spaces they live in. As such, Gypsies and Travellers disrupt settled environments by moving through boundaries that are invisible to them or at least, are inconsequential to their way of living.

The tensions between Gypsies and Travellers and settled communities were augmented by the influx of New Traveller communities in the late 1970s and early 1980s. The New Travellers, or 'New Age' Travellers as they were originally known, were borne of the music festival culture of the 1970s, inspired by traditional Gypsy lifestyles. However, research has shown that they were commonly originally 'pushed' into a travelling lifestyle through poverty or exclusion (Martin 2002) and they are now recognised as a diverse group (Webster and Millar 2001) that has been nomadic for four generations (Clark 1997). The origins of this community and their links to environmental protest movements and 'rave' festivals meant that they were associated with dissent by government. In 1985, a substantial police operation was put in place to prevent a gathering of New Travellers for a festival at Stonehenge in southern England.

That police operation led to what is colloquially known as the 'battle of the beanfield', wherein police in full riot apparel set upon a convoy of New Traveller vehicles that had been ushered by them into a bean field near the Stonehenge festival. On that day 440 New Travellers were arrested, none of whom were convicted of offences. Of those arrested, 24 New Travellers won cases against Wiltshire police for their treatment on that day (Worthington 2005).

The use of paramilitary public order policing techniques against New Travellers in 1985 set a precedent for policing Gypsy and Traveller communities (James 2006) that remains in place in contemporary society as was seen in 2011 when, again in full riot gear and this time using tasers, over a hundred police officers aided the eviction of the Dale Farm Traveller site in Essex. Until the 1980s the key tool utilised to manage Gypsy and Traveller communities had been provision of accommodation as an assimilating process. In other words, government policy had aimed to assimilate Gypsies and Travellers through the provision of housing for them in bricks and mortar accommodation. In 1994 however, the Criminal Justice and Public Order Act created provisions that placed all Gypsies and Travellers within a remit of public order control (Hester 2000; James 2004). That is not to say that government no longer aimed to assimilate Gypsies and Travellers via housing, but rather that when this was unsuccessful, they could be controlled via public order law and policing tactics that are usually associated with managing dissent. Indeed, the assimilation aims of government remain, described by McVeigh (2007: 100) as 'cultural genocide'.

The Criminal Justice and Public Order Act 1994 revoked the requirement of the Caravan Sites Act 1968 for local authorities to provide sites for Gypsies and Travellers. Further, it provided enhanced powers for police and local authorities to evict Gypsies and Travellers from land that they were not legally residing on. The 1994 Act effectively criminalised Gypsies' and Travellers' traditional lifestyles (Bancroft 2000). In the post-1968 period eviction from land had become a more regular experience for Gypsies and Travellers. However, there remained the duty for local authorities to provide sites and as such, failure to do so meant that eviction was often delayed or deferred and there was, at least, a formal recognition of the need for the provision of space for Gypsies and Travellers. In the period following the 1994 Act, evictions from land increased concomitantly with a reduction in site provision, as local authorities were no longer required to ensure site provision (Murdoch and Johnson 2004). All Gypsies and Travellers were therefore encompassed within the changes to the law that the 1994 Act brought about and conflict between Gypsy and Traveller communities themselves heightened alongside the existing tensions between Gypsies and Travellers and the settled community. In the eyes of traditional Gypsy and Traveller communities, New Travellers had been culpable in the criminalisation of their lifestyle (James 2004).

The conflict between Gypsies and Travellers that arose following the enactment of the Criminal Justice and Public Order Act 1994 augmented existing discord between traditional Gypsies and Travellers who were descended from

Romany Gypsies, Irish Travellers or Showmen. Romany Gypsies are recorded as having lived in England since the fifteenth century, Irish Travellers are recognised as having come to England and Wales since the nineteenth century and Showmen have had ancient charter for fairs since the twelfth century (Murdoch and Johnson 2004). Within a society that has been organised through sedentary boundary setting since the Enclosure Acts of the eighteenth century, the nomadic lifestyle of Gypsies and Travellers has proved problematic for state agencies to manage and control. Gypsies and Travellers have always therefore existed on the margins of society and fought for recognition and space. Despite a short period of time during and immediately after the Second World War, when sedentarists lived alongside Gypsies and Travellers relatively harmoniously (Kenrick and Clark 1999), the late twentieth century increasingly pitted Gypsies and Travellers against each other within the margins of their existence. Recent research by Foley (2010) specifically explored feuding within and between Gypsy and Traveller communities. In her thesis Foley identifies forms of 'Gypsy justice' that negate processes of justice provided by the state that will be returned to further below.

As the Criminal Justice and Public Order Act 1994 was utilised against all Gypsies and Travellers, a shift of emphasis in their traditional conflicts occurred, wherein the commonalities of those groups were increasingly recognised by them, rather than their differences. Traditional Gypsies and Travellers particularly came together in support of their mutual cause for recognition by the state as requiring appropriate accommodation and services (Morris and Clements 2002). The culmination of this coming-together of Gypsy and Traveller communities was the creation of the Gypsy and Traveller Law Reform Coalition in 1999 that made some headway in bringing Gypsies' and Travellers' welfare issues to the sight of government and eventually placed on the agenda of the last New Labour government via the Housing Act 2004. As the 1990s had drawn on and site provision increasingly diminished, so Gypsies and Travellers' had suffered worse welfare outcomes. Compelling evidence of the high mortality rates for Gypsy and Traveller infants (Parry *et al.* 2004), their poor achievement at school (OFSTED 1996, 1999) and their low life expectancy (Parry *et al.* 2004) proved hard to ignore. However, the gains made during this period, particularly through the lobbying activity of the Gypsy and Traveller Law Reform Coalition, were short lived.

As was noted above in this chapter, the completion of GTAAs that were required by the Housing Act 2004 did not lead to increased provision of Gypsy and Traveller sites in England and Wales (Brown and Niner 2009). Indeed, the Anti-Social Behaviour Act in 2003 actually increased police powers for eviction of Gypsy and Traveller sites. The Criminal Justice and Public Order Act 1994 had provided local authorities and the police with the power to evict Gypsies and Travellers who gathered with six or more vehicles. The Anti-Social Behaviour Act increased this power by allowing police eviction powers where Gypsies and Travellers gathered with three or more vehicles. The additional powers laid down by the Anti-Social Behaviour Act 2003 were justified by their power being derived only in circumstances where pitches for Gypsies and Travellers were available on sites within the local area. Thus the broad aims of the New Labour government of the time, to balance the rights and responsibilities of individuals as part of communities (Hughes 2007), were fulfilled as the right to accommodation for Gypsies and Travellers was coupled with their responsibility to remain settled and the assimilation aims of the state again became apparent.

Eviction of Gypsies and Travellers from illegal encampments did not diminish with the additional rights provided by the Anti-Social Behaviour Act 2003 however. The availability of a pitch on a local site was unlikely to move a family or group of Gypsies and Travellers into that space. As noted above, differences between communities would place certain sites beyond the reach of certain groups. So, it is unlikely that an Irish Traveller family, for example, could move on to a Romany Gypsy site and feel at all comfortable or at home. In reality, such settlement could cause conflict between those communities. Further, groups of Gypsies and Travellers moving and living together rely on their own support networks that are definitive of their culture. To break them up in order that they could settle on available pitches in scattered places would again prove problematic to those communities and culturally insensitive. Post-1994 evidence showed (Bucke and James 1998) that Gypsies and Travellers were often travelling together in larger groups than previously, meaning it would be unlikely for sufficient pitches to be available for them. Finally, the notion of placing Gypsies and Traveller on available pitches negates their cultural mobility. Families of Gypsies and Travellers commonly travel together with a purpose, to carry out work, to visit family, go to a funeral, to attend a wedding or a fair. Given these circumstances, it was unlikely that Gypsies and Travellers offered local pitches would take them and therefore, their eviction, or at least statutory agency requirements for them to move on in lieu of eviction, was inevitable.

It is extremely difficult to measure the extent to which Gypsies and Travellers are moved on or evicted under the police or local authority powers of the Criminal Justice and Public Order Act 1994. This is due to there being no formal requirement to record the use of such powers, whether formal eviction takes place or not (Bucke and James 1998), although it should be noted that more recent guidance from ACPO (2011) encourages recording. The police can evict unauthorised Gypsy and Traveller sites at short notice; however in most situations, Gypsies and Travellers are provided with a warning or direction to move on from the police, local authority or other agency involved prior to their formal eviction. Indeed, local authorities are required to consider the welfare needs of Gypsies and Travellers prior to eviction and therefore unauthorised sites are commonly visited by numerous agencies on multiple occasions in order that formal eviction can occur (James and Richardson 2006).

Surveillance of Gypsy and Traveller sites (both authorised and unauthorised) by multiple agencies and information gathering on site occupants by police has become commonplace as policing agencies have increasingly been required to measure risk and share intelligence within and between agencies (James 2004; James and Richardson, 2006). Gypsies' and Travellers' details are recorded by the police on site visits by neighbourhood officers, they are more often stopped and searched by police than their (white) sedentary neighbours (Bowers, undated, Greenfields 2006), car and helicopter video surveillance of sites is gathered (James 2004; Bowers n.d.) and welfare agencies record their family circumstances via education and health assessment visits on site (Cemlyn *et al.* 2009). This process of information gathering informs police and local authority decisions to evict Gypsies and Travellers from unauthorised sites, whether they are short term, long term, tolerated (under previous 2004 ODPM guidance) or unauthorised development sites. Sites considered most problematic to policing agencies are often those that are short term encampments that arise in spaces that are highly visible to the settled population, such as parks and roadside lay-bys. Police action to move on, or evict such sites is likely to be swift in order to ease community tensions. Long term sites that are illegal due to unauthorised development are similarly risky to policing agencies however, as has been evidenced by the case of Dale Farm in Essex. As mentioned above, the policing of this site culminated in an extensive multi-agency operation which incorporated use of paramilitary public order policing tactics to enact eviction. The lack of available sites for Gypsies and Travellers and their cultural need to live amongst their own community is demonstrated by the numbers of evicted Gypsies and Travellers from the Dale Farm site continuing to live in the environs of the authorised site that remains there (Tomlinson 2012).

Statutory agencies are loath to engage in full eviction processes in most cases due to the high cost such evictions involve (Morris and Clements 1999). Previous research (James and Richardson 2006) has shown that the police are instead prepared to 'threaten' use of their powers of eviction against Gypsies and Travellers in order to get them to move from land without need for full eviction. Additionally, and more dramatically, other threats by a range of agencies have been made to Gypsies and Travellers in order to provoke their movement prior to formal eviction. Such threats have included threats to remove children, to destroy animals and seize vehicles (Greenfields 2006; James 2004). Gypsies and Travellers therefore commonly move on from illegal encampments prior to full eviction occurring, particularly in light of threats made to their homes and families (James 2006). Additionally, Gypsies' and Travellers' prior experience of eviction as a traumatic event means that they avoid such action as much as possible.

Analysis of the GTAAs shows that 'voluntary' movement from an area prior to formal eviction was reported in a large majority of areas surveyed. However the GTAAs lack clarity on whether a formal eviction of Gypsies and Travellers had taken place, or simply an '*enforcement action*' (GTAA 7) had occurred, which may have been the delivery by police or local authority of a warning or direction to leave land prior to using their powers of eviction.

It is clear from the GTAAs that the majority of Gypsies and Travellers living on unauthorised sites had experienced some formal action by statutory agencies, including formal eviction, within the last year. Reference to enforced movement by Gypsies and Travellers themselves in the GTAAs includes use of terms such as, *'horrific'* (GTAA 6), *'made to feel like criminals'* (GTAA 1), and *'authorities treat you terrible'* (GTAA 9). The impact of forced movement on Gypsies and Travellers is evidenced in the GTAAs by their suspicion of formal agencies and general fear of eviction. For example, the following quote exemplifies the concerns of Gypsies and Travellers, *'It looks like we're going to get moved on really soon, We're really anxious about threat of eviction and worried about when it'll happen and where we will be able to go next'* (GTAA 13). Within Gypsies' and Travellers' cultural psyche, the notion of enforced movement by eviction looms large and tales of previous large scale evictions and use of paramilitary policing tactics in eviction such as described above at the 'battle of the beanfield' in 1985 and at Dale Farm in 2011 augment the fears of the wider communities of Gypsies and Travellers (James 2014, forthcoming).

The report for the Commission for Racial Equality (2006: 4) suggests that Gypsies and Travellers experience 'enforced nomadism through constant eviction' and previously researchers have referred to the process of enforced movement as a 'merry-go-round' (Morris and Clements 1999) for Gypsies and Travellers. As Shubin and Swanson (2010) note, the mobile or nomadic habit of life for Gypsies and Travellers is not necessarily manifested by constant movement, but rather is an emotional mobility. Kabachnik (2012) has suggested that in fact, 'place' is as important to Gypsies and Travellers as 'mobility'. As one GTAA states, *'Our study found an urgent need to balance the cultural needs of Gypsy and Traveller families to maintain a mobile life style, with their need to develop some measure of security in terms of their accommodation'* (GTAA 12). In his analysis, Kabachnik (2012) argues that the media has fed sedentarists' lack of understanding of Gypsies' and Travellers' use of place by presenting them as 'invaders'. As such, policing of Gypsies and Travellers via enforced movement fulfils the desires of an ill-informed settled society whose fears are amplified by media stories (Cohen 1972) which do not recognise that Gypsies and Travellers need places to stop and stay, from which they can be mobile.

Patterns of enforced movement of Gypsies and Travellers in the GTAAs vary widely across and between areas surveyed. On initial reading of the GTAAs it could be implied that different areas enforce movement more or less, but this finding may simply be an artefact of the process of information gathering and reporting practice by agencies; as noted above there is a lack of comparability between GTAAs, despite the guidance provided by the ODPM and there is no requirement for agencies to report actions carried out under the Criminal Justice and Public Order Act 1994. The bounded nature of policing practice according to police force areas and within them basic command units, can also impact on levels of enforcement. Despite the requirement of the National Intelligence Model for police areas to effectively communicate intelligence in order to facilitate 'joined up' proactive policing, in the case of Gypsies and Travellers the police are unwilling to share knowledge beyond their specific area boundaries. Previous research (James 2004) has shown that police areas have been unwilling to pass intelligence on Gypsy' and Traveller' movements to neighbouring police areas. This was due to resultant pre-emptive strategies having been put in place to block Gypsies and Travellers entry into the neighbouring area due to their potential costs. Police areas therefore weigh the costs of retaining Gypsies and Travellers in their area against the cost of sharing intelligence with their neighbouring police area and consider the use of intelligence as disproportionate (Maguire 2000) to the potential costs of heightened community tensions, welfare assessments, enforced movement and eviction that Gypsies and Travellers bring.

Overall then, I have outlined here how Gypsies and Travellers are managed by statutory agencies as offenders due to their accommodation status. While there are some authorised Gypsy and Traveller sites across England and Wales, provision of accommodation is largely lacking and even for those Gypsies and Travellers who live on authorised sites, their cultural mobility means that they are likely to experience some sort of enforcement while on the move. Surveillance of Gypsy and Traveller sites is common, both of sites that are authorised and those that are unauthorised; the governmental gaze has increasingly focused on Gypsy and Traveller communities in the late twentieth century and into the twenty-first century (Richardson 2006). The association of all Gypsies and Travellers with dissent, that the Criminal Justice and Public Order Act 1994 formalised, reinforced the notion of Gypsies and Travellers as a dangerous other that the police must control in order to retain the status quo of sedentarism (James 2006). As such Gypsies and Travellers are treated by statutory agencies as offenders when they stop and stay anywhere, as they must in the process of their mobility.

The management of Gypsies and Travellers as offenders outlined here shows that they are constantly subject to enforced movement, either as a consequence of threats of enforcement action or by actual eviction. If Gypsies and Travellers choose to remain on an illegal encampment, the Criminal Justice and Public Order Act 1994 allows for their vehicles (i.e. their homes) to be seized as part of the eviction process. The criminalisation of Gypsies' and Travellers' mobility therefore feeds into the long-established assimilationist aims of the state. This 'over-policing' of Gypsies and Travellers as offenders is reminiscent of other minority groups' experiences (for example, Hall *et al.* 1978; Macpherson 1999; Webster 2004). Despite their 'whiteness' Gypsies and Travellers are demonised as a cultural other, apart from when the romantic idyll of the Romany Gypsy is evoked (Holloway 2005). Interestingly, Gypsies and Travellers have largely not been recognised within academic studies of minority communities until more recently, despite their continued existence in England since at least the fifteenth century. This might be explained by the intersection of their mobility and their whiteness. When mobile Mulcahy (2012) has suggested that Gypsies' and Travellers' legitimacy is negated by their existence outside the moral community that sedentarism represents and thus they live beyond the acceptable parameters of all of settled society, even those that are marginalised. When assimilated into bricks and mortar accommodation however, Gypsies and Travellers have been invisible due to their whiteness; there has been a lack of recognition until the late twentieth century of their racial identity and Gypsies and Travellers have been reluctant to identify themselves as racially distinct for fear of victimisation. It is now appropriate therefore to consider Gypsies' and Travellers' experiences of victimisation, police management of their victimisation and the associated issues of identity that this raises.

## Gypsies and Travellers as victims

Gypsies' and Travellers' experiences of victimisation are relatively unknown in quantitative terms. There have been no academic studies of Gypsies' and Travellers' victimisation rates and the British Crime Survey explores the victimisation of 'households', without visiting Gypsies and Travellers on sites. Further, the British Crime Survey does not classify Gypsies and Travellers as a distinct category for analysis and therefore would not be able to distinguish between Gypsies and Travellers and other white communities living in bricks and mortar accommodation. Indeed, it was only in 2011 that the population of Gypsies and Travellers was measured at all when the Census created a category for them of Gypsy/Roma/Traveller. As noted above, estimates of the Gypsy and Traveller population are borne of the annual caravan count, which is problematic in itself. Hence the degree of victimisation of Gypsies and Travellers is not a 'dark figure' of crime (Hough and Mayhew 1983), but rather, an invisible figure.

We do, however, know that Gypsies and Travellers are commonly victims of crime, anti-social behaviour and harassment, due to the wealth of qualitative evidence provided by studies of Gypsies' and Travellers' lives (for example, Okely 1983; Fraser 1992; Bancroft 2005; Bhopal and Myers 2008). Such studies have largely discussed victimisation of Gypsies and Travellers as an artefact of their lifestyle and have therefore rarely explored it as a specific issue. Greenfields (2006) does consider the experiences of Gypsies and Travellers with legal matters specifically in her work, but this discussion is couched within a broader conceptualisation of Gypsies and Travellers as offenders as described above and I, likewise, have addressed their victimisation within broader studies of policing (James 2007, 2014, forthcoming). Studies thus far, have therefore failed to distinguish how Gypsies and Travellers have specifically experienced victimisation that is targeted at them due to their minority status.

Focused studies of minority group victimisation have burgeoned in the last ten years as research on 'hate crime' has developed in England and Wales, following the lead of research and study in the United States (Hall 2005). Two particular cases of Gypsy and Traveller victimisation have influenced the recognition of Gypsies and Travellers as a specific group who suffer such hate crimes. In 2003 the murder of a 15-year-old Irish Traveller boy, Johnny Delaney, drew attention to the severe consequences of racism against Gypsies and Travellers. As Johnny was brutally kicked and beaten to death, the teenagers who carried out the assault made racist comments that included referring to him as 'only a ... Gypsy' (Greenfields 2006). The police treated this case as a racist incident, but the conviction did not enhance sentence on the basis of the racism, as is allowed for hate crimes. At the time, the Chair of the Commission for Racial Equality questioned the lack of recognition of race as a motivating factor for the crime, though no further action regarding the case, nor publicity followed. Given the climate of concern regarding race issues following the Macpherson Inquiry (1999) into the racist murder of Stephen Lawrence at the time, it seems incongruous that further attention was not given to this case. Greenfields (2006) argues that this lack of action exemplifies the lack of status given to Gypsies and Travellers by the state, media and within race debates.

In 2003 a further incident of hate crime against Gypsies and Travellers drew some attention, at least amongst hate crime scholars, to their victimisation. A small village in Sussex held their annual bonfire night celebrations, at which they burnt an effigy of a Gypsy caravan. The effigy was a large cardboard construction of a caravan that contained images of children inside and a licence plate of 'P1 KEY'. The burning of this effigy led to a complaint by a resident of the village, who was then herself subject to threats and intimidation. Finally, after a lengthy process, in which the police were accused of dragging their feet and the Commission for Racial Equality intervened to provoke action, the police did charge 12 villagers with the offence of incitement to racial hatred. The crown prosecution service did not eventually pursue the charges in court however, citing a lack of evidence as their rationale for withdrawal of the charges. Again, Greenfields (2006) questions the likelihood of such a case against any other minority community being dealt with similarly.

The cases cited above have been recognised to some degree as 'racist' hate crimes. As hate crime research and policy has developed, so it has aimed to identify different types of hate crime that can be clearly defined. Such definition then allows cases to be dealt with appropriately by the police, crown prosecution service and courts, with the majority of sanctions provided to hate crime offenders via enhanced sentencing. To date hate crimes are defined in policy as crimes or incidents that are motivated by either 'hate or prejudice' (ACPO 2005) or 'hostility or prejudice' (Home Office 2009) as perceived by the victim or any other person. Despite the breadth of this definition of hate crime, both the ACPO (2005) and Home Office (2009) guidance specifies minority groups who may be victimised in this way and should be protected. Therefore, the guidance refers to race, sexual orientation, religion, disability and transgender status as protected identities. Academic debate continues to ensue as to the appropriateness of the specific groups protected by hate crime policy (for example, Garland and Chakraborti 2006; Dixon and Gadd 2006), particularly given that they differ from the nine protected characteristics outlined by the Equality Act 2010.

The police record hate crimes, as do the crown prosecution service, and statistics are published annually on their monitored prevalence (Home Office 2012). These statistics show that by far the greatest number of hate crimes recorded are those committed on the basis of race hate. This is likely to be due to the original premise of the development of hate policy and legislation having grown out of the Macpherson Inquiry (1999). Further, police forces are more used to addressing issues of race, rather than other areas of diversity in their communities. The police commonly struggle to embed an understanding of diversity into their practice (Rowe 2004; James 2007), which may explain why they have not responded to hate crime comprehensively in the past (Cronin *et al.* 2007; Hall 2010). In relation to hate crimes committed against Gypsies and Travellers, policy has recognised their victimisation, with the Home Office (2009) guidance specifically referring to Gypsies and Travellers as victims in need of protection.

The inclusion of Gypsies and Travellers within hate crime policy represents a positive outcome of the GTAA process, given that the core evidence represented of hate victimisation against Gypsies and Travellers in the Home Office (2009) guidance was based on two GTAAs (Southern and James 2006; Greenfields *et al.* 2007). However, the inclusion of Gypsies and Travellers within the guidance is based on the notion of hate crime being a racist event which raises two particular issues. Firstly, not all Gypsies and Travellers are recognised legally as racial groups. Romany Gypsies were recognised as an ethnic group under the Race Relations Act 1976 following case law in 1989, but it was not until 2000 that Irish Travellers gained the same recognition. New Travellers and Showmen are not recognised by race relations legislation. Therefore, only certain groups of Gypsies and Travellers have recourse to the law as protected groups under the hate crime definitions, despite their having experienced hate crimes similarly to other groups (James 2007; Clark 2006). Secondly, the definition of Gypsies and Travellers in law relating to accommodation, including the Caravan Sites Act 1968 and the Criminal Justice and Public Order Act 1994, does not refer to racial groups, but defines Gypsies and Travellers according to their 'nomadic habit of life' (Barton 2004).

The broad definition of Gypsies and Travellers within legislation relating to accommodation allows enforced movement of any Gypsies and Travellers from areas as identified in this chapter above. However, when Gypsies and Travellers are persecuted in some way for their lifestyle, mode of living or ethnic origins, only Romany Gypsies and Irish Travellers are protected under the law. This inconsistency in the law has the capacity to confuse Gypsies and Travellers themselves, as well as those agencies that are tasked with managing them. Given that Gypsies and Travellers are largely treated as problematic due to their mobility, their victimisation as vulnerable communities is less likely to be recognised as only some of those communities are protected in law. This is likely to be particularly problematic for the police who struggle to engage with issues of diversity in managing hate crime (Hall 2010), especially when it is being dealt with by officers who are not specialists in the area (James and Simmonds 2012). The identity of Gypsies and Travellers therefore becomes central to their experience of the criminal justice system, with Romany Gypsies and Irish Travellers being placed higher on a hierarchy of authenticity than other groups. This situation feeds in to the commonly held image of Romany Gypsies as ethnically 'pure', which is not a true representation of their community (Hancock 1976) or other Gypsy and Traveller groups. As Holloway (2005) notes in her research on relations between a settled community and an annual influx of Gypsies and Travellers to their area for a horse fair, the demonisation of Gypsies and Travellers occurs when they do not fulfil the romantic notion of the Romany myth.

Analysis of the GTAAs for this chapter provides information on Gypsies' and Travellers' hate victimisation beyond that which has been gathered previously. By drawing together evidence from the sample of GTAAs it is possible to see that hate crime is a problem experienced by Gypsies' and Travellers' across England. Although the findings here are not wholly representative or quantifiable due to the differences in recording practices in the GTAAs as discussed above, it is possible to provide a little light on to the problem of hate crime committed against Gypsies and Travellers. Following the good practice of the Cambridgeshire GTAA, as recommended by the ODPM, many GTAAs asked Gypsies and Travellers about their experiences of crime, anti-social behaviour and harassment, including whether they had reported such problems to authorities and how they had been dealt with.

All GTAAs sampled, bar one, contained some information on Gypsies and Travellers having been victimised as a consequence of their identity. That victimisation ranged from minor incidents of name calling through to serious physical assaults. Examples of the kinds of activities carried out against Gypsies and Travellers were: stone throwing; name calling including, '*gypo*', '*pikey*' and '*dirty Gypsy*'; shouting of abuse; broken windows; vandalism of vehicles; and physical assault. One GTAA referred to the '*endemic level of hostility towards Gypsies and Travellers*' (GTAA 4) shown from settled communities. Examples of the victimisation here are best shown in the words of Gypsies and Travellers themselves: '*one night a group of local lads came around and were rocking my trailer and when I came out one of them hit me with a stick so I had to move off at two in the morning to get away*' (GTAA 14) and '*I got my windows put out, they threw petrol bombs at us, we had to leave*' (GTAA 9).

It is clear from the examples cited above, that Gypsies and Travellers experience a range of hate crimes similar to other minority communities (Chakraborti and Garland 2009). In particular, bullying and harassment is reported in the GTAAs that might be referred to as hate 'incidents', rather than crimes. Policy on hate crime acknowledges the relevance of hate victimisation commonly occurring via repeated incidents of hate, rather than more serious crimes necessarily. The cumulative impact of such harassment and bullying impacts on whole communities, as well as on the individuals involved. However, policing does not necessarily recognise this process and therefore, the police are often loath to deal with minor incidents, which may prevent them from addressing the problem of hate crime effectively and lead to a lack of reporting (Bowling 1999). Indeed, analysis of the GTAAs showed that Gypsies and Travellers rarely reported problems to the police, despite their severity in some cases. Low reporting of crime problems is common in wider society, but reporting of hate crime is particularly low (Christman and Wong 2010). In the case of Gypsies and Travellers, it is possible that low reporting levels can be explained by their mobility. As cited in the examples above, hate victimisation may lead Gypsies and Travellers to simply move on, rather than attempt to address the problem. Indeed, higher levels of victimisation were found in the GTAAs amongst those Gypsies and Travellers who lived on unauthorised encampments, who are potentially more mobile than those living on authorised sites. Additionally, the GTAAs identify that one of the core reasons for Gypsies and Travellers having left their last site, whether authorised or unauthorised, was due to harassment they had experienced there.

Other reasons for low levels of reporting of hate crime to the police or other agencies were cited in the GTAAs as due to a lack of trust in those services. The policing experiences of Gypsies and Travellers, particularly in relation to eviction as discussed above, led them to lack confidence in the police more broadly. Comments made about the police in GTAAs included, '*They don't want to listen*' (GTAA 17), '*I don't have any faith in the police, they didn't do anything when we had problems here*' (GTAA 16), '*Don't take our emergency calls seriously; Gypsy people don't trust the police*' (GTAA15). As can be seen from these quotes, Gypsies and Travellers associate the police with a lack of action, again similar to other minorities who have complained that they are under-policed as victims (Bowling 1999). However, it should be noted that Gypsies and Travellers are used to resolving conflict within their own communities.

Low levels of reporting hate victimisation may also be associated with Gypsies' and Travellers' fear of exposure in some way. Having lived on the margins of sedentary society for so long, Gypsies and Travellers are used to hiding their identity in order to protect themselves. In the GTAAs Gypsies and Travellers commonly refer to their unwillingness to identify themselves to agencies for fear of poor treatment, as the following quote describes, '*When I have told people how I live, their whole manner will change from being polite and friendly, into being impolite, blunt and cold, while making me feel like dirt, as if I don't have any right to be taking up their time with my questions, so I find it very difficult to go to any organisations*' (GTAA 13). Therefore Gypsies' and Travellers' lack of trust of the police goes beyond them to other agencies and organisations. Previous research has similarly found a reluctance from Gypsies and Travellers to engage with advice services for example, such as the Citizens Advice Bureaux (James and Simmonds 2010). It is unlikely then, that Gypsies and Travellers will utilise third party reporting centres that have been introduced to increase hate crime reporting. As Christman and Wong (2010) suggest, it would seem more pertinent to tackle hate crime reporting by Gypsies and Travellers in a way that would address their cultural mistrust of agencies and services and be sympathetic to their cultural expectations.

Interestingly, Gypsies' and Travellers' mistrust of services may be explained by other evidence gained from the GTAAs. In addition to the victimisation described above, Gypsies and Travellers commonly reported to GTAAs that they suffered exclusion from a range of environments and services. Gypsies and Travellers said that they had been refused access to shops, public houses, nightclubs and activity centres. They had been refused access to doctors' surgeries, midwife services and site waiting lists. Further, they had been refused access to their benefit entitlements, insurance services and their right to be on the electoral roll. The exclusion of Gypsies and Travellers from these environments and services that are both publically and privately owned, may explain their lack of trust in agencies that aim to support them. Again, the marginalised environment in which Gypsies and Travellers live, due to their nomadic or mobile lifestyle sets them apart from sedentary society creating a boundary that they are as fearful to breach as the sedentarists who created it.

As mentioned briefly above, a significant proportion of victimisation of Gypsies and Travellers as noted in the GTAAs occurred between and within different Gypsy and Traveller communities, as opposed to them being targeted by the settled community. Such incidents were rarely reported to the police, similar to those hate crimes discussed above. The reasons for these problems not being reported to the police may be twofold. First, the trust that Gypsies and Travellers have in authorities is limited, as again noted above. In relation to conflict between Gypsy and Traveller communities, the perception of the police shifted slightly however, so that rather than perceiving the police as generally uninterested and uncaring, Gypsies and Travellers perceived them as allowing vigilantism, as identified in the following quote, '*The police come on the sites and see a bit of trouble and just drive off. They think, "they're only Gypsies, let them kill themselves"'* (GTAA 5). Second, Gypsies and Travellers in the GTAAs occasionally stated their desire to be '*left alone*' (GTAA 19). This may be due to their cultural expectation to resolve their own problems and conflicts within and between Gypsy and Traveller communities as identified above, within their marginal existence. As has been discussed by Foley (2010), feuding between Gypsies and Travellers is often resolved through a process of 'Gypsy justice', which provides those communities with a sense of justice having been served. Given that the spatial boundary between Gypsies and Travellers holds firm when they are victimised, as the police and other agencies do not act to support them, their sense of justice is only served through vigilantism. However, this is problematic for Gypsies and Travellers who do not want to conform to traditional notions of Gypsy justice and more broadly to those who are victimised by settled society that is beyond the reach of Gypsy justice. The hate victimisation of Gypsies and Travellers is not resolved or provided justice by either the state system or by cultural resolution processes (Foley 2010).

# Conclusion

This chapter has presented the findings of research and analysis carried out to explore the policing experiences of Gypsies and Travellers as offenders and victims. In doing so it has identified the ways in which Gypsies and Travellers have historically been perceived as offenders through the provision of legislation that criminalises their cultural lifestyle which is nomadic or mobile. The chapter has gone on to consider the degree to which Gypsies and Travellers are victimised as a consequence of their identity and the lack of support they have attained as victims of hate crime.

The chapter has shown that Gypsies' and Travellers' experiences of policing are focused around their enforced movement and the fear of formal eviction from sites. The lack of accommodation provided to Gypsies and Travellers throughout England and the lack of understanding of Gypsy and Traveller identities means that they commonly live as illegal campers on the margins of society. As such, they are vilified by settled society as deviant others and subjected to hate crimes that reinforce their difference. The police perceive Gypsies and Travellers primarily as offenders and manage them accordingly. Working with other agencies they carry out surveillance of Gypsies and Travellers and move them on and out of their police area as swiftly as possible. Confusing definitions of Gypsies and Travellers as both recognised ethnic groups and nomads have created a hierarchy of authenticity that feeds in to mythical notions of the legitimate Gypsy or Traveller. The failure of Gypsies or Travellers to conform to this idyllic notion reinforces police perceptions of them as offenders, or at least as worthy of suspicion.

Gypsies and Travellers do not report their experiences of hate crime to the police or other agencies, due to their negative experiences of policing via enforced movement, surveillance and non-response to previous victimisation. The police therefore fail to address the needs of Gypsies and Travellers as victims of hate crime due to their conflicting perception of them as offenders. As they are not supported in their experiences of hate crime, Gypsies and Travellers retreat further to the margins of society where they live illegally and become more likely to experience enforcement from policing agencies. A vicious cycle of enforcement and victimisation is augmented by policing practice that cannot ratify the paradox presented by Gypsies and Travellers who are concomitantly offenders and victims due to the two underpinning factors of their accommodation and identity that create spatial boundaries between them and sedentary society.

# References

Association of Chief Police Officers (ACPO) (2000) *Guide to Identifying and Combating Hate Crime.* London: ACPO.
——(2005) *The ACPO Hate Crime Manual – 2010.* London: Home Office Police Standards.

——(2011) *Guidance on Unauthorised Encampments*. London: ACPO.

Bancroft, A. (2000) '"No Interest in Land": Legal and Spatial Enclosure of Gypsy-Travellers in Britain', *Space and Polity*, 4 (1): 41–56.

——(2005) *Roma and Gypsy-Travellers in Europe*. Aldershot: Ashgate.

Barton, S. (2004) 'Race Discrimination', in C. Johnson and M. Willers (eds) *Gypsy and Traveller Law*. London: Legal Action Group.

Bhopal, K. (2011) '"What about us?" Gypsies, Travellers and "White Racism" in Secondary Schools in England', *International Studies in Sociology of Education*, 21 (4): 315–29.

Bhopal, K. and Myers, M. (2008) *Insiders, outsiders and others: Gypsies and Identity*. Hatfield: University of Hertfordshire Press.

Bowers, J. (n.d) *Prejudice and Pride: The Experiences of Young Travellers in Cambridgeshire*. Cambridgeshire: Ormiston Children and Families Trust.

Bowling, B. (1999) *Violent Racism: Victimisation, Policing and Social Context*. Oxford: Oxford University Press.

Brown, P. and Niner, P. (2009) *Assessing local housing authorities' progress in meeting the accommodation needs of Gypsy and Traveller communities in England*. London: EHRC.

Bucke, T. and James, Z. (1998) T*respass and Protest: Policing Under the Criminal Justice and Public Order Act 1994*. London: Home Office.

Casciani, D. (2004) 'Prejudice Defeated Gypsy Reform', BBC News. Online. Available at http://news.bbc.co.uk/1/hi/uk/3704167.stm (accessed 21 October 2004).

Cemlyn, S., Greenfields, M., Burnett, S., Matthews, Z. and Whitwell, C. (2009) *Inequalities Experienced by Gypsy and Traveller Communities: A Review*. London: EHRC.

Chakraborti, N. and Garland, J. (2009) *Hate Crime: Impact, Causes and Responses*. London: Sage.

Christman, K. and Wong, K. (2010) 'Hate Crime Victims and Hate Crime Reporting: Some Impertinent Questions', in Chakraborti, N. (ed.) *Hate Crime: Concepts, policy and future directions*. Collumpton: Willan.

Clark, C. (1997) '"New Age" Travellers: Identity, Sedentarism and Social Security', in Acton, T. (ed.) *Gypsy Politics and Traveller Identity*. Hatfield: University of Hertfordshire Press.

——(2006) 'Who are the Gypsies and Travellers of Britain?', in: Clark, C. and Greenfields, M. (eds) *Here to Stay: The Gypsies and Travellers of Britain*. Hatfield: University of Hertfordshire Press.

Clark, C. and Greenfields, M. (eds) (2006) *Here to Stay: The Gypsies and Travellers of Britain*. Hatfield: University of Hertfordshire Press.

Cohen, S. (1972) *Folk Devils and Moral Panics: The Creation of the Mods and Rockers*. London: MacGibbon and Kee.

Commission for Racial Equality. (2006) *Common Ground: Equality, Good Race Relations and Sites for Gypsies and Irish Travellers*. London: CRE.

Cronin, S. W., McDevitt, J., Farrell, A. and Nolan III, J. J. (2007) 'Bias-Crime Reporting: Organizational Responses to Ambiguity, Uncertainty, and Infrequency in Eight Police Departments', *American Behavioral Scientist*, 51 (2): 213–31.

Dixon, B. and Gadd, D. (2006) 'Getting the Message? 'New' Labour and the Criminalization of 'Hate'', *Criminology and Criminal Justice*, 6 (3): 309–28.

Foley, A. (2010) 'Trailers and Tribulations: Crime, Deviance and Justice in the Gypsy and Traveller Community', unpublished thesis, Cardiff University.

Fraser, A. (1992) *The Gypsies*. Oxford: Blackwell.

Garland, J. and Chakraborti, N. (2006) 'Recognising and Responding to Victims of Rural Racism', *International Review of Victimology,* 13 (1): 49–69.

Greenfields, M. (2006) 'Gypsies, Travellers and Legal Matters', in Clark, C. and Greenfields, M. (eds) (2006) *Here to Stay: the Gypsies and Travellers of Britain.* Hatfield: University of Hertfordshire Press.

Greenfields, M., Home, R., Cemlyn, S., Bloxsom, J. and Lishman, R. (2007) *West of England; Gypsy Traveller Accommodation (and Other Needs) Assessment 2006–2016.* Buckinghamshire: Chilterns University College.

Hajioff, S. and McKee, M. (2000) 'The Health of the Roma People: A Review of the Published Literature', *Journal of Epidemiology and Community Health,* 54: 864–69.

Halfacree,K. (1996) 'Out of Place in the Country: Travellers and the "Rural Idyll"', *Antipode,* 28 (1): 42–72.

Hall, N. (2005) *Hate Crime.* Collumpton: Willan.

——(2010) 'Law Enforcement and Hate Crime: Theoretical Perspectives on the Complexities of Policing "Hatred"', in Chakraborti, N. (ed.) *Hate Crime: Concepts, policy and future directions.* Collumpton: Willan.

Hall, S., Critcher, C., Jefferson, T., Clarke, J. and Roberts, B. (1978) *Policing the Crisis: Mugging, the State and Law and Order.* London: Macmillan.

Hancock, I. (1976) 'Romance vs. Reality: Popular Notions of the Gypsy', *Roma,* 2: 7–23.

Hawes, D. (1997) *Gypsies, Travellers and the Health Service: A Study on Equality.* Bristol: The Policy Press.

Hester, R. (2000) 'Social Control of New Age Travellers', unpublished thesis, University of Birmingham.

Holloway, S. L. (2005) 'Articulating Otherness? White Rural Residents Talk about Gypsy-Travellers', *Transactions of the Institute of British Geographers,* 30 (3): 351–67.

Home Office. (2009) *Hate Crime – The Cross-Government Action Plan.* London: Home Office.

——(2012) *Hate crimes, England and Wales 2011/12.* London: Home Office. Available at www.homeoffice.gov.uk/counter-terrorism/uk-counter-terrorism-strat/ (accessed: 20 August 2012).

Home, R. and Greenfields, M. (2006) *Cambridge Sub-Region Traveller Needs Assessment.* Cambridge: Anglia Ruskin University.

Hough, M. and Mayhew, P. (1983) *The British Crime Survey: First Report,* Home Office Research Study 76. London: HMSO.

Hughes, G. (2007) *The Politics of Crime and Community.* Basingstoke: Palgrave Macmillan.

James, Z. and Simmonds, L. (2010) 'The Advice Needs of Gypsies and Travellers in Plymouth: Final Report', *Crimes and Misdemeanours: Deviance and the Law in Historical Perspective,* 4 (1): 53–56.

James, Z. (2004) 'New Travellers, New Policing? Exploring the Policing of New Traveller communities under the Criminal Justice and Public Order Act 1994', unpublished thesis, University of Surrey.

——(2005) 'Eliminating Communities? Exploring the Implications of Policing Methods Used to Manage New Travellers', *International Journal of the Sociology of Law,* 33 (3): 159–68.

——(2006) 'Policing Space: Managing New Travellers in England', *British Journal of Criminology,* 46 (3): 470–85.

——(2007) 'Policing Marginal Spaces: Controlling Gypsies and Travellers', *Criminology and Criminal Justice: An International Journal,* 7 (4): 367–89.

——(2011) 'Gypsies and Travellers in the Countryside: Managing a Risky Population', in Yarwood, R. and Mawby, R. I. (eds) *Constable Countryside? Policing, Governance and Rurality*. Aldershot: Ashgate.

——(2014, forthcoming) *Policing Gypsies and Travellers: Managing Identity and Controlling Nomadism*. Bristol: The Policy Press.

James, Z. and Richardson, J. (2006) 'Controlling Accommodation: Policing Gypsies and Travellers', in Dearling, A, Newburn, T. and Somerville, P. (eds) *Housing and Crime*, Chartered Institute of Housing.

James, Z. and Simmonds, L. (2010) 'The Advice Needs of Gypsies and Travellers in Plymouth: Final Report', *Crimes and Misdemeanours: Deviance and the Law in Historical Perspective*, 4 (1): 53–56

——(2012) *Exploring Prejudice: Mapping Hate Crime in the South West*. Plymouth: Plymouth University.

Kabachnik, P. (2009) 'To Choose, Fix or Ignore Culture? The Cultural Politics of Gypsy and Traveller Mobility in England', *Social and Cultural Geography*, 10 (4): 461–79.

——(2010) 'Place Invaders: Constructing the nomadic threat in England', *The Geographical Review*, 100 (1): 90–108.

——(2012) 'Nomads and Mobile Places: Disentangling Place, Space and Mobility', *Identities: Global Studies in Culture and Power*, DOI: 10.1080/1070289X.2012.672855. Online access 10/05/12.

Kenrick, D. and Clark, C. (1999) *Moving On: The Gypsies and Travellers of Britain*. Hatfield: University of Hertfordshire Press.

Macdonald, K. (1993) 'Using Documents', in Gilbert, N. (ed.) *Researching Social Life*. London: Sage.

Macpherson, W. (1999) *The Stephen Lawrence Inquiry*. London: HMSO.

Maguire, M. (2000) 'Policing by Risks and Targets: Some Dimensions and Implications of Intelligence-Led Crime Control', *Policing and Society*, 9 (4): 315–36.

Martin, G. (2002) 'New Age Travellers: Uproarious or Uprooted?', *Sociology*, 36 (3): 723–35.

McVeigh, R. (2007) 'The "Final Solution": Reformism, Ethnicity Denial and the Politics of Anti-Travellerism in Ireland', *Social Policy and Society*, 7 (1): 91–102.

Morris, R. and Clements, L. (1999) *Gaining Ground: Law Reform for Gypsies and Travellers*. Hatfield: University of Hertfordshire Press.

——(2002) *At What Cost? The Economics of Gypsy and Traveller Encampments*. Bristol: The Policy Press.

Mulcahy, A. (2012) 'Alright in their Own Place: Policing and the Spatial Regulation of Irish Travellers', *Criminology and Criminal Justice*, 12 (3): 307–27

Murdoch, A. and Johnson, C. (2004) 'Introduction', in Johnson, C. and Willers, M. (eds) *Gypsy and Traveller Law*. London: Legal Action Group.

Niner, P. (2003) *Local Authority Gypsy/Traveller Sites in England*. London: Office of the Deputy Prime Minister.

——(2007) *Preparing Regional Spatial Strategy Reviews on Gypsy and Travellers by Regional Planning Bodies*. London: DCLG.

——(2004) *Counting Gypsies and Travellers: A Review of the Gypsy Caravan Count System*. London: Office of the Deputy Prime Minister.

ODPM (2006) *Gypsy and Traveller Accommodation Assessments: Draft Practice Guidance*. ODPM: Gypsy and Traveller Unit.

OFSTED (1996) *The Education of Travelling Children: A Survey of Educational Provision for Travelling Children*. London: OFSTED Publications Centre.

——(1999) *Raising the Attainment of Minority Ethnic Pupils.* London: OFSTED Publications Centre.

Okely, J. (1983) *The Traveller-Gypsies.* Cambridge: Cambridge University Press.

Parry, G., Van Cleemput, P., Peters, J., Moore, J., Walters, S., Thomas, K. and Cooper, C. (2004) *The Health Status of Gypsies and Travellers in England,* Report of Department of Health Inequalities in Health Research Initiative Project 121/7500. London: Department of Health.

Richardson, J. (2006) 'Talking about Gypsies: The Notion of Discourse as Control', *Housing Studies,* 21 (1): 77–96.

Robinson, V. (2002) '"Doing Research" with Refugees and Asylum Seekers', *Swansea Geographer,* 37: 61–67.

Rowe, M. (2004) *Policing, Race and Racism.* Collumpton: Willan

Shubin, S. and Swanson, K. (2010) '"I'm an Imaginary Figure": Unravelling the mobility and marginalisation of Scottish Gypsy Travellers', *Geoforum,* 41: 919–29.

Sibley, D. (1994) 'The Sin of Transgression', *Area,* 26 (3): 300–303.

Simmel, G. (1971) *On Individuality and Social Forms: Selected Writings of George Simmel.* Chicago, IL: University of Chicago Press.

Southern, R. and James, Z. (2006) *Devon-wide Gypsy & Traveller Housing Needs Assessment.* Plymouth: University of Plymouth.

Tomlinson, S. (2012) 'Travellers Evicted from Notorious Dale Farm Site "are Suffering from Mental Illness as a Result of Stress"', *Mail Online,* 21/10/12.

Webster, C. (2004) 'Policing British Asian Communities', in Hopkins-Burke, J. (ed.) *Hard Cop, Soft Cop: Dilemmas and Debates in Contemporary Policing.* Collumpton: Willan.

Webster, L. and Millar, J. (2001) *Making a Living: Social Security, Social Exclusion and New Travellers.* Bristol: Policy Press.

Worthington, A. (ed.) (2005) *The Battle of the Beanfield.* Teignmouth: Enabler Publications.

# 9   Inside white – racism, social relations and ethnicity in an English prison

*Rod Earle*

What are the terms for groups of people from different cultural, religious, linguistic, historical backgrounds, who have applied to occupy the same social space, whether that is a city or a nation or a region, to live with one another without either one group [the less powerful group] having to become the imitative version of the dominant one – i.e. an assimilationism – or, on the other hand, the two groups hating one another, or projecting images of degradation? In other words how can people live with difference?

(Stuart Hall, 'Rethinking the cultural question' – a video conversation with
Nira Yuval-Davis, presented at the 'Racisms, Sexisms and Contemporary
Politics of Belonging' Conference, London, August 2004)

## Prison: signs of trouble, symbols of order

Prisons are strange and difficult social spaces, at once familiar, because they are part of an everyday vocabulary of punishment, and remote because what goes on inside a prison is rarely the stuff of lived experience for the majority of the population. Prisons are the stuff of legend and nightmares, myths and movies. They symbolise the state's authority, order and the rule of law. They are its ultimate sanction demonstrating, short of the death penalty, the state's power over a person's life. A prison sentence, particularly a long one, is referred to as a 'civil death' with good reason. Prisons can be tombs as well as cages. As such, the fascinations they provoke in social scientists can be simultaneously profound, morbid and instrumental. For some people however, prisons are more routine, a fate lurking not so far around the corner. This is particularly the case if you are a young man and not of the majority population in terms of ethnicity.

From the time of Gresham Sykes's (1958) seminal study, *The Society of Captives*, the institution of prison has been recognised as a political device of the state's creation, a decisive instrument in the arbitration of social power, and the archetype of its 'exclusionary enclosure' (Wacquant 2007). As Sykes (1958: 8) reminds us 'we must keep this simple truth in mind if we are to understand the prison'. According to Loic Wacquant (2009a, 2009b) the racial configurations of western penal systems are now so stark they represent a significantly novel development in neo-liberal statecraft. He suggests the 'blackening' of the carceral population in the US at a time of declining crime rates should be recognised as a mechanism for managing the marginalised populations of an expanding neo-liberal order. The state, he argues, is engaged in the social and moral excommunication of its racialised and ultimately expendable 'others'. Although Wacquant's complex theoretical propositions have been met with a combination of guarded welcome and some scepticism in the UK (Newburn 2010; Squires and Lea 2012) the data on levels of incarceration according to ethnicity on both sides of the Anglophone Atlantic are stark. For the US in 2008, of the 1.54m imprisoned for over a year in federal and state prisons, 34 per cent were white, 38 per cent were black and 20 per cent were Hispanic (Sabol *et al.* 2009). The composition of the general population of the US in 2004 was 80 per cent white, 13 per cent black, 4 per cent Asian with the remainder made up of other minority ethnic groups (US Census Bureau 2005, cited in Sabol 2009). With an incarceration rate of 760 per 100,000 in the US the sheer number of the Black minority ethnic group in the US prison population is as staggering as it is exceptional (Pratt 2011). Going to prison has become a commonplace, 'a modal event' as Megan Comfort (2008) puts it. For some young African American men, going to prison after high-school is as likely as going to college, more likely if they happen to occupy public housing.

The astonishing scale of the US penal nightmare tends to overshadow the fact that racial disproportionality in prison populations is *even more* marked in England and Wales (and Australia) than in the US, and has been skewed that way for some time (Phillips 2012; Tonry 1994). Based on 1990 data the black: white ratio was 7.1:1 in England and Wales compared with 6.44:1 in the US and this pattern continues (see Phillips 2012). The most recent available comparison from 2000 shows a black:white (male and female) incarceration ratio of 8.5:1 in England and Wales compared to 7.7:1 for men and 6:1 for women in the US (Home Office 2000; Becker and Harrison 2001).

If you are black and male prison is likely to feature in your life as something other than a remote symbol. If not a haunting presence touching friends and family, it will be a direct and forceful reality. Similarly, if you are male, white and working class your experience of prison is less likely to be one of fascination or theoretical speculation than fateful or fatalistic dread. It is now, as it ever was, that prisons are filled with men from the social and economic margins of society. The extraordinary growth of penal populations in Anglophone democracies, but particularly the US, confounds penal theorists' explanations (Garland 2001; Simon 2007). It is almost as if the ultimate force of imperialism that once extended the reach of the State beyond its boundaries, is now, in post-colonial societies, turned inward. Where the armies of the State projected its influence beyond its borders, prisons are now raised to secure the State from internal threat and pacify the unruly enemies within (Christie 2004). For many young men the priorities of the neo-liberal security state are the ones they are most likely to encounter. Increasingly, they find themselves engaged not by a State recognised for its provision of housing, hospitals and schools, but by a hostile force they need to avoid or confront as it pursues them through the economic margins. This hostile state is to many young men what 'interfering' tax authorities are to their super-rich equivalents at the other end of the social hierarchy, only a lot more extensive, militarised and difficult to dodge (Earle 2011a).

## Prison: perspectives on everyday life?

In this chapter I discuss some aspects of a two-year research project into men's social relations in two prisons in SE England between 2006 and 2008. The research explores the salience of ethnicity and gender to the lived realities of being in prison. The dynamics of ethnicity in men's prisons, prior to this study, were largely absent from the prison research literature. Some of the impetus behind the study derives from the disproportionality referred to above, the persistence of this disproportionality and the need for deeper, clearer and more local understandings of the ways in which 'race' and ethnicity are implicated in the contemporary carceral process (see Phillips 2012).

The research adopted qualitative research methods involving extended visits to two prisons in S.E. England where I, along with Coretta Phillips, the Principal Investigator, spent as much time as we could talking with prisoners and hanging around the wings, workshops and restricted social spaces of the prisons. Over the course of eight months in each prison, a total of 110 semi-structured interviews were conducted with men in the prisons, and fieldnotes recorded our observations, interactions and feelings during the research period.

This extract from my field journal indicates how some of the preoccupations alluded to above, and that I develop further here, began to emerge:

> I sometimes think, abstractly as I'm conducting fieldwork, travelling to the prison, or away from it, that the prison order is the order of a police state, i.e. a society of almost total control where there is only the (aberrant, dangerous, lonely) Individual (man) and The State (men). I don't know what to do with this dystopian image that haunts me. Is it the spectre that haunts the Western, the Late Modern, social imagination? (following De Certeau – 'Believing is running out, being exhausted, leaving only seeing, seeing like a state').
>
> (Fieldnote, 4 November 2007)

It is tempting to see 'the prison' as a microcosm of a whole society. Such thinking is at least partly shaped by being consumed by the fieldwork process, the compelling strangeness of prison life and the power prisons hold over the sociological imagination. De Certeau (1984), for example, finds an analogy for the constraints of modern life in the similarities between a train and a prison: you can't get out, except at your allotted time, and because 'inside' real life is suspended, life is simple, reduced to a functionality that is accepted on the basis of the separation and compartmentalisation necessary for the journey.

If you imagine being locked in a train compartment for about three months with the same people and that the train never moves, but all around you the world whirls and moves on, you have something of the disorienting stasis I experienced as a prisoner in my twenties. That's the sentence I got through and the impression it left with me.

Prison is a place so removed from the real world that temporality (experienced time) is distorted in such a way that a sense of 'the future', which should be an open horizon, becomes all-but-inoperative while you are in prison. There is no future within a prison sentence, nothing between going in and coming out but the pre-established routines, the prison timetable, to drift through. As gang leader, Avon Barksdale, remarks in the television series The Wire (Season 3, Episode 7) 'you only do two days inside, the day you go in and the day you come out'. A prison sentence blocks what Merleau-Ponty (1968) has called the originary power of 'I can', the innate power to realise the formation of human possibilities. The recognised 'pains of imprisonment' close off conventional existential horizons but through their closure, they are, ironically and painfully, made more apparent. The possibility of possibilities is made real by their withdrawal (Nakagawa 1993). I think many prisoners contend, at various levels, with such ontological dilemmas of who they are, and how they want to be; they work on themselves and their possibilities even as the prison does the same. You are often your own best company in prison. I don't know if after three years in prison I'd feel the same about it, let alone if I did more, but now some 30 years later, De Certeau's train image resonates powerfully with my experience as a prisoner and conveys the peculiar, cramped, immobilisations and separations from more regular living conditions that prison imposes.

For other social theorists the prison provokes more portentous analogies. For Jerome Miller (2000, cited in Shalev 2009: 28) 'prisons and jails are an early warning system for society. They constitute the canary in the coalmine, providing an omen of mortal danger that often lies beyond our capacity to perceive.' For Zygmunt Bauman (1993: 122) prisons are fertile ground for sociological research because ' … penal practice may serve as a laboratory where the tendencies attenuated and adulterated elsewhere can be observed in their pure form; after all control and order are the outspoken objectives of the prison system.' These ominous perspectives suggest prisons offer premonitions of social processes otherwise obscured or impending, as if prison relations can be scaled up to model those of wider society, or that they are stripped down forms of those operating in society at large, revealed from their social camouflage.

Within the more prosaic ambitions of penal research itself, two theoretical frames have guided most qualitative studies of prisoner's social relations. The first, derived from Sykes' (1958) study, is known as the 'indigenous model'. It suggests men's identities are subsumed by a master prisoner status imposed by the grim routines and regimentation of prison life. These formally strip the individual of their erstwhile identity and impose what Foucault (1975) liked to think was a 'recoding of their existence'. The second 'importation model', derived from Jacobs' (1979) study, suggests prison identities are less discrete and draw more from external, racialised identities. These largely pre-existing identities from outside the prison structure its social hierarchies, its informal economy and most religious activity. As is perhaps obvious, both these influential models derive from dated US research.

In the UK, empirical studies of race and ethnicity in prison have been scarce and limited, the exception being Genders and Player's (1989) study, drawing from fieldwork in the early 1980s. This described primarily same-race solidarities within three English prisons, with a racially stratified social hierarchy in one institution, headed by white professional 'gangsters', with black and 'terrorist prisoners' in the middle echelons and sex offenders at the bottom of the hierarchy. Bosworth's (1999) analysis of women's prisons has explored how intersecting identities of race, ethnicity, gender, class, and nationality provide a mechanism for resisting institutional power and control, whilst Wilson (2003) found strong black prisoner solidarity in response to racism in a YOI. Crewe's (2009) and Drake's (2012) rich and detailed studies concentrate on reconfigurations of power, security and legitimacy in prison. In most recent contemporary prison research a hybrid model is acknowledged that synthesises elements of both the 'importation' and 'indigenous' models.

## Modern, multicultural prison

At the time of this study in 2006 27 per cent of male prisoners in England and Wales were of minority ethnic origin and 15 per cent were foreign nationals (Ministry of Justice 2009). The two prisons were chosen to reflect this. HMP Maidstone and HMYOI Rochester in Kent were selected for having an ethnically mixed population of prisoners from both urban and semi-rural settings. Each of the prisons holds approximately 400 men convicted in the Greater London area courts, where Black and minority ethnic men are over-represented in the criminal justice system, and from courts, or other prisons, in the neighbouring counties of Kent, Essex and Sussex where white ethnicities predominate. The minority ethnic population of Inner London registers somewhat above 34 per cent, while the corresponding figure for Kent and Essex, to the north, is approximately 3 per cent).

The research, briefly summarised here (see Phillips 2012 for a full account), reveals a complex and contradictory picture of social relations among prisoners in which ethnic differences were frequently seen as quite an ordinary and unremarkable aspect of their lives, both inside and outside the prison. Black and minority ethnic men tended to have stronger senses of ethnic identity, sometimes expressed in styles of hair care, idioms of speech, modes of greeting, social interaction and ways of wearing prison-issue clothes. Trousers, for example, worn beltless and low over the backside represented an ironic transatlantic echo of young men's street fashions that draw from the iconography of US prison dress codes (the enforced removal of trouser belts resulted in such low slung, apparently ill-fitting habits of dress). Some white prisoners also felt comfortable with such stylings, but for others they seemed challengingly defiant of convention and were resented. However, many white and ethnic minority prisoners told us they preferred to ignore ethnic differences and focus on a sense of 'common humanity' in which differences of skin colour and culture were dismissed in favour of a kind of dissolute egalitarian humanism. Following Gilroy (2004) we have dubbed these relations as expressions of a tentative con-viviality (Earle 2011b; Earle and Phillips 2009), elements of which transcend conventional habits of racialisation.

Both researchers observed how many social groupings and forms of association gathered around ethnicity, but this did not appear to be rigid, overtly antagonistic or actively exclusionary. By way of contrast, expressions of explicit racism or racialised antagonism were vehemently condemned by prisoners, many of whom were prepared to confront it with force. Overt racism was not tolerated among the men in the limited open social spaces of the prison but we found signs that though suppressed, it had not disappeared. It had retreated 'behind closed doors'. Personal expressions of racism had been privatised rather than being rendered entirely obsolete as a social currency or an ontological resource. For some white prisoners feelings of hostility toward black and minority ethnic prisoners continued to be expressed in private, away from 'mixed company'. These expressions drew on the conventional racial fetish of innate white superiority, national mono-culture and essential differences (Hage 1998).

Some white prisoners expressed frustration at the impact of race equality and diversity policies which they felt unfairly offered some prisoners a form of leverage against the prison regime that they could not operate. As the case study discussed below indicates, this 'race card resentment' had considerable momentum and currency among white men who appeared unaware, or dismissive, of widespread and empirically sustained complaints of unfavourable differential treatment of black and minority ethnic men by prison officers in particular and the criminal justice system in general.

For many of the younger men interviewed in the HMYOI Rochester whether you were black or white was of less significance than where you were from. Area-based identification or a sense of locality seemed at times to displace senses of identity based on conventional ideas of race or ethnicity. This sense of 'postcode pride' (Earle 2011a) seemed less significant to the older men in the adult prison, but was a material practice that fashioned a localised kind of territorial, working class masculinity similar to that identified by Robins and Cohen (1978).

Though they are more comprehensively explored by Phillips (2012) these summary findings indicate a variety of significant features of men's prison experiences that can contribute helpfully to understanding neglected aspects of ethnicity and social relations in English prison life. In the next sections I concentrate on how some aspects of prison conditions and contexts can sharpen the anxieties that occupy contemporary white English identities (Ware 2009).

## What white is that?

It is quite common for white people to want not to acknowledge racialised differences. As Ruth Frankenberg (1993) has pointed out to be 'colour-blind' constitutes an organised effort not to acknowledge such differences. It has become the 'polite' way of doing racialised difference by appearing not to. Although this stance has complex and sometimes honourable antecedents (see Gilroy 2000) it is, inevitably, an insufficient account of race, not least because it sustains the confusion that to be 'caught in the act of seeing race [is] to be caught being prejudiced' (Frankenberg 1993: 145). As the brief account of prisoner social relations above indicates, the colour-blind disavowal of racialised difference by white prisoners proved functional at a number of different levels, but also floundered in the contested and fractured domain of the late modern, multicultural prison described by Phillips (2008, 2012). Phillips argues that conventional hegemonies of race in Britain, in prison or otherwise, are so thoroughly disrupted by the volatile dynamics of globalisation that it is frequently difficult to recognise or identify the proliferating replacements and multicultural re-combinations emerging in people's practice and social relations. As Hall notes above, the terms of reference are unclear, the language and social spaces contested.

The fieldwork itself, conducted by a white man (myself) and a mixed race woman (Coretta Phillips), was not free of such 'blind-spots'. Being white and male, my 'ways of seeing' social relations, and doing the research frequently contrasted with those of Coretta, and it was sometimes only by 'comparing notes' and seeking to acknowledge differences of ethnicity, gender and class that we could appreciate how they shaped the data we were collecting (see Phillips and Earle 2010). The following fieldnote of our joint observation of men returning across the prison compound to their cells blocks from the prison workshops is a case in point:

> Today it seems like one big group, maybe 100 prisoners, all together moving loosely. It's more tightly packed than the one I saw previously, and there is less calling. Coretta nudges me and says, 'See, how it is grouped according to race' or something like that and I feel myself snap to a different kind of attention; where I had been noticing a tighter knit whole group, she had seen ethnic grouping, and I wonder what is wrong with my way of looking that what leapt to her attention, leapt over my head. I look again, and in the crowd, which is loosening as people peel off to Medway [prison wing block] while others proceed to Weald [prison

wing block], it is obvious that black guys are bunched together and white and white-ish guys are also in groups, 3–4, or 4–5, with little overlaps here and there.

(Fieldnote, 4 July 2007)

In subsequent theorising of ethnicity and social relations in the prison my identification with evidence for post-colonial con-viviality in the prisons is, I am sure, at least partially mediated by those aspects of my whiteness that correspond with Frankenberg's formulations (Earle and Phillips 2009). The pursuit of equanimity and conflict-avoidance are frequent leitmotifs of white 'colour-blind' perspectives on race. Although these pursuits acquire added resonance in prison's brittle contexts, an unintended consequence is to implicitly privilege racialised conflicts and disturbance. These become the pre-eminent 'signal crimes' (Innes and Fielding 2002) of racism, such that they can be taken as the benchmark that defines the issue at the expense of recognising more pervasive, banal and ambient racism that frequently only occupies the margins of the white field of vision. As such racism remains deeply implicated in the dynamics of prison life but, as elsewhere, it survives in countless 'hidden injuries' (Sennett and Cobb 1993; Gadd 2010) inflicted by the lattice work of an ethnically undifferentiated social power, whiteness, that has often escaped scrutiny (Garner 2006). Just as many men commonly find it hard to recognise gender privilege and the patriarchal dividend that accrues to them through hegemonic masculinity because it is the norm for them to occupy its social spaces (Connell 2006), so whiteness appears as intelligible to white folk as wetness does to a fish. This is not to say that whiteness is natural, only that, like masculinity, one of its most potent social privileges is to render them as such, natural and thus invisible to the bearer.

According to Hage (1998, 2003) such blinkered perspectives are particularly characteristic of a white bourgeoisie whose relationships with the conventional structures of political power are being redrawn. Historically neglectful of race and racism these relationships are now complicated by the waning pre-occupations of nation states toward their publics and the declining welfare priorities of modern statecraft. One consequence of this redrafting is the concomitant decline of the post-war welfare settlement between the British state and its publics, such that it is now more likely to eschew the material implications of redistributive demands for racial and sexual equality.

## Prisons and publics, ghosts and phantoms: the state of the prison(er)

Hage (2003) recalls 'the Lippmann Question' in which the celebrated American journalist, Walter Lippmann, disillusioned by media manipulation of public opinion in World War I and alarmed by the rise of fascism in Italy, declared the idea of 'the public' to be a phantom (Lippmann 1925). Preceding Margaret Thatcher's notorious dismissal of 'society' by about 60 years, Lippmann regarded the idea of a civil public sphere as a dangerous illusion, a theoretical fiction conjured into place by sociological busy-bodies intent on justifying state interference in people's lives. Hage's analysis works with the conjoined dynamics of race and nation, racism and nationalism, to speculate on the predicament of post-war welfare states as they encounter the full force of neo-liberalism's globalising, fragmenting and disorienting momentum. The welfare state, he argues, once stood for a conception of public and social life, the organisation and trajectory of its hopes that surfaced after the defeat of fascism in Europe and the exposure of its genocidal ambition:

> When the society of the past saw the possibility of social death, the welfare state intervened to breath in hope, for there was a perception that all society was at stake wherever and whenever this possibility arose. Today, not only does the state not breathe in hope, it is becoming an active producer of social death, with the bodies rotting in the spaces of chronic underemployment, poverty and neglect. We seem to be reverting to the neo-feudal times analysed by Norbert Elias, where the boundaries of civilisation, dignity and hope no longer coincide with the boundaries of the nation, but with boundaries of upper-class society, the societal spaces inhabited by an internationally delineated cosmopolitan class.

Hage (2003: 18) does not refer to prisons, perhaps because his work precedes Wacquant's (2007, 2009a, 2009b) evolving analysis of the emergence of a penal security state, but his examination of the ways in which white ethnicities, nationalism and racism have been implicated in state projects or statecraft (in Wacquant's terminology) in Australia has much to offer an understanding of contemporary English prisons. Like Wacquant he finds the changes that are emerging around nation-states to be epochal in scale, creating new hybrids of pre-modern feudal orders and modern cosmopolitan ones. In this schema, the twenty-first century increasingly resembles 'an amalgam of the sixteenth and the nineteenth' (Retort 2004: 12). The 'social death' Hage sees as the state's novel and increasing output in these new times is heavily rehearsed in the prison's civil death. It is a fate reserved for those unruly elements that cannot be otherwise contained to the expanding social margins of the privileged, cosmopolitan core.

Hage's psycho-social theorising draws creatively from both Klein and Winicott to explore how the nation-state provides for personal attachments, senses of belonging and care out of which publics grow. In this schema the nation offers citizens ontological as much as material security but, asks Hage, 'what happens when the nation starts hurting you?'; what happens when its apparatus becomes security-minded rather than care-minded? Hage suggests that as the state's ambitions to provide shrink and its orientations toward the future become narrower it triggers, particularly in white middle class people, avoidant, 'worrying' and blaming strategies that result in defensive, paranoid character formulations, not dissimilar to those originally analysed by Frankfurt School Freudo-Marxist theorists such as Erich Fromm, Herbert Marcuse and Wilhelm Reich (see also Gadd 2010). Although it is probably too speculative to call prison the character armour of the emerging neo-liberal state, the characters in prison, and their relationship to the state, their formulations of ethnicity and race, can be revealing of such a process because being a prisoner generates a paradoxical condition of almost total dependency on the state. In prison, like nowhere else in society, the state is your keeper and you are its property (Ruggiero 2010).

Even as the British Government affirms the 'civil death' status of its prisoners through its exceptional resistance to the European Court of Human Rights' ruling regarding the denial of prisoner's voting rights, it also pursues an assertive, innovative and largely progressive approach to diversity in prison and prisoner management. Before going on to analyse this further I present a case study from HMP Maidstone in an attempt to flesh out the issues being raised as they were encountered in the prison.

### A case in point: 'Barry', racism and care in the (nanny) state

Barry (not his real name) is an articulate, middle-aged, university educated white man. As a prisoner at HMP Maidstone he became something of a wing advocate, organising for better facilities and volunteering to provide prisoner-led activities. He deeply resents his incarceration for 'white-collar crimes' and holds the prison in the same kind of contempt which he reserves for the State. In the course of a long and thoughtful interview his ideas about ethnicity, race, racism and diversity seemed to encapsulate many of the paradoxical, contradictory accounts and experiences we encountered in the prison from white prisoners.

In the following composition extracts from Barry's interview are woven together to present a single continuous narrative that offers insights into aspects of the kind of white ethnicities Hage insists require urgent analysis. While this composition is an analytical artefact the words are almost entirely his own and have been put together from the interview transcript by removing my questions and connective interjections. Although this case study composition is an unconventional rendition of respondent perspectives it provides a way of linking sometimes disjointed discussions of ethnicity threaded through an extensive interview (Gomm *et al.* 2000; Gadd and Jefferson 2007; Gadd 2010). It is deliberately condensed and constructed to convey those aspects of a longer discussion and presented in this way to convey something of the person's narrative account of themselves that would be lost in fragmentary interview extracts (see Crewe and Bennett (2012) where this case study and approach was first deployed). Barry's perspectives on race and ethnicity are then discussed and contextualised as aspects of whiteness more fully in the remainder of the chapter.

BARRY:  Well you have ethnicity jammed down your throat all the time don't you. I'm a Samaritan for the prison, a Listener, so I do have to speak to a lot of people and or rather, have them speak to me. They're sometimes quite distressed. There was one about six months ago when I got referred to somebody who was trying to kill himself. And he said he didn't want to talk to me cos 'you're a white racist motherfucker'. And he would not speak to me. So the other racists in here do throw one's Caucasian background down your throat all the time. They play the race card even more in here.

You find that people stick together in here for language reasons quite a lot. If there's three Dutch people on the wing, you'll find they play cards all the time. The West Indians stick together cos that's the way they are. I'm not being racist there, but they are, and they're the cause of an awful lot of trouble in here. They're the most racist bunch of bastards in the world. The Asians stick together.

It brings back the old question which is whether the racial and cultural barriers and difference should be celebrated or broken down. I don't think you could ever break them down. And if you celebrate them too strongly then it becomes racism. They have to be accepted and appreciated for what they are. Diversity is always a great thing. It's enriching for everybody who's in the melting pot. But it has to be tempered with reason. On one wing there was a period where the Muslims complained so much about people cooking bacon that it was banned completely from the self-cook. And they tried to make that stick on another wing, and in this one. I wouldn't have it, neither would any of the others. Fuck off, if you don't like it mate. I'm sorry, we can always fall back to the old baseline that this is a Christian country and if you want to be here, come and fit in. If I go and live in Dubai, I fit in with the Arabs, I observe Ramadan. I don't walk down the street with a beef burger. And you observe the traditions of the country that you're in, you don't try and impose your own traditions on them. I know that sounds a bit hard-line.

With the bacon ban, it didn't last long at all, but that's what they can do, they play the race card, they say 'he's being racist, he's cooking bacon where I want to'. Fuck off. They try it on all the time, they try and play the race/religion/Muslim card all the time. It has made them so unpopular. I mean I've heard people on the wing saying openly that they do not want Muslims on this wing. And that's not healthy.

On the other wing I couldn't get down to self-cook because the West Indians are the only ones allowed to cook. Nobody else is allowed to. It's the fact that the West Indians are the ones who take over. Again, I'm sounding racist. I'm not at all, it's just an observation. If you're not West Indian you can't cook on that wing, full-stop, that's it, end of the line. You try, you have a fight. If you're not West Indian you have to queue for your dinner as well on the servery. If you're West Indian you don't need to queue, you just go straight to the front, and the officers turn a blind eye because they can't argue with them because they're West Indian. That causes resentment. But the West Indians are a minority obviously, but they're one of the bigger minorities, they are very strong, they're not afraid to have a fight because they pull the race card straightaway. If you hit a black guy, you'll get shipped off the wing because you've assaulted him in a racist manner. That's the way it always goes. It's reverse racism.

It's the same as it is outside the prison. There'll always be ethnic inter-mingling and ethnic separation as well. I had a flat once in Stoke New-ington, big Turkish area [in north London]. Everybody was Turkish round there. I was one of the few English people in the street. And they just stick together, it's a ghetto. You go up to Stamford Hill [north London] and it's a Jewish area. It's a funny thing in here and it's a funny thing in society in general. Pure diversity and lack of racism involves not noticing the other person's diversity, the other person's race. It's irrelevant, it's irrelevant that you're black and I'm white, that you're from somewhere else to me. And yet the first thing they do when you come in here is 'what's your ethnic code'. That's disgusting. How dare they! It's none of their business what my ethnic code is. I put myself down as a black Afro-Caribbean Chinese cross usually, just to piss them off. It is none of their business. It's disgusting that they even ask. And I always tell them it's none of your business, 'make a guess' I say.

The prison service is not working, particularly because of the social worker input as I call it. The fact that they're forced to record one's ethnic code and all the rest. Even mentioning that somebody is Chinese or Norwegian should be a sackable offence. Nanny state again. 'We seem to have some-body from Laos on the Wing', so they'll have to reprint every sign in the jail with Laos as an option. Fuck off! This is England. These people they're all one great big bunch of ethnic foreigners or English ethnic different background, but nevertheless they're in England. Keep the signs in English, supply some translators and pretend not to notice that they're from a dif-ferent country. That's the only way to do it. And anything beyond that is racism in itself. It's only a problem in England. What is it with the English? And the more these PC [political correctness] idiots try, and do, to solve the problems, the worse they make them.

## Unhappy bedfellows: penal and political corrections

In prison being the same as each other, wearing a prison uniform and being assigned a number have, traditionally, been seen as providing a simple 'us prisoners' v. 'them officers' set of relations and identities. Although it is a largely mythical image, albeit with more than a grain or two of truth to it, there was much more going on in the two prisons of this research. Modern British prisons no longer address prisoners by their number or insist on prison uniform but they remain a paradoxical exercise in the degradation of what it is to be human (punishment) and in the imagination of what it is to be human (rehabilitation). Just as 'race' is premised on a similar kind of perverse, con-flicted humanism (Young 1992), so too is the prison. It involves a similar kind of 'Enlightened' conjunctural practice where philanthropy meets misanthropy, often with the most terrible consequences.

Unsurprisingly, most people sent to prison resist being cast as 'all the same', 'all trash', and this can make personal projects in identity management more urgent and explicit. Prisons are places with obvious designs on men and in them, men design their own responses. Difference and distinction are needed by prisoners to discount the historical effort to reduce their humanity and rehabilitate them into more manageable units of society. Dehumanisation is an intensely deconstructive business, resisting it, a very personal affair.

Both HMP Maidstone and HMYOI Rochester had active, widely promoted and energetically developed diversity policies (Phillips 2012). There were obvious provisions for the substantial minority of Muslim prisoners, multi-faith facilities, and corresponding, if limited, dietary options. Religious and cultural festivals, such as Christmas, Passover, Ramadan and Eid, were accommodated in prison schedules and calendar activities. The prison administration's diversity panels and committees met regularly and reviewed complex, computer-assisted monitoring data that mapped the allocation of significant decisions and actions against prisoner's recorded ethnicity. The software operated a 'traffic-light' warning system indicating the presence of ethnic disparities and the urgency of addressing them as they emerged. These high-profile procedures were a prominent feature of prison administration, as Barry's account indicates. In these complex and necessarily pervasive procedures, white English prisoners, such as Barry, appear to recognise a provision, even a sense of care, for people 'not like them', ethnic people. At the same time they both resist and resent their own apparently inconsequential 'ethnification', not least because it is encountered as a fait accompli, presented to them by default (their fault!), rather than shaped by them. They are presented with a white ethnic identity that, if it cannot distinguish itself by an external nationality, such as Irish, or Polish, becomes intensely troubled and troubling (Ware 2009).

Barry resorts to an assimilative, colour-blind English national identity, but it is a besieged, defensive and plaintive position, an identity far removed from the empowered positions he sees in other prisoners' identities. It holds none of the attractions, and little correspondence with, the identities that emerged from the popular movements of minority ethnic people in many Western countries from the late 1960s. These 'traditionalist' identities provided a sense of security, even salvation, in times of turbulence and crisis. The character of these 'old ethnicities' was 'fixed and ascribed' and provided a medium for engagement in larger imagined collectivities, such as the nation state. In some cases they offered 'a set of standards, values, rules for living' (Friedman 1994: 243). They are associated with a kind of essentialism and traditionalism expressed in the desire for roots, 'the rise of the fourth world, the return to religion and stable values' (ibid.: 243). As Brah (1992: 144) quizzically notes, essentialism is 'not easy to deal with' and the problems of such 'strategic essentialism' have left lasting legacies in the recognition and management of new diversities.

Among white people the beleaguered, resentful response to the new management of diversity ('everyone else gets all the advantages, we're abandoned'), is so pervasive as to be becoming constitutive of a new whiteness in contemporary Britain (Garner 2012, personal comm.). It implicitly signals the displaced racial status quo in which minorities that were once discounted and discriminated against with impunity, and English imperial aspirations imposed across the globe, no longer holds. The apparently 'tolerant' 'live and let live', 'when in Rome … ' account proffered by Barry depends on, and can only be sustained by, a wilful historical amnesia. Barry says, 'If I go and live in Dubai, I fit in with the Arabs, I observe Ramadan. I don't walk down the street with a beef burger. And you observe the traditions of the country that you're in, you don't try and impose your own traditions on them. I know that sounds a bit hard-line.'

Unfortunately, for most of the eighteenth, nineteenth and half of the twentieth century 'ramming it down people's throats', imposing English traditions, law, language, customs and habits was pretty much business as usual from Ireland to Africa, Australia and south east Asia. Barry's evocation of the equable, white Englishman abroad respecting local custom and culture represses this history and substitutes a more palatable inversion of contemporary cosmopolitanism (see Wemyss 2008; Tyler 2012). Barry's account also discretely implies an equivalence to the way he behaves as a visitor in a foreign country with the behaviour of a British citizen in their own country because, in his eyes, they would not be, could not be, a Muslim: 'Fuck off' or 'fit in' as he puts it to those he regards as badly behaved guests rather than fellow citizens. These unstable tensions energise the confused antagonism he has toward those he feels are failing to abide by his enlightened standards of international, inter-ethnic understanding. To the extent that this also represents Barry's middle class whiteness, his resentment is racialised (Aughey 2012; Fenton 2012).

## History and prison: no escape, no short cuts

Stuart Hall's (1992: 254) acute evaluation that the political consequences of what he called 'the end of the innocent notion of the essential black subject' had not been 'fully reckoned with' is as true now as it was when he made it. And so it continues. Gilroy's (2006) account traces how these seductive 'certainties' of 'race thinking' allow white Britons to keep their bearings in a world they experience as increasingly confusing. Barry's account offers a compelling mixture of indignant exasperation and reluctant engagement as he is drawn into that same 'old question' that Hall diagnosed as so elusive but so central to the social and cultural life of modern societies. In the enclosed proximities and shrunken social possibilities of the prison ducking the question is rarely an option.

Barry's account reflects the melancholic (Gilroy) and paranoid (Hage) tendencies that surface as he grapples with difference and searches for hope in the flattened, abbreviated hierarchies of the society of captives. Here he, and other prisoners in HMP Maidstone and HMYOI Rochester, encounter some of the 'feral beauty' (Gilroy 2004: 157) of unruly post-colonial hybridity, the paradoxical and disorienting glamorisation of racial difference and the banal, 'ragged-edge vitality' (Irwin 1980) of an undeniably multicultural prison. Barry's whiteness is as hidden from him as the injuries of racism endured by non-white prisoners, all those subtle and not so subtle difficulties, experiential anomalies and obstacles thrown up against the life course that are obscured by the material and ontological privileges of whiteness (Sennett and Cobb 1993; Gadd 2010). Alongside this uneven multicultural experience of diversity (con-viviality) white prisoners also encounter multiculturalism as a prescription for the management of such diversity. Boxed into the confined spaces of wings, courtyards and workshops prisoners are manifestly 'all in it together' in all the ways that the rest of us in David Cameron's Big Society manifestly are not. Here the state has them locked in and locked out of society and presents them with its own paradoxical vision of diversity, of 'how people can live with difference', and how it can react to the systemic discrimination and prejudice of racism that propelled so many of them there in the first place. For prisoners it is as challenging, enigmatic and ironic as that.

As both Phillips (2012) and Hage (1998, 2003) argue, contemporary formulations of racism in policies and personal practice commonly present the issue in zero sum binary terms – you are (a) racist or you are not, you are a victim or a perpetrator. The implied morality of this liberal anti-racism, sometimes conveyed in prison diversity programmes, threatens white prisoners, not just for portraying them as potentially evil perpetrators (convicted again!), but also casting non-white prisoners as victims and virtuous (un-like them). The reductive moralism of this discourse implicitly projects virtue onto the victims and sets up a bogus hierarchical difference that is deeply resented (Ware 2008). Hence, perhaps, the vehemence of Barry's protestations and inversions that 'black people are the most racist people in here' while he is the victim of 'reverse racism'.

Looking for answers to the questions posed by Stuart Hall at the start of this chapter on how we can live with difference inevitably involves working beyond the boundaries of conventional Anglophone criminology. Expecting to find them in prison is perhaps naïve but, following Bauman (1993), in the multicultural prisons of this research the 'tendencies' of both a penal humanism and a more planetary humanism (Gilroy 2000) could be found, alongside and within the reconfigured racisms.

Henry Giroux (2008) insists that the meanings and definitions of racism alter for each generation, and that the challenge for scholars is to develop a new language for understanding how race redefines social relations between people. Stuart Hall's remarks suggest this process and his work around new ethnicities (Hall 1992) remains the most viable starting point. Hage (1998, 2003), Gilroy (2004, 2006) and Gadd (2010; Gadd and Jefferson 2007) all provide evidence, empirical and theoretical, that psychosocial, intersectional analyses are providing resources for this language. Whiteness, as Garner (2006, 2007) notes, is now part of the vocabulary and helps us to identify and trace its variable trajectories. Among these are the elusive 'ghostly forms' that enable people, such as Barry, to 'see themselves as unfairly dealt with simply because they are white' (ibid. 2006: 178).

## Acknowledgment

The author acknowledges the generosity and co-operation of staff and prisoners at HMYOI Rochester and HMP Maidstone, and the ESRC Identities and Social Action research programme. Coretta Phillips' fieldwork and analysis have influenced my own in innumerable ways, and I am fortunate to have worked with such a generous and collaborative academic and Principal Investigator. Steve Garner, Vron Ware and Colin Webster provided insightful comments on earlier drafts. All remaining errors and shortcomings are my own.

## References

Aughey, A. (2012) 'Englishness as Class: A Re-examination', *Ethnicities*, 12 (4): 394–408.

Bauman, Z. (1993) *Postmodern Ethics*. Cambridge: Polity Press.

Becker, A. J. and Harrison, P. M. (2001), *Prisoners in 2000. NCJ 188207*. Washington, DC: Bureau of Justice Statistics.

Bosworth, M. (1999), *Engendering Resistance: Agency and Power in Women's Prisons*. Aldershot: Dartmouth Publishing Company Limited.

Brah, A. (1992) 'Difference, Diversity and Differentiation' in Donald, J. and Rattansi, A. (eds) *'Race', Culture and Difference*. London: Sage.

Christie, N. (2004) *A Suitable Amount of Crime*. London: Routledge.

Comfort, M. (2008) *Doing Time Together: Love and Family in the Shadow of the Prison*. Chicago, IL: University of Chicago Press.

Connell, R. (2006) *Gender*. Cambridge: Polity Press.

Crewe, B. (2009) *The Prisoner Society: Power, Adaptation and Social Life in an English Prison*. Oxford: Oxford University Press.

Crewe, B. and Bennett, J. (2012) *The Prisoner*. Abingdon: Routledge.

De Certeau, M. (1984) *The Practice of Everyday Life*. Berkeley: University of California Press.

Drake, D. (2012) *Prisons, Punishment and the Pursuit of Security (Critical Criminological Perspectives)*. Basingstoke: Palgrave Macmillan.

Earle, R. (2011a) 'Boys' Zone Stories: Perspectives from a Young Men's Prison', *Criminology and Criminal Justice*, 11 (2): 129–43.

——(2011b) 'Ethnicity, Multiculture and Racism in a Young Offenders' Instittion', *Prison Service Journal*, 197: 32–38.

Earle, R. and Phillips, C. (2009) '"Con-viviality" and Beyond: Identity Dynamics in a Young Men's Prison', in M. Wetherell (ed.) *Identity in the 21st Century*. Basingstoke: Palgrave Macmillan.

Fenton, S. (2012) 'Resentment, Class and Social Sentiments about the Nation: The Ethnic Majority in England', *Ethnicities*, 12 (4): 465–83.

Foucault, M. (1975), *Discipline and Punish: The Birth of the Prison*. Harmondsworth: Penguin Books Ltd.

Frankenberg, R. (1993) *White Women, Race Matters: The Social Construction of Whiteness*. Minneapolis: University of Minnesota Press.

Friedman, J. (1994) *Cultural Identity and Global Process*. London: Sage.

Gadd, D. (2010) 'Racial Hatred and Unmourned Loss', *Sociological Research Online*, 15 (3): 9.

Gadd, D. and Jefferson, T. (2007) *Psychosocial Criminology*. London: Sage.

Garland, D. (2001) *The Culture of Control*. Oxford: Oxford University Press.

Garner, S. (2006) 'The Uses of Whiteness: What Sociologists Working on Europe Can Draw from Us Research on Whiteness', *Sociology*, 40 (2): 257–75.

——(2007) *Whiteness: An Introduction*. London: Routledge.

——(2012) 'A Moral Economy of Whiteness: Behaviours, Belonging and Britishness', *Ethnicities*, 12 (4): 445–464.

Genders, E. and Player, E. (1989), *Race Relations in Prison*. Oxford: Clarendon Press.

Gilroy, P. (2000) *Between Camps: Nations, Culture and the Allure of Race*. London: Allan Lane.

——(2004) *After Empire: Melancholia or Convivial Culture?* London: Routledge.

——(2006) 'Multiculture in Times of War: An Inaugural Lecture Given at the London School of Economics', *Critical Quarterly*, 48 (4): 27–45.

Giroux, H. (2008) *Against the Terror of Neoliberalism: Politics Beyond the Age of Greed*. Boulder, CO: Paradigm Publishers, University of British Columbia Press.

Gomm, R., Hammersley, M. and Foster, P. (eds) (2000) *Case Study Method*. London: Sage.

Hage, G. (1998) *White Nation: Fantasies of White Supremacy in a Multicultural Society*. Annandale, NSW: Routledge.

——(2003) *Against Paranoid Nationalism: Searching for Hope in a Shrinking Society*. London: The Merlin Press.

Hall, S. (1992) 'New Ethnicities', in Donald, J. and Rattansi, A. (eds) *'Race', Culture and Difference*. London: Sage.

Home Office (2000) *Prison Statistics England and Wales 1999*. London: Home Office.

Innes, M. and Fielding, N. (2002) 'From Community to Communicative Policing: "Signal Crimes" and The Problem of Public Reassurance', *Sociological Research OnLine*, 7 (2).

Irwin, J. (1980) *Prisons in Turmoil*. Boston, MA: Little, Brown and Company.

Jacobs, J. B. (1979) 'Race Relations and the Prisoner Subculture', in N. Morris and M. Tonry (eds) *Crime and Justice*. Chicago, IL: The University of Chicago Press.

Lippmann, W. (1925) *The Phantom Public*. New York: Transaction Publishers.

Merleau-Ponty, M. (1968) *The Visible and the Invisible: Followed by Working Notes*. Evanstown: Northwestern University Press.

Ministry of Justice (2009) *Statistics on Race and the Criminal Justice System 2007/08*. London: Ministry of Justice.

Nakagawa, G. (1993) 'Deformed Subjects, Docile Bodies: Disciplinary Practices and Subject-constitution in Stories of Japanese American Internment', in Dennis K. Mumby (ed.) *Narrative & Social Control – Critical Perspectives*. London: Sage.

Newburn, T. (2010) 'Diffusion, Differentiation and Resistance in Comparative Penality', *Criminology and Criminal Justice*, 10 (4): 341–52.

Phillips, C. (2008) 'Negotiating Identities: Ethnicity and Social Relations in a Young Offenders' Institution', *Theoretical Criminology*, 12 (3): 313–31.

Phillips, C. and Earle, R. (2010) 'Reading Difference Differently? Identity, Epistemology and Prison Ethnography', *British Journal of Criminology*, 50 (2): 360–78.

Phillips, C. (2012) *The Multicultural Prison*. Oxford: Clarendon Press.

Pratt (2011) 'The International Diffusion of Punitive Penality: Or, Penal Exceptionalism in the United States? Wacquant v Whitman', *Australian and New Zealand Journal of Criminology*, 44 (1): 116–128.

Retort (2004) 'Afflicted Powers: the State, the Spectacle and September 11', *New Left Review*, 27 May/June.

Robins, D. and Cohen, P. (1978) *Knuckle Sandwich; Growing Up in the Working Class City*. London: Penguin.

Ruggiero, V. (2010) *Penal Abolitionism*. Oxford: Oxford University Press.

Sabol, W. J., West, H. C. and Cooper, M. (2009) *Correctional Populations in the United States, 2008*. Washington, DC: US Department of Justice.

Sennett, R. and Cobb, J. (1993) *The Hidden Injuries of Class*. New York: Norton and Co.

Shalev, S. (2009) *Supermax: Controlling Risk through Solitary Confinemen*, Cullompton: Willan.

Simon, J. (2007) *Governing through Crime: How the War on Crime Transformed American Democracy and Created a Culture of Fear. Studies in Crime and Public Policy*. New York: Oxford University Press.

Squires, P. and Lea, J. (eds) (2012) *Criminalisation and Advanced Marginality: Critically Exploring the Work of Loic Wacquant*. Bristol: Policy Press.

Sykes, G. M. (1958) *The Society of Captives: A Study of a Maximum Security Prison*. Princeton, NJ: Princeton University Press.

Tonry, M. (1994) 'Racial Disproportion in US Prisons', *British Journal of Criminology*, 34 (Special Issue): 97–115.

Tyler, K. (2012) *Whiteness, Class and the Legacies of Empire: On Home ground*. Palgrave Macmillan.

Wacquant, L. (2007) *Urban Outcasts: A comparative study of advanced marginality*. Cambridge: Polity Press.

——(2008) *Urban Outcasts: A Comparative Sociology of Advanced Marginality*. Cambridge: Polity Press.

——(2009a) *Punishing the Poor: The Neoliberal Government of Social Insecurity*. Durham, NC: Duke University Press.

——(2009b) *Prisons of Poverty*. Minneapolis, MN: University of Minnesota Press.

Ware, V. (2008) 'Towards a Sociology of Resentment: A Debate on Class and Whiteness', *Sociological Research Online*, 13 (5). Available at www.socresonline.org.uk/13/15/19.htm (accessed 2 October 2012).

——(2009) 'The Ins and Outs of Anglo-Saxonism', in Perryman, M. *Breaking Up Britain: Four nations After a Union*. London: Lawrence & Wishart.

Wemyss, G. (2008) 'White Memories, White Belonging: Competing Colonial Anniversaries in "Postcolonial" East London', *Sociological Research*, 13 (5): 8. Available at www.socresonline.org.uk/13/5/8.html (accessed 2 October 2012).

Wilson, D. (2003) '"Keeping Quiet" or "Going Nuts": Some Emerging Strategies Used by Young Black People in Custody at a Time of Childhood Being Re-Constructed', *Howard Journal of Criminal Justice*, 42 (5): 411–25.

Young, R. (1992) 'Colonialism and Humanism' in Donald, J. and Rattansi, A. (eds) *'Race', Culture and Difference*. London: Sage.

# 10 New directions and new generations – old and new racism?

*Coretta Phillips and Colin Webster*

To take a new direction one must understand where we have come from and why. In the Introduction to this book we argued that we have already taken some very necessary steps to understand the complex relationship between race, ethnicity, offending and criminal justice outcomes. Official data from the 1990s stoked an important, but ultimately narrow, debate about whether black disproportionality in the prison population was the result of elevated rates of offending or discrimination in the criminal justice process, or indeed both. Moreover, for some scholars official statistics concealed as much as they have revealed (FitzGerald 2009; Stenson 2011), and in the ensuing years the identification of conceptual and methodological weaknesses with these data have challenged their validity. While sympathetic to these dissenting voices, we reiterate our view that they still require our vigilant attention and engagement, not least to refute the loud assertions of uninformed ideologues. More positively, in putting together this volume, we believe we have been able to move beyond these data in presenting new work in the field of race, ethnicity and crime, which has transcended most of these difficulties.

When a new generation – of scholars and 'subjects' of research study – emerges we are enabled to see and learn from new ways of looking at old and new problems, and we begin to sketch out our future. This requires being open to perceiving change where it has occurred but also not being blind to persistent continuities. In this regard it is sobering to read Elijah Anderson's (2011) reflections on 'The Nigger Moment' in his recent book, *The Cosmopolitan Canopy*. Not unlike Paul Gilroy's (2004) work here, Anderson is cautiously optimistic about the nature of civility and social relations in ethnically mixed settings in the US where segregation is not practiced. Notwithstanding, the 'Nigger Moment' is where African Americans, regardless of their class position and status, are painfully reminded that they are always vulnerable to being degraded, humiliated, demoralised by their treatment at the hands of the white majority, that 'there is no protection, no sanctuary, no escaping from this fact' (Anderson 2011: 253). Anderson uses several case studies to illustrate these enlightening moments, including the story of Shawn, a student at a prestigious law school, who is publicly embarrassed by a stop and frisk in his middle class neighbourhood. Eventually Shawn is released from handcuffs and he learns that the police suspicion of him as a robbery suspect was informed by his white neighbours contacting the police when they heard of the robbery. For Shawn there was then the traumatic realisation that racism has not entirely gone away, even in our cosmopolitan, multicultural societies, and significantly also within the middle classes.

The chapters in this volume point to continuing racial inequities in the treatment of minority ethnic groups, which we will come to in a moment. However, in order for us to move in new directions within the discipline of criminology we must also recognise the culpability of our discipline and academia in general. One of us (Coretta Phillips), as a minority ethnic scholar, has also experienced 'nigger moments' in academic life. One particularly telling incident occurred at an editorial board meeting. Conversing with colleagues over lunch, I was met by a criminologist who repeatedly asked me whether she could give me some documents relating to the administrative business of the meeting. It took a while before it dawned on me that she had assumed that I was attending as an administrative representative of the publisher, rather than as a fellow criminologist, and she had been sure enough not to doubt this assumption. In another incident, I attended an invited seminar where delegates were staying overnight in a plush conference centre. As I left my room on the way to go for breakfast I saw several cleaning trolleys in the corridor outside my room as the cleaning staff began the unenviable job of making beds in guests' rooms. At the same time, a Research Officer also came out of her bedroom. She looked along the corridor, noticed me leaving a room, saw the cleaning trolleys, and she helpfully offered to leave her room door open for me so that I could clean her room! Evidently, it did not seem possible to her that I might be her professional (and senior) colleague and not her cleaner (see Anderson (2011: 263) for references to similar experiences among African American professionals). Thus, lest we become complacent that racialised thinking resides externally, only in the actions of agents of social control, as Palmer reminds us in her chapter, 'we should also be attuned to the 'imprint of slavery and colonialism on the *psyche of criminologists* [our emphasis]'. This seems apt given the experiences described here. And indeed, Palmer acknowledges how black scholars, including herself, seek 'objective validation' of their qualitative work with black participants in a way which is not expected when white scholars research white people.

It will undoubtedly be no surprise to readers that such encounters were also recalled by research participants in the chapters of this volume, exemplifying old and familiar forms of racist thought. Ishtaq, one of Alpa Parmar's interviewees, for example, told her of his 'nigger moment': 'Obviously it's not just bad luck or random that I am targeted. It's because of how I look, who I am. I've lived here all my life, but feel like an outsider. I said to the police that my race is British Muslim, not British or Muslim.' This poignantly signified the power of his exclusion within the nation of which he was a citizen. Such potent and painful statements provide a lens for understanding enduring patterns, but also new configurations, of exclusion and racism in the globalised twenty-first century. Real and imagined fears of terrorist violence from Muslims born in Britain and abroad frame policing tactics, particularly stop and search powers which are seemingly in equal measure, revered by policing professionals and reviled by those vulnerable to their reach. In this the question of racial profiling remains, to use Palmer's phrase, the 'elephant in the room'. Yet Palmer also implores us to seek to understand the links between the historical and the contemporary, in perception and action. Some of her African Caribbean participants viewed offending in the black community as rooted in their internalisation of racist ideologies which were operationalised in slavery and colonialism. Deeply embedded feelings of self-hatred and inferiority seemed to fuel aggressive predatory behaviour which harmed other black community members. Palmer urges us to recognise the distinctive racial dynamics of late modern society and not simply assume a trumping of race by class relations.

The fault-line of belonging, in an absolute sense of formal citizenship, but also in an emotive sense of human rootedness, also features heavily in this volume, and can be seen as a new mechanism of racialised sorting. It is not that criminal justice is no longer implicated in this process, but just that state control begins and is policed as frequently at the border of nation states today (De Giorgi 2006; Bosworth and Guil 2008). Here, Bosworth and Kellezi's chapter presents an evocative account of physical confinement and women detainees' desperate need to belong to Britain, to establish a legitimate equivalence of British citizenship to which they had been denied. For Fraser and Piacentini's Francophone African refugees and asylum seekers, there is a similar sentiment in which mobility and immobility is inscribed in everyday life. Forcible dispersal has followed initial migration to Britain, with further uncertainty etched into people's lives as they are relocated into 'foreign' parts of Glasgow, despite attempts at local integration and participation in British society. These forms of social stratification take troubling questions of identity, race, faith, and culture to the global stage as we see the profound inequalities between migrant-receiving countries of the global North and sending countries of the global South, often tied politically and symbolically to Britain by colonial links. Political discourses routinely and regularly underpin and reinforce precisely these boundaries of inclusion and exclusion. At the time of writing, for example, prime minister David Cameron offered this to an electorate concerned about Britain being regarded as a welfare magnet: 'Ending the something for nothing culture is something that needs to apply in the immigration system as well as the welfare system ... you put into Britain, you don't just take out' (Speech at University Campus Suffolk, 25 March 2013). Not lost is the irony for Fraser and Piacentini's asylum seekers who face state restrictions and controls on their ability to work, thus maintaining their liminal and welfare-dependent status.

The subjects of Zoë James' chapter, Gypsies and Travellers, have a far longer history of being marginalised on the edge of society, their sense of belonging refuted by their nomadism, and they are often despised in local settled communities. Regarded as unwelcome invaders of public space, they easily fit the role of dangerous Other, which legitimises them being forcibly moved on by the police and local authorities. 'Horrific' experiences as the 'authorities treat you terrible', making them 'feel like criminals'; such comments peppered Gypsy and Traveller accounts in James' research. Similarly, as Paul Iganski observes in his chapter, the contested presence of Jewish people in the contemporary period presents a potential paradox of spatial and political relations. After centuries of pogroms and persecution, of which the Nazi Holocaust was only the most 'successful', recent, anti-Jewish incidents have been assumed to relate to Israeli Jews' poor treatment of Palestinians in their disputed homeland. Indeed, it is precisely because they are seen to belong and not belong elsewhere (Israel) that their right to belong in several European countries, including Britain, is challenged. As it turns out, Paul Iganski finds a more banal racism, a common or garden variety, where abuse, harassment, and sometimes violence is meted out by young men, who more than anything are characterised by their own marginality, social exclusion, and significantly, their whiteness.

It is from a similar position that Rod Earle's white prisoners argue the validity of their colour-blindness, perverted in their minds by the explicit focus on race in the prison's race equality regime. His case study of Barry reveals a troubled and plaintive narrative in which whiteness is perceived to have been rendered culturally inferior, inadequate, and his and other prisoners' talk is laden with cultural loss. Here there is a suggestion of an inverted binary; not white racist-black victim, but instead the other way around, as white people are victimised by the racism and preferential treatment of black and Muslim prisoners. The distinctive psycho-social attributes of racism are clearly indicated here, and represent a late, but welcome turn towards the psycho-social in criminology (see for example Gadd and Dixon 2011; Gadd and Jefferson 2007; Gelsthorpe 2007). None of this should be seen to deny the economic and spatial marginalisation of poor white ethnicities, captured vividly in Alistair Fraser and Teresa Piacentini's chapter. Glasgow's Langview Boys are confined to a physical space, which assumes symbolic significance, as an area to be proudly defended and emotionally invested in, as the gang tag provides a vessel for this local patriotism or 'neighbourhood nationalism'. Yet this pride is undermined as the boys' spatial boundedness is overlaid with stigma, inscribed with danger, threat, and very real economic disadvantage. It would be a nonsense to claim that the materiality of class is not writ large in many of the boys' life experiences.

Du Bois' (1903) conceptualisation of racial segregation as *the* problem of the twentieth century in US society has, in Elijah Anderson's (2011) view, shifted to a state of instability, tension, and negotiation, where the colour line is blurred, submerged, and uncertain, particularly in cosmopolitan settings. Effusive demonstrations of the vitality of British multicultural society are contained in several chapters in this volume: explicitly in Webster's account of young people reflecting on their interactions in multicultural and multi-faith

Bradford and London where difference was mostly tolerated or negotiated in relatively benign ways; in Bosworth and Kellezi's discussion of everyday life in Yarl's Wood Immigration Removal Centre; and such sentiments infused the narratives of Rod Earle's prisoners too. Nevertheless, in all cases a residual of underlying anxieties about race and faith remained. We must, therefore, remember that crude forms of racialised stereotyping have not disappeared from social relations, and also that such forms are not the preserve of only the white majority. Bosworth and Kellezi found dispiriting the belittling, racist comments *within* the immigrant detainee community – the Jamaicans and Nigerians cruelly mimicking the Chinese women whose own views portrayed the familiar, derogatory motifs of blackness, and so on.

Inevitably, given the subject matter of criminology, the theme of formal social control is foregrounded in many chapters in this book. This exercise of state power and authority is underlaid by familiar racial tropes of danger, which in a Foucauldian (1975) sense, legitimises increased penality. Bosworth and Kellezi find immigration detention officers making distinctions on the basis of 'cultural traits' deemed helpful or problematic from a control and security perspective. These understandings conditioned categorical views about which women were deserving and undeserving of the right to remain and participate in British society. The racialised elements of this practice are obscured by a simple binary of citizenship. The same can be said of the use of paramilitary public order techniques combined with legislative powers to evict or contain Gypsy and Traveller communities and the securitised policing of Asian men as potential terrorist suspects. For all groups subject to these shows of state authority the sense of injustice is palpable.

The response to this sense of unfair treatment can develop into different forms of resistance. There is the passive resistance exhibited by one of the women in Bosworth and Kellezi's study. A long-term British resident but not a citizen, she resists the inferior notion of her citizenship status by perceiving herself as a valuable worker and a responsible mother, as a net contributor to British society. There is also a more active resistance which may prove counterproductive for state control. Fraser and Piacentini use Soja's (1998) concept of 'thirdspace' to understand the physical and symbolic spaces in which 'gang' boys entertain an autonomous sense of self and shape a positive, agential, collective identity. The problem, of course, is that the defence of space makes for 'tyrannical relations' which in no way confront the problems of the boys' economic immobility, and may even serve to entrench them. There also always remains the possibility that the challenging or demeaning of identities by the state shapes them into oppositional ones. Thus, for some of Parmar's Asian young men, the vulnerability of their racialised status as Muslims, led them to assert a positive Muslim identity among others, to assuage and resist their criminalisation. State practices thus served to essentialise and reify ethnic identities, constraining the opportunities to identify across multiple categories, instead upholding a singular sense of race, ethnicity, of faith or nationality which prevents other possibilities. In the case of

Gypsies and Travellers, an identity of victim was denied. For asylum seekers only a foreign national identity can prevail. This erasure of subjectivity pains all involved; for as Anderson (2011: 259) has observed, reflecting on Du Bois, the colour line 'diminishes everyone it touches'.

The continuing racial inequities in the treatment of minority ethnic groups evidenced by our contributors should guard us against complacency encouraged by claims about the demise of race thinking in the present compared to the past. Themes of belonging and borders, rootedness and global migration, immobility and mobility, feature strongly in the accounts collected here while marking the future areas that the race and crime debate will most likely address, likely because migration has once again come to the fore, mobilised in political discourse and generalised anxieties, as part of the ways we are governed through race and crime. Just as white ethnicities and their marginalisation have emerged as an area of interest to the debate about race and crime so too has the blurring of racial and ethnic boundaries, and again this is seen at different points across the contributions here. Recognising that the developing story of racism from a situation whereby racist attitudes and behaviour were a 'normal', everyday aspect of life in Britain to the present situation whereby such behaviour is much less likely to be tolerated, even if that is less clear in relation to attitudes (except perhaps among the young), we welcome such a turning point. This transitional moment in the history of postcolonial Britain, as we have implied and our contributors show, is by no means settled and future developments can go in new directions different to a long-term decline in race thinking and racism.

Before we go on briefly to review the evidence about longer-term changes in race thinking here we remind readers about what we have thought was inadequate about the race and crime debate as traditionally conceived. Although important, confining the debate to a narrow and sole concern to seek a resolution to the question whether minorities offend or are victimised at a higher rate or are discriminated against does not go far enough and needs refreshment and widening, specifically, in terms of geographical reach and focus, new substantive topics, and the use and refinement of racial and ethnic categories. As Bosworth *et al.* (2008: 270) have argued:

> ... we must take seriously the global context of crime and justice, the importance of 'within group' differences and 'between group similarities', the growing relevance of mixedness and hybridity and the intersections between geographical, economic, cultural, religious, ethnic and racial stratification.

## Old and new racism?

There is quite strong evidence that 'old racism' has sharply declined in Britain among generations who have grown up since mass immigration began in the

1950s. For example, opposition to contact with black and Asian minorities in both the family and workplace was markedly lower in the mid-1990s than it was in the early 1980s. Not only does residual racism tend to remain and reside among older people not younger people, it continues to rely on race-based rather than perceived cultural differences. 'New racism' or cultural racism has not replaced 'old racism' based on visible difference. Ford (2008: 630) concludes, on the basis of questions about white racial prejudice against black and Asian Britons asked in successive British Social Attitudes surveys from 1983 to 2010 that, 'a large and growing segment of Britain's white population is at ease with racial diversity ... A major generational shift in white attitudes towards ethnic minorities is the most important driver of this trend.' Further, unlike American commentators' claims of 'new racism' in the United States, preferences in the British marriage and housing markets are quite different and in Britain shifts in attitudes reflect a genuine increase in the social acceptance of British minorities.

The reasons for this apparent sea change in attitudes may be found in recently analysed data from the same attitude surveys that shows a rise in individualism, strikingly so among younger people. As attitudes to collective welfare provision and group solidarity have become negative so has there been a weakening of ascriptions of individuals by virtue of their membership of racial, cultural and social groups. Attitudes to immigrants as a group however are less sanguine and more complicated. Public anti-immigration attitudes are not uniform and do not see immigrants as a homogeneous group. British people are in fact net supporters of well qualified professional migrants, regardless of their circumstances or origins, but are strongly opposed to unskilled labour migration, again regardless of circumstances or origins (Park *et al.* 2012).

Of course the data reported here are about public attitudes and not behaviour and the extent to which a striking decline in racial prejudice – mostly inter-generational among the young – translates into changed behaviour, particularly among key decision-makers and gatekeepers such as employers, the police and the courts is a difficult to answer empirical question. Only to note here that evidence about changes in public perceptions of fairness in the ways minorities are treated by the police and the criminal justice system have not mirrored the changes described above, possibly because these changes are still in the making among younger rather than older people. Indeed surveys have shown that black people have trusted the police and prisons less and expected to be treated worse than whites by a very considerable margin (Smith and Gray 1985; FitzGerald *et al.* 2002; DCLG 2008) and from 1981 to 2000 a belief that the police discriminate has grown (Hough 2007).

## New directions

The methods traditionally associated with the race, ethnicity and crime field of study although capturing disparities in the treatment of, and outcomes for ethnic minorities in police and criminal justice processes have been less able to document close-up, the processes and decision making by which such out-comes are arrived at. They have certainly been unable to capture the nature and dynamics of the racial aspects of these behaviours. Not only may people hold contradictory ideas about race but the racialisation processes by which 'race' accrues meaning in given situations require for their understanding, a qualitative, ethnographic approach to their study. In seeking to uncover or describe disproportionality, discrimination or different offending and victimi-sation patterns, surveys and statistical studies often seem static or too general and the categories and relationships uncovered too simple, fixed and binary. Although showing the continuing significance of race and ethnicity and their effects on crime and justice they tell us little about why these effects continue or are even strengthened despite the appearance of a decline in race thinking.

Our new directions then take us to a more considered and serious view of the complexity of ethnic identities, the changing and negotiated nature of identities – their blurring *and* simplification through reduction in racialisation processes. How racial, religious and ethnic boundaries are created and dis-solved, and their meaning change. Another new direction is a greater ambi-guity about race, particularly a shift in race thinking and racist expression and assumption to the individual, private realm where its covert forms occur behind closed doors. Regarding public institutional spaces, these too may be experiencing continuing yet more covert forms of prejudice, especially among their older members unaffected by liberal individualism's embrace of Britain's multicultural legacy and reality.

## Things to do

We cannot list all the things that have been neglected and remain to be done in understanding race and crime. Leaving aside the long-standing call for institutional ethnographies of street policing and current criminal justice pro-cessing, we focus here, to end, on newly marginalised white groups and EU white migration. An important source and means of understanding racism in the police, the criminal justice system and wider society is understanding white ethnicity. Studies show how white ethnicities have a dynamic relation-ship with class and gender, and how white racism and the paradoxes of race and class among poor whites show 'white privilege' to be often meaningless in this context. In particular white racism is strongly linked to place and class resentment, humiliation and shame born from slurs on poverty and degraded forms of white working-class identity (Moss 2003; Wray 2006). These and similar studies perhaps take us to where we began at the opening to this book seen in David Starkey's use of the term 'chav'. This and other proxies for poor whites show how flexible, adaptable and ingenious racist insults, slurs and abuse have been and are.

It is hopefully not too grand a claim to say that the field of race and crime has come of age. It has developed a maturity, borne of engagement with different conceptual, methodological, epistemological and theoretical tools. It has pulled away from the narrow statistical moorings of official data to situate our understandings within social theory, within insights from the sociology of race and ethnicity, and within other academic disciplines, such as human geography, anthropology, and philosophy.

## References

Anderson, E. (2011) *The Cosmopolitan Canopy: Race and Civility in Everyday Life.* New York: W.W. Norton & Company.

Bosworth, M., Bowling, B. and Lee, M. (2008) 'Globalization, Ethnicity and Racism: An Introduction', *Theoretical Criminology,* 12 (3): 313–31.

Bosworth, M. and Guil, M. (2008) 'Governing through Migration Control: Security and Citizenship in Britain', *British Journal of Criminology,* 48 (6): 703–19.

De Giorgi, A. (2006) *Re-Thinking the Political Economy of Punishment: Perspectives on Post-Fordism and Penal Politics.* Aldershot: Ashgate.

Department for Communities and Local Government (DCLG) (2008) *The Drivers of Black and Asian People's Perceptions of Racial Discrimination by Public Services: A Qualitative Study.* London: Communities and Local Government.

Du Bois, W. E. B. (1903) *The Souls of Black Folk.* Harmondsworth: Penguin.

FitzGerald, M., Hough, M., Joseph, I. and Qureshi, T. (2002) *Policing for London.* Cullompton: Willan Publishing.

FitzGerald, M. (2009) '"Race", Ethnicity and Crime', in C. Hale, K. Hayward, A. Wahidin and E. Wincup (eds) *Criminology. Second Edition.* Oxford: Oxford University Press.

Ford, R. (2008) 'Is Racial Prejudice Declining in Britain?', *British Journal of Sociology,* 59 (4): 609–36.

Foucault, M. (1975) *Discipline and Punish: The Birth of the Prison.* Harmondsworth: Penguin Books Ltd.

Gadd, D. and Jefferson, T. (2007) *Psychosocial Criminology: An Introduction.* London: Sage.

Gadd, D. and Dixon, B. (2011) *Losing the Race: Thinking Psychosocially About Racially Motivated Crime.* London: Karnac.

Gelsthorpe, L. (2007) 'The Jack-Roller: Telling a Story?', *Theoretical Criminology,* 11 (4): 515–42.

Gilroy, P. (2004) *After Empire: Melancholia or Convivial Culture?* London: Routledge.

Hough, M. (2007) 'Policing London 20 Years On', in A. Henry and D. Smith (eds) *Transformations of Policing.* Aldershot: Ashgate.

Moss, K. (2003) *The Color of Class: Poor Whites and the Paradox of Privilege.* Philadelphia, PA: University of Pennsylvania Press.

Park, A., Clery, E., Curtice, J., Phillips, M. and Utting, D. (2012) (ed.) *British Social Attitudes: The 29th Report.* London: NatCen Social Research.

Smith, D. J. and Gray, J. (1985) *People and Police in London.* London: Gower.

Soja, E. (1998) *Thirdspace: Journeys to Los Angeles and Other Real and Imagined Places.* Cambridge, MA: Blackwell.

Stenson, K. (2011) 'Review of Race, Crime and Criminal Justice: International Perspectives', *Global Crime,* 12 (1): 87–92.

Wray, M. (2006) *Not Quite White: White Trash and the Boundaries of Whiteness.* Durham, NC: Duke University Press.

# Index